Who's Who in Science Fiction

BRIAN ASH

Who's Who in
SCIENCE FICTION

Taplinger Publishing Company
NEW YORK

First published in the United States in 1976 by
TAPLINGER PUBLISHING CO., INC.
New York, New York

Library of Congress Catalog Number: 76-11667
ISBN 0-8008-8274-1 (cloth)
ISBN 0-8008-8279-2 (pbk)
Printed in the United States of America

For Jolyon and Jane—
may it enrich them!

Contents

Introduction and acknowledgements 9

US and UK sf magazines and editors 21

Chronological guide 25

A–Z of contributors 29

Bibliography 217

'Everything is determined, the beginning as well as the end, by forces over which we have no control. It is determined for the insect as well as for the star. Human beings, vegetables or cosmic dust, we all dance to a mysterious tune, intoned in the distance by an invisible piper.'

ALBERT EINSTEIN

'A psychotic is a guy who has just found out what is going on!'

WILLIAM BURROUGHS

Introduction

ANY effort to compile a popular 'Who's Who?' is bound to be selective; this one is no exception. It is designed to provide a comprehensive guide for the newcomer to science fiction, to widen the horizon for those who already know something of the genre, and to be a useful, but less than exhaustive source of reference for the scholar and the committed devotee. Its four-hundred-odd entries have been chosen to give an overall picture of the noted writers, editors, illustrators and other contributors, and also to include as many lesser—but still significant—names as space allows. Given that intention, the winnowing process is most evident among the early pulp-magazine writers and their later counterparts, and among recent arrivals whose importance is still to be judged. Of these last, some may have produced a handful of good stories or a single novel of promise. Drawing the line between those who could be included and those who for the time being can only be mentioned in passing was difficult, and the final choice is clearly open to argument. However, the purpose of this guide is to detail the writers firmly established in the genre.

Many people have speculated on what exactly the term 'science fiction' means. A review of the numerous definitions offered over the years would itself occupy several pages. It is probably better to say what, for the purposes of this book, the expression does not mean. There is a minimum of reference to pure fantasy, weird tales, horror stories and other minority areas in the entries that follow. Where a fantasy author is mentioned, it is because he or she has also produced some science fiction or has been an admitted influence on other more relevant writers. By this yardstick the immensely popular 'Middle Earth' sagas of J. R. R. Tolkien, and such delights as Charles Finney's *The Circus of Dr Lao* and the writings of Clark Ashton Smith, have to be excluded. Similarly, what might be called the occasional 'genuine' sf stories by writers more usually associated with other branches of literature do not automatically earn their authors an individual entry, unless—as in the case of Orwell's *Nineteen Eighty-four*—their impact has been great.

There seems little to be gained in arguing that writers of the calibre of L. P. Hartley, Robert Graves and E. M. Forster have produced one or two stories which might be classed as science fiction, any more than there is in suggesting that a handful of science fiction authors have also provided some examples of particularly fine writing. The techniques and thematic approaches employed in science fiction are available to all who wish to exercise their imaginations on paper; this compilation is concerned with those who have employed them regularly, and to some effect. However, for the benefit of anyone interested in the labelling game, a list of probable contenders outside the main field is included towards the end of this introduction.

In the same way that this 'Who's Who?' is deliberately less than exhaustive, so too are its individual entries. Potted biographies, however intriguing, take second place to a useful representation of the writer's achievement. Bibliographic details are normally confined to the first appearance of short stories in magazines and to the first publication of novels *in book form*, together with the year and country of origin. Where this general approach meets with problems, as in the case of title changes or when book versions have only appeared many years after original magazine serializations, the discrepancies are usually made clear. Expressions such as 'first published story' indicate first identifiable *science fiction* stories and not necessarily a writer's actual début in print. A list of US and UK magazines referred to is given before the start of the entries, together with a chronological table of one hundred leading names which should help to guide the newcomer. There are now many awards made in the sf field. The two most notable referred to in the entries are the Hugo (awarded at the annual World Conventions) and the Nebula (chosen annually by the Science Fiction Writers of America).

*

Science fiction can be seen as the modern equivalent of a type of speculative endeavour which reaches back to the very beginnings of the written word. Its study is already overburdened with the attempts of enthusiasts to link medieval and even earlier stories with their present-day counterparts. While these may all be good grist to the historical mill, they really say no more for today's genre than that it was anticipated by the likes of Francis Godwin's *The Man in the Moone* (1638), where the hero ascended into the blue harnessed to a team of long-suffering geese. If the term 'science fiction' means anything at all, it must be firmly related to eras in which a widespread knowledge of science and its applications has a significant influence on the lives of ordinary human beings, and in which extrapolations regarding future scientific, technological and social effects can be worked out with some degree of plausibility. Jules Verne lived in such an era, so did H. G. Wells. Francis Godwin, although he had heard of Copernican theory but was sensible enough—since he was a Bishop—to keep quiet about it, did not.

When science-based technology began to make its impact on common folk towards the beginning of the nineteenth century, some of the basic themes of modern science fiction soon appeared. Mary Shelley dreamt of the artificial creation of life in *Frankenstein* and Edgar Allan Poe of the personality 'scientifically' sustained beyond physical death in 'The Facts in the Case of M. Valdemar'. More basically, Verne conjured machines which allowed his characters to indulge Man's search for individual freedom in a series of *voyages extraordinaires*, while Wells took the archetypal 'little man' and propelled him into no end of unfamiliar surroundings and unexpected events. The prevailing reaction to the scientific achievements of the times was an openminded 'Sense of Wonder', and much of Verne's and Wells's work was stuffed with it. So were the stories of the indefatigable contributors to the early pulp magazines in the 1920s and 1930s.

As the modern genre matured, the themes became categorized and took on labels, as also did many of the special effects which had become part of the sf writer's stock-in-trade. A newcomer to the literature might be forgiven for expressing bewilderment over such shorthand terms as 'space opera', 'BEMs' and 'travelling arks'. Since they appear very regularly in the following entries, they are worth explaining here—the more so because, taken in all, they present a concise picture of the preoccupations and scope of science fiction. Here is a glossary of the most commonly-used terms, with one or two suggestions regarding entries which have some bearing on them:

Aliens and extraterrestrials
All forms of life originating beyond Earth and unconnected with the activities of Man. Usually they consist of protoplasm and are carbon-based. Occasionally they are silicone-based, but this is now known to be a highly unlikely life-form. The interaction between humans and aliens is the basis of many plots. They may fight, co-operate, or sometimes simply ignore each other. A ripe area for allegories of human behaviour and speculative treatments of the nature of perception and communication. It also provides scope for illustrating the relative importance or insignificance of Man when he encounters beings of lesser or greater intelligence. (See entries for Blish, Arthur C. Clarke, Niven, Tenn, Weinbaum and James White.)

Alternate worlds
Other Earths existing in different space-time continuums. They may vary only marginally from our own and include the same individuals, or they may differ greatly in historical details according to the position of their continuum in what is seen as an infinite progression of such states of existence. They can be reached by devious means—stepping into space warps, entering black holes, or sometimes just sitting and dreaming. They may also be called 'parallel worlds', although that expression can cover planets very unlike Earth. (See entries for Aldiss, Farmer, Laumer and Wells.)

Alternative histories
Tales of Earth with usually one historical detail changed in the past, and chronicling the resulting effects today. If, for instance, Lincoln had not been shot, or Queen Elizabeth I had been, how would those events have changed history as we think we know it? (See entries for Ward Moore and Roberts.)

Androids
Chemically-built beings usually indistinguishable physically from humans. Normally they cannot reproduce. They can, however, be programmed—not often with much success—and most android tales tell of their resentment towards their makers. Occasionally their brains are electronic rather than organic. (See entries for Čapek, Cooper, Dick and Wilhelm.)

Awareness of reality
An intriguing category. The central characters discover in the course of the story that things are not what they seem—often including themselves. Who for example, is or is not a robot? Or is Man somebody else's property, and if so, for what purpose? (See entries for Dick, Disch (*The Genocides*) and Russell (*Sinister Barrier*).)

Bug-eyed monsters (BEMs)
What most aliens were seen as in the early stories—and the nastier the better. They are still around, but much less often. (See entries for Leinster, Weinbaum and Wells (*The War of the Worlds*).)

Cataclysms and dooms
A class of story associated with overwhelming disasters, either cosmic, man-made or instigated by aliens. Anything, in fact, from suns going nova and moons which disintegrate, to floods, plagues, scientific experiments getting out of hand and nuclear wars. A favoured 'end of the world' theme among pulp writers. (See entries for Ballard, Roshwald, Serviss and Wells ('The Star').)

Cloning
A technique for breeding large numbers of animals or humans of identical type by the division of fertilized ova and other methods (now a practical possibility). It ties in with genetic engineering and presents the sf writer with a variety of plot developments. (See entries for Cowper, Huxley (*Brave New World*) and Mitchison.)

Cyborg
Abbreviation of 'cybernetic organism'—the bonding of human with machine. Cyborgs range from computers housing human brains to mechanical limb extensions operated by direct impulses from the brain. (See entries for Caidin and McCaffrey.)

ESP and psi-powers
Anything related to the mentally paranormal. Telepathy, mind control, telekinesis (moving objects by the power of thought) and communicating across the depths of space without radio lag. A popular collection of themes in the early 1960s, but always in some demand. (See entries for Bester, John W. Campbell, Arthur C. Clarke (*Childhood's End*) and Van Vogt (*Slan*).)

Force-field
A protective shield set up by energizing matter or altering the configuration of sub-atomic particles. A means of defence, but also a way of warping space to facilitate interstellar travel in some stories. An allied concept is a 'stasis field', in which everything is held in a permanent state of inanimation. (See entries for Duncan (*Occam's Razor*) and Williamson.)

Future histories
Occasional groups of stories by individual writers presenting a logical historical sequence. They may cover a few decades or range far into the future. (See entries for Asimov, Heinlein and Stapledon.)

Heroic barbarian
A recurrent concept, either set on other worlds or in a future where science and technology have declined. Sometimes reminiscent of Arthurian myths, sometimes of Norse and other legends. Epic battles and not a little bloodshed. Another term is 'romantic primitivism'. It borders on all-out 'Sword and Sorcery' fantasy, which runs the full gamut of magic weapons, herculean feats and more of the inevitable carnage. (See entries for Anderson, Bradley, Carter, de Camp, Howard and Merritt.)

Inner space
Not the inside of Earth, but the inside of the head. Stories with psychological angles, investigations into perception and altered states of awareness—an area particularly associated with the 'New Wave' writers of the 1960s who abandoned hardware gadgetry in favour of the software in the skull. Not always a very popular theme with some of the diehards who maintain that much of it isn't science fiction. (See entries for Aldiss (*Barefoot in the Head*), Ballard and Moorcock.)

Machine intelligence
The whole field of computers and cybernetics, with 'thinking' machines being ever more advanced and sometimes becoming genuinely 'awake'. In which case they begin to experience emotions, rarely of the untroubled variety. An important theme, which explores the nature of intelligence and the definitions of 'personality' and 'soul'. (See entries for Arthur C. Clarke (*2001*) and Heinlein.)

Mutants
Often conceived as monstrosities following the escape of atomic radiation, the genetic pattern in the reproductive cells having been damaged. On other occasions they are presented as evolutionary advances, capable of telepathy and other gifts. Whichever the case, they are usually abhorred and hounded by 'normals'. (See entries for Huxley, Walter M. Miller (*A Canticle for Leibowitz*), Sturgeon and van Vogt.)

Pantropy
A form of biological engineering which entails breeding or shaping people to allow them to survive on very alien worlds. (See entries for Abé and Blish.)

Post-catastrophe worlds
Commonly-used term to denote the aftermath of nuclear wars, with the struggle of the survivors to adjust. Frequently complicated by the appearance of mutants and ascetic religions, descents into tyranny and barbarism, and thwarted attempts to rebuild civilization. It can also describe the effects of natural cataclysms. (See entries for Cooper (*All Fools' Day*), Walter M. Miller and Wyndham.)

Pulp magazines
Not intended as a description of the contents, although it was sometimes accurate enough, but a reference to the type of cheap paper on which they were printed.

Robots
The metal servo-mechanisms of the future. They are programmed to obey men and protect them from harm, but they get into difficulties if orders are not precise. Some of them 'think' better than others, and consequently get into bigger trouble. Another useful means to present allegories of human nature. (See entries for Asimov, Bayley, Binder, Čapek, del Rey, Goulart and Williamson.)

Spacecraft and spacedrives
An ever-popular area—ranging from early moon-flights to advanced starships colonizing the galaxy. An abundance of faster-than-light drives has been invented to cut down travelling time and to enable

the establishment of interstellar empires. Many involve the jump through 'hyperspace' (which takes advantage of the curvature of space proclaimed by Einstein) to avoid going the long way round. 'Space warps' follow this idea and can be natural or produced by force-fields. In some stories space would appear to be so bent that it ends up resembling Chinese crispy noodles. For those who stay this side of the light barrier there remains the 'travelling ark'—a ship designed for centuries of flight (often in order to escape from a doomed Earth), in which several generations live and die before eventual landfall. Anti-gravity devices are another means of space-flight. (See entries for Anderson, Blish, Arthur C. Clarke, Cooper, E. E. Smith, Wells (*The First Men in the Moon*) and Verne.)

Space opera
What is regarded by people who take science fiction seriously as being akin to 'soap opera' if it were taking place on Earth. Nevertheless, it is immensely popular. Mile-long spaceships, fast-moving action with blasters and death-rays, BEMs—and generally 'cow-boys-and-indians-in-the-sky'. (See entries for Hamilton, Harrison, Niven, E. E. Smith, Williamson, and many, many others.)

Symbiosis
Generally applied to alien invaders which literally cling to Man in the form of parasites. But otherwise the condition is portrayed in groups of humans, either physically or mentally linked, who attain advanced states of ability and perception: the *Homo gestalt* of the future. (See entries for Heinlein, Pohl and Sturgeon.)

Time travel
Very much what the expression implies. The journey through time, either to the future or the past. A universal theme, particularly in the intellectual puzzles involved in working out the paradoxes which may result—the most common being the man who travels back to murder a direct ancestor before he or she has produced any children. Since the basis for his own existence is thereby destroyed, where does that leave the time traveller? Moving into other dimensions is a close neighbour, and brings us back to alternate and parallel worlds. (See entries for Asimov, Disch (*Echo Round His Bones*), Heinlein, Leiber, Leinster and Wells.)

Utopias and anti-utopias
One of the largest and most important areas in the genre. Any future state of Man can be presented within these opposing poles. So-called 'utopian' paradises can turn into nightmares *overnight*. All human aspirations are bound up in the visions of a brighter tomorrow; and both the bright and the dark aspects of the utopian story are probably science fiction's most relevant contribution to the modern culture. The warnings are there, alongside the dreams. The nature of oppression, of good and evil, the need for population control and ecological harmony—all fall into this category. (See entries for Brunner, Harrison, Huxley, Orwell, Pohl, Wells and Vonnegut.)

These are many of the principal themes of science fiction. There are others, and new ones occur—or resurface—continously; the variety is infinite. If a further definition of the genre were needed, it might as well say that science fiction is a current mode of literary expression in which every element of past literature can co-exist with every element of present and imagined future literature. It is the written interpretation of the past, present and future human culture fused into one—to exist here and now. And it is unique.

*

It is bad to end introductions with eye-wearying lists of names, but they are better here (if they are read at all) than in valedictory appendices. The following stories are those of 'outside' writers which have been claimed, amongst others, for the canon of science fiction. They are given in no particular order, since no particular order applies. They include: Robert Ardrey's *World's Beginning*, J. Jefferson Farjeon's *Death of a World*, Nigel Balchin's *Kings of Infinite Space*, L. P. Hartley's *Facial Justice*, Evelyn Waugh's 'Love Among the Ruins', Constantine Fitzgibbon's *When the Kissing Had to Stop*, Jack London's *The Scarlet Plague*, William Golding's *The Inheritors* and *Lord of the Flies*, Robert Graves's *Seven Days in New Crete*, E. M. Forster's 'The Machine Stops', William Morris's *News From Nowhere*, Samuel Butler's *Erewhon*, Edward Bellamy's *Looking Backward*, Richard Jefferies' *After London*, Sir Compton Mackenzie's *The Lunatic Republic*, Nevil Shute's *In the Wet* and *On the Beach*, R. C. Sherriff's *The Hopkins Manuscript* (later revised as *The Cataclysm*), G. K. Chesterton's *The Man Who was Thursday*,

J. B. Priestley's various time plays and *The Magicians*, B. F. Skinner's *Walden Two*, J. D. Beresford's *The Hampdenshire Wonder*, Karen Boye's *Kallocain*, André Maurois' *Les Mondes Impossibles*, Mark Twain's *A Connecticut Yankee in King Arthur's Court*, Anatole France's *Penguin Island*, John Jacob Astor's *A Journey in Other Worlds*, Alun Llewellyn's *The Strange Invaders*, Lin Yutang's *The Unexpected Island*, David Karp's *One*, James Hilton's *Lost Horizon*, Robert Louis Stevenson's *The Strange Case of Dr Jekyll and Mr Hyde*, Albert Joseph Guerard's *Night Journey*, Thea von Harbou's *Metropolis*, George R. Stewart's *Earth Abides*, Thomas Pynchon's *Gravity's Rainbow*, Gore Vidal's *Messiah*, Rudyard Kipling's 'With the Night Mail', Howard Fast's collections *The Edge of Tomorrow* and *A Touch of Infinity*, and Robert Merle's *The Day of the Dolphin* and *Malevil*.

Finally, of the newer writers, and some less recent, who have no individual entries in this 'Who's Who?', but have certainly not gone unnoticed, the following are among those worthy of attention: Colin Anderson, T. J. Bass, Michael Bishop, Edward Bryant, Angela Carter, William E. Cochrane, L. P. Davies, Peter Dickinson, Hugh Dirac, Joe Haldeman, Lee Harding, James B. Hemesath, H. H. Hollis, Langdon Jones, Vincent King, Sterling Lanier, Ken McCullogh, George R. R. Martin, Martin Padway, Doris Piserchia, Jerry Pournelle, Kit Reed, Frank Riley, William Rotsler, James Sallis, Pamela Sargent, Josephine Saxton, Philip Strick, J. Thacker, Gene Wolfe, Will Worthington, Lan Wright, Chelsea Quinn Yarbro, George Zebrowski and Pamela Zoline.

One must end on a note of caution. The current record of background facts about sf writers and their work is in a state of dreadful muddle. Errors perpetrated by individual compilers have been taken as facts by others (the books mentioned in the Acknowledgements below are no exception). Doubtless there may be some such howlers in this present work, but a number of long-standing offenders have at least been corrected here. The Compiler invites the constructive criticism and help of every reader and reviewer who can produce reliable evidence where facts are in dispute. Such a cooperative undertaking is needed if the accuracy surely demanded in reference works on science fiction is to be achieved.

BRIAN ASH
Summer 1976

Acknowledgements

Much of the research undertaken for this book was carried out at the Science Fiction Foundation, which is housed in the Barking precinct of the North East London Polytechnic. Warm thanks are due to the governing council and to the administrator, Peter Nicholls, for the enjoyment of this facility.

Many of the reference works and other studies consulted are included in the bibliography at the end of this 'Who's Who?'. However, two books must be singled out as exceptionally helpful: Donald H. Tuck's *The Encyclopedia of Science Fiction and Fantasy*, Vol. I, and Robert Reginald's *STELLA NOVA: The Contemporary Science Fiction Authors*. Much information has been drawn from them, but verified elsewhere when possible. Though exhaustive in their own ways, they have their limitations. Both are inclusive only to the end of 1968. *STELLA NOVA* covers only living writers and gives no annotations regarding the contents of their stories. Tuck covers everyone, including the horror merchants, and provides many annotations; but his Vol. II, which will feature the M–Z of authors, has still to appear at the time of writing. These are not criticisms, simply statements of fact to show how the books differ from the present volume. Their existence has been invaluable in the compilation of numerous entries included here and the debt is gratefully acknowledged.

Thanks are also due in appreciation of those recently established authors who personally provided details of their backgrounds and work—and to Wally Gillings and Mike Ashley for invaluable help at proof stage.

SF magazines and editors

(These magazines are referred to in the A–Z. This is not an exhaustive list, but simply details editors mentioned in the entries.)

US magazines:

Air Wonder Stories
  Hugo Gernsback

Amazing Stories
  Hugo Gernsback
  Harry Harrison
  Raymond A. Palmer
  T. O'Conor Sloane
  Ted White

Amazing Stories Quarterly
  Hugo Gernsback
  T. O'Conor Sloane

Astonishing Stories
  Alden H. Norton
  Frederik Pohl

Astounding Stories
(became *Analog Science Fiction/
Science Fact* in 1960)
  Harry Bates
  Ben Bova
  John W. Campbell Jr
  F. Orlin Tremaine

Beyond
  Sam Merwin Jr

Captain Future
  Oscar J. Friend
  Leo Margulies
  Mort Weisinger

Comet Stories
  F. Orlin Tremaine

Cosmic Stories
  Donald A. Wollheim

Famous Fantastic Mysteries
  Alden H. Norton

Fantastic Adventures
  Harry Harrison
  Raymond A. Palmer
  Ted White

Fantastic Story Magazine
  Sam Merwin Jr
  Samuel Mines
  Alexander Samalman

Fantastic Universe
  Leo Margulies
  Sam Merwin Jr

Fantasy Fiction
  Lester del Rey

Future (Science) Fiction
  Charles D. Hornig
  R. W. Lowndes

Galaxy Science Fiction
  H. L. Gold
  Sam Merwin Jr
  Frederik Pohl

If
  Damon Knight
  Frederik Pohl
  James Quinn

Imagination
  Raymond A. Palmer

*The Magazine of Fantasy and
Science Fiction*
  Anthony Boucher
  Avram Davidson
  Edward L. Ferman
  J. F. McComas
  Robert P. Mills
  Ted White

Marvel (Science) Stories
Daniel Keyes

Miracle Science & Fantasy Stories
Elliot Dold

Other Worlds
Raymond A. Palmer

Planet Stories
Jerome Bixby

Satellite Science Fiction
Leo Margulies
R. W. Lowndes·

Science Fiction
Charles D. Hornig

Science Fiction Adventures
Lester del Rey

Science Fiction Quarterly
Charles D. Hornig
R. W. Lowndes

Science Wonder Stories
Hugo Gernsback

Space Science Fiction
Lester del Rey

Space Stories
Samuel Mines

Startling Stories
Oscar J. Friend
Leo Margulies
Sam Merwin Jr
Samuel Mines
Alexander Samalman
Mort Weisinger

Stirring Science Stories
Donald A. Wollheim

Strange Stories
Mort Weisinger

Strange Tales
Harry Bates

Super Science Stories
Alden H. Norton
Frederik Pohl

Thrilling Wonder Stories
(originally *Wonder Stories*)
Oscar J. Friend
Leo Margulies
Sam Merwin Jr
Samuel Mines
Alexander Samalman
Mort Weisinger

Unknown (Worlds)
John W. Campbell Jr

Venture
Robert P. Mills

Weird Tales
Farnsworth Wright

Wonder Stories
(amalgamation of *Air Wonder Stories* and *Science Wonder Stories*)
Hugo Gernsback
Charles D. Hornig

Wonder Story Annual
Sam Merwin Jr
Samuel Mines

Worlds Beyond
Damon Knight

Worlds of Tomorrow
Frederik Pohl

UK magazines:

Authentic Science Fiction
  Herbert J. Campbell
  E. C. Tubb

New Worlds
  E. J. Carnell
  Michael Moorcock

Science Fantasy
(became *Impulse* in 1966)
  Kyril Bonfiglioli
  E. J. Carnell
  Walter Gillings
  Keith Roberts

Science Fiction Adventures
  E. J. Carnell

Science Fiction Monthly
  Julie Davis

Tales of Wonder
  Walter Gillings

Chronological guide

100 leading writers and editors in their main periods of production

1800–1900

Ambrose Bierce	Luis Senarens
George Griffith	Garrett P. Serviss
Kurd Lasswitz	Mary Shelley
Fitz-James O'Brien	Jules Verne
Edgar Allan Poe	H. G. Wells

1900–1920

Edwin L. Arnold	W. H. Hodgson
Edgar Rice Burroughs	Luis Senarens
Ray Cummings	Garrett P. Serviss
George Allan England	Jules Verne
Hugo Gernsback	H. G. Wells

1920s

Edgar Rice Burroughs	Murray Leinster
Karel Čapek	E. E. Smith
Ray Cummings	John Taine
George Allan England	H. G. Wells
Hugo Gernsback	Jack Williamson
Edmond Hamilton	Evgenii Zamyatin
David H. Keller	

1930s

Otto O. Binder	David H. Keller
Edgar Rice Burroughs	Henry Kuttner
John W. Campbell Jr	Fritz Leiber
Karel Čapek	Murray Leinster
Ray Cummings	C. L. Moore
L. Sprague de Camp	Raymond A. Palmer
John Russell Fearn	Eric Frank Russell
Hugo Gernsback	Clifford D. Simak
H. L. Gold	E. E. Smith
Edmond Hamilton	Olaf Stapledon
Aldous Huxley	John Taine

1930s—cont.

Donald Wandrei
Stanley G. Weinbaum
H. G. Wells
Jack Williamson

Donald A. Wollheim
Philip Wylie
John Wyndham

1940s

Poul Anderson
Isaac Asimov
Alfred Bester
James Blish
Anthony Boucher
Ray Bradbury
Fredric Brown
Edgar Rice Burroughs
John W. Campbell Jr
E. J. Carnell
Arthur C. Clarke
Hal Clement
Groff Conklin
L. Sprague de Camp
Lester del Rey
John Russell Fearn
Hugo Gernsback
H. L. Gold
Edmond Hamilton
Robert A. Heinlein
Aldous Huxley
C. M. Kornbluth

Henry Kuttner
Fritz Leiber
Murray Leinster
C. L. Moore
George Orwell
Raymond A. Palmer
Frederik Pohl
Eric Frank Russell
Idris Seabright (Margaret St Clair)
Clifford D. Simak
E. E. Smith
Olaf Stapledon
Theodore Sturgeon
Wilson Tucker
Jack Vance
A. E. van Vogt
Donald Wandrei
Jack Williamson
Donald A. Wollheim
Philip Wylie
John Wyndham

1950s

Brian W. Aldiss
Poul Anderson
Isaac Asimov
J. G. Ballard
Alfred Bester
James Blish
Leigh Brackett
Ray Bradbury
Fredric Brown
John Brunner
Algis Budrys
Kenneth Bulmer
John W. Campbell Jr
E. J. Carnell

John Christopher
Arthur C. Clarke
Hal Clement
Groff Conklin
Edmund Cooper
Avram Davidson
L. Sprague de Camp
Lester del Rey
Philip K. Dick
Harlan Ellison
Philip José Farmer
John Russell Fearn
H. L. Gold
James Gunn

26

Edmond Hamilton
Harry Harrison
Robert A. Heinlein
Frank Herbert
Damon Knight
C. M. Kornbluth
Henry Kuttner
Fritz Leiber
Murray Leinster
Stanislaw Lem
Richard Matheson
Judith Merril
Walter M. Miller Jr
C. L. Moore
Andre Norton
Raymond A. Palmer
Frederik Pohl
Eric Frank Russell

Idris Seabright (Margaret St Clair)
Bob Shaw
Robert Sheckley
Robert Silverberg
Clifford D. Simak
Cordwainer Smith
E. E. Smith
Theodore Sturgeon
William Tenn
Wilson Tucker
Jack Vance
A. E. van Vogt
Kurt Vonnegut Jr
Jack Williamson
Donald A. Wollheim
Philip Wylie
John Wyndham

1960s

Brian W. Aldiss
Poul Anderson
Isaac Asimov
J. G. Ballard
James Blish
Ben Bova
Leigh Brackett
John Brunner
Algis Budrys
Kenneth Bulmer
John W. Campbell Jr
E. J. Carnell
John Christopher
Arthur C. Clarke
Groff Conklin
Edmund Cooper
Avram Davidson
L. Sprague de Camp
Samuel R. Delany
Lester del Rey
Philip K. Dick
Thomas M. Disch
Harlan Ellison
Philip José Farmer
James Gunn
Edmond Hamilton
Harry Harrison

Robert A. Heinlein
Frank Herbert
Aldous Huxley
Damon Knight
Ursula K. Le Guin
Fritz Leiber
Stanislaw Lem
Judith Merril
Walter M. Miller Jr
Michael Moorcock
Larry Niven
Andre Norton
Frederik Pohl
Keith Roberts
Eric Frank Russell
Idris Seabright (Margaret St Clair)
Bob Shaw
Robert Sheckley
Robert Silverberg
Clifford D. Simak
Cordwainer Smith
E. E. Smith
Boris & Arkadi Strugatski
Theodore Sturgeon
William Tenn
James Tiptree Jr
Jack Vance

1960s—cont.

A. E. van Vogt
Kurt Vonnegut Jr
Kate Wilhelm
Jack Williamson

Donald A. Wollheim
John Wyndham
Roger Zelazny

1970s:

Brian W. Aldiss
Poul Anderson
Isaac Asimov
J. G. Ballard
Alfred Bester
James Blish
Ben Bova
John Brunner
Kenneth Bulmer
Arthur C. Clarke
Edmund Cooper
Samuel R. Delany
Thomas M. Disch
Gordon Eklund
Harlan Ellison
Philip José Farmer
Harry Harrison

Robert A. Heinlein
Frank Herbert
Ursula K. Le Guin
Stanislaw Lem
Barry Malzberg
Michael Moorcock
Larry Niven
Bob Shaw
Robert Silverberg
Clifford D. Simak
James Tiptree Jr
Wilson Tucker
Jack Vance
A. E. van Vogt
Jack Williamson
Roger Zelazny

A-Z of contributors
(through mid-1976)

Kobo Abé

Kobo Abé is a leading Japanese writer, born 1924, whose occasional forays into the realm of science fiction reached a high point in 1959 with the publication of *Inter Ice-Age 4*. The novel deals with a world rapidly disappearing beneath the seas as the polar ice-caps melt. Man is being compulsorily adapted to fit biologically for a sub-aquatic life. The distasteful necessity for experimenting on human beings, and the possibility of conflict with computers, are the book's major themes. *The Ruined Map* (UK translation 1972) is a further example of Abé's distinguished sf work.

Forrest J. Ackerman

Winner of a Hugo Award in 1953 as 'Number One Fan Personality', Forrest Ackerman is very much what the title denotes. Born in 1916, he is an American editor, authors' agent, film adviser—and a life-long sf fan who has attended numerous conventions. During the 1930s he worked on a very early fan magazine, *The Time Traveller*, and on *Science Fiction Digest*. He was a founding member in 1934 of The Los Angeles Science Fantasy Society, reputedly the most long-lived of all the fan organizations.

Towards the end of the 1950s he became editor of *Famous Monsters of Filmland* magazine, and much of his home is now a museum devoted to the bizarre props which have adorned countless horror films and many best-forgotten sf movies. He has also edited selections from the magazine, appropriately titled: *Best From Famous Monsters of Filmland* (US 1964), *Son of Famous Monsters of Filmland* (US 1964) and *Famous Monsters of Filmland Strike Back* (US 1965).

George Adamski

Born in Poland in 1891, George Adamski moved with his family to the US two years later. He has been a lecturer in philosophy, and is a keen astronomer and photographer. He came to prominence by claiming to have talked with Venusians in *Flying Saucers Have Landed* (UK 1953, in collaboration with D. Leslie), a book which caused some stir at the time, as well it might. Some suggested that he had written more science fiction than he thought, while others succeeded in replicating his alleged photographs of alien spacecraft using mundane household objects. Unabashed, he went on to produce several further offerings on the same theme: *Inside the Space Ships* (US 1956), *Flying Saucers Farewell* (US 1961) and *Behind the Flying Saucer Mystery* (US 1967).

Mark Adlard

Mark Adlard was born in the North East of England in 1932. Educated at Trinity College, Cambridge, he later also took a degree in economics and spent twenty years in the steel industry, occupying various managerial posts. He wrote a number of short stories in the sf idiom during the 1960s before he realized that the genre existed. Having discovered it, he saw it as a literary technique with which business life could be shown in a larger context—to underline its effects on the economy, society and the individual. His three novels, *Interface* (UK 1971), *Volteface* (UK 1972) and *Multiface* (UK 1975), form a trilogy designed to illustrate those effects in a future setting.

Brian W. Aldiss

Voted the UK's most popular sf writer by the British Science Fiction Association in 1968, Brian Wilson Aldiss was born in Norfolk in 1925. He served in the British Army in the Far East during the Second World War, later becoming literary editor of the *Oxford Mail* after a number of years in the bookselling trade. His first published sf story, 'Criminal Record', appeared in *Science Fantasy* in 1954. He won joint-Second Prize in the *Observer* newspaper's sf competition *AD 2500*. Since then he has become known for his prolific output, the fecundity of his ideas, and his ability to comment imaginatively on the genre. He became the President of the British Science Fiction Association in 1960, and was Guest of Honour at the 23rd World Science Fiction Convention in 1965. He also edited the Penguin sf novels paperback series during 1961–64.

Among his early stories are a mutant variation, *Non-Stop* (UK 1958); two accounts of the exploitation of Earth by aliens, *Vanguard from Alpha* (US 1959) and *Bow Down to Nul* (US 1960); and a tale dealing with emotions and sexual attraction, *The Primal Urge* (US 1961). *Hothouse* (UK 1962) was the novel-length version of his

Hugo-winning short-story series of the same title, telling of Man's struggle to exist in the sweltering environment of Earth in the far future (he had won an earlier Hugo in 1959 as 'The Most Promising New Author').

There followed a number of impressive books. *The Dark Light-Years* (UK 1964) featured encounters with a race of physically repellent, but socially highly-evolved aliens, while both *Greybeard* (UK 1964) and *Earthworks* (UK 1965) looked ahead to times when humanity and Earth itself are respectively becoming sterile. *An Age* (UK 1967) dwelt on the hazards of time travel, and *Report on Probability A* (UK 1968) proved a novel, if over-extended variation on the parallel worlds theme. Followers of the 'New Wave' claimed *Barefoot in the Head* (UK 1969) for their very own—it recounts the mind-blown actions of a Europe suffering from a hallucinogenic-gas attack by the Middle East. *The Eighty-Minute Hour: a Space Opera* (UK 1974) provided the kind of joyride its subtitle denotes.

For something like a decade Aldiss worked on a grand design for a genuine history of the genre. When it arrived, *Billion Year Spree* (UK and US 1973), proved that history writing should not lightly be attempted in the confines of a single book where coverage of the most recent period is starved for lack of space. Nevertheless, much of it is well handled, and its author's advocacy of Mary Shelley's *Frankenstein* as the first 'true' sf novel was reflected in his subsequent *Frankenstein Unbound* (UK 1973), a fantasy involving time travel back to the original motivation for Mary Shelley's tale. Other works dealing with the ideas and creative concepts of science fiction include *The Shape of Further Things* (UK 1970) and *Hell's Cartographers* (UK 1975), the latter a compilation of personal histories by several sf writers, and jointly edited by Harry Harrison, with whom Aldiss has also produced a number of anthologies (*see under* Harry Harrison). He has also edited *Science Fiction Art* (UK and US 1975), selected from a half century of good, bad and normally colourful illustrations.

Many of his short stories can be read in the collections: *Space, Time and Nathaniel* (UK 1957), *Airs of Earth* (UK 1963), *Intangibles Inc., and Other Stories* (UK 1969) and *Moment of Eclipse* (UK 1971). The title story of *The Saliva Tree* (UK 1966), written as a celebration of the centenary of H. G. Wells, won a Nebula in the previous year.

Kingsley Amis

Kingsley William Amis is an English writer and critic who was born in London in 1922. Educated at City of London School and St John's College, Oxford, he served in the British Army during the Second World War. A noted novelist in other fields, he made an important contribution to science fiction with the publication of *New Maps of Hell* (US 1960), based on a series of lectures he had given at Princeton during the previous year. The book drew the attention of conventional critics and academics to the genre and went some way to establishing its respectability in eyes situated beneath suitably elevated brows. At the same time he succeeded in persuading the staid British periodical, *Spectator*, to run his sf short story, 'Something Strange'.

Since 1961 Amis has compiled the *Spectrum* series of sf anthologies jointly with Robert Conquest. They contain many excellent stories by well-known writers, and *Spectrum 4* (UK 1965) also includes an illuminating introductory discussion between Amis, Brian Aldiss and the late C. S. Lewis (first published in *SF Horizons No. 1* (UK 1964).) The series ended with the fifth book.

Poul Anderson

A prolific American writer and much-lauded prize-winner, Poul William Anderson was born in Pennsylvania in 1926. He graduated with an honours degree in physics from the University of Minnesota in 1948, but chose to write as a career—his work also includes both historical and conventional fiction. He first appeared in the sf field with 'Tomorrow's Children' in *Astounding* (1947) and has maintained a consistently high output ever since.

The versatility and sheer volume of his work, coupled with a realistic approach and generally straightforward literary style, have enhanced his popularity as an author. He has exercised some influence in the sf world, particularly in the introduction of new ideas regarding the future development of science and technology. He is also noted for several series, among them the 'Flandry' stories featuring a secret space agent, and the 'Hoka' tales (in collaboration with Gordon R. Dickson) which tell of intelligent bears and have been collected in *Earthman's Burden* (US 1957). The Flandry saga can be found in *We Claim These Stars* (US 1959), *Earthman Go Home!* (US 1960), *Mayday Orbit* (US 1961), *Agent of the Terran*

Empire (US 1965), *Ensign Flandry* (US 1966) and *Flandry of Terra* (US 1966). Another series, the chronicles of 'Trader Nicholas Van Rijn', appears in *War of the Wing-Men* (US 1958), *Trader to the Stars* (US 1964), *The Trouble Twisters* (US 1966) and *Satan's World* (US 1969).

Anderson's Nordic parentage is reflected in several of his stories, including *The High Crusade* (US 1960), which tells of an alien space-ship landing on a medieval Earth where the knights cheerfully outwit the invaders, and *Let the Spacemen Beware* (US 1963), telling of a refuelling base built on a planet inhabited by a Celtic-type civilization. His preoccupation with time is recorded in the 'Time Patrol' collection, *Guardians of Time* (US 1960), in *The Corridors of Time* (US 1965) and in the further collections: *Time and Stars* (US 1964) and *The Horn of Time* (US 1968).

Interplanetary exploration and colonization are handled in *Planet of No Return* (US 1956), *The Snows of Ganymede* (US 1958), *Orbit Unlimited* (US 1963), *Three Worlds to Conquer* (US 1964), *The Star Fox* (US 1965), *World Without Stars* (US 1966) and *Tau Zero* (US 1970), the last of these being one of the best thought out descriptions of a spaceship in the genre. On the post-catastrophe theme he has produced *After Doomsday* (US 1962), relating the search through space for human survivors after the destruction of Earth, and *Twilight World* (US 1961).

Other stories of note include *Brain Wave* (US 1954), *The Enemy Stars* (US 1958), *War of Two Worlds* (US 1959), *Shield* (US 1963) and *The Byworlder* (US 1971)—also the collection *The Un-Man and Other Novellas* (US 1962). His non-fiction work is represented by *Is There Life on Other Worlds?* (US 1963).

Among Anderson's awards are Hugos in 1961, 1964, 1969, 1972 and 1973—respectively for 'The Longest Voyage', 'No Truce with Kings', 'The Sharing of Flesh', 'The Queen of Air and Darkness' (which also won a Nebula in 1971), and 'Goat Song' (another Nebula winner in 1972). He was Guest of Honour at the 17th World Science Fiction Convention in 1959.

Piers Anthony

Piers Anthony Dillingham Jacob was born in Oxford in 1934 and became a US citizen in 1958. He spent three years as a technical writer for a communications company and subsequently taught

35

English at Admiral Farragut Academy in the US. A relative new-comer to science fiction, he has been likened (by Arthur C. Clarke) in originality and inventiveness to Delany and Algis Budrys. He received the $5000 Pyramid Award for his novel *Sos the Rope* (US 1968)—a warrior and empire saga set in a post-catastrophe world which was the first part of a trilogy that also included *Var the Stick* (US 1973) and *Neq the Sword* (US 1975).

Among Anthony's other stories are *Chthon* (US 1967), which verges on fantasy but contains powerful poetic imagery, and *Macroscope* (US 1969). *The Ring* (US 1968, in collaboration with Robert E. Margroff) deals with a device for rehabilitating criminals which produces unexpected social side effects; and *Prostho Plus* (US 1971) records the comic adventure of a twentieth-century dentist kidnapped by extraterrestrials.

Christopher Anvil

Pen-name of US writer Harry C. Crosby who first appeared in *Astounding* in 1956 with 'The Prisoner'. His 'Pandora' series in 1956–61 was popular in *Astounding/Analog* and his novel *The Day the Machines Stopped* (US 1964) relates the chaos experienced when electrical energy fails planet-wide. His latest, *Warlord's World* (US 1975), is a deliberately hilarious space opera.

Edwin L. Arnold

Edwin Lester Arnold (1857–1935) is now best remembered for his novel *Gulliver of Mars* (UK 1905). Its account of the adventures on the red planet of Lieut. Gulliver Jones has been seen by some as a prelude to Rice Burroughs' epic Martian series which began seven years later. Son of Sir Edwin Arnold, whose *Light of Asia* introduced Victorian readers to the teachings of Buddha, he bred cattle in Scotland and worked in forestry in India before taking up a literary career. His best-known fantasy, *Phra the Phoenician* (US 1890), was revived in *Famous Fantastic Mysteries* in 1945.

Isaac Asimov

The Gibbon of the rise and fall of future history, and advocate-in-chief of the Three Laws of Robotics, Isaac Asimov may not be the most prolific of sf authors, but his total literary output is well in excess of a hundred books. For thirty-five years his name has been among the foremost in the genre, since the time when his 1940 story 'Nightfall' captured the imaginations of *Astounding* readers. Many still regard it as the most outstanding work in modern science fiction.

Asimov was born in Russia in 1920 and emigrated with his family to the US when he was three. By the age of ten he was already an avid reader of the early sf pulps. Leaving high school at sixteen, he studied chemistry at Columbia University, at the same time beginning his first attempts at sf writing. He was rewarded in 1939 with the publication of 'Marooned off Vesta' in *Amazing*, but within a year he was safely gathered into Campbell's fold at *Astounding*. During the Second World War he worked for the Navy aircraft research complex in Philadelphia, and also served in the post-war US Army before returning to his studies.

On receiving his doctorate in 1949 he joined the faculty of the Boston University School of Medicine, his doctoral thesis being simply: 'The Kinetics of the Reaction Inactivation of Tyroserose During Its Catalyzing of the Aerobic Oxidation of Catechol'. By that time, he had already completed the series in *Astounding* which was later to emerge in book form as the trilogy *Foundation* (US 1951), *Foundation and Empire* (US 1952) and *Second Foundation* (US 1953). The series was hailed as a landmark; and although it contained elements of space opera, its galactic view of a million-world empire threatened with a collapse into thirty thousand years of strife was a far cry from 'Doc' Smith's epic sagas. Rather belatedly, it won its author a Hugo as 'The Best All-Time Series' in 1966. He was Guest of Honour at the 13th World Science Fiction Convention in 1955.

Against the backdrop of 'Foundation's' vast empire Asimov set three further novels: *Pebble in the Sky* (US 1950), *The Stars Like Dust* (US 1951) and *The Currents of Space* (US 1952) where, unlike the trilogy, he recorded the struggle of individual men (the three were collected in *Triangle* (US 1961)). Drawing back from the remote future, he returned to Earth with *The Caves of Steel* (US 1954) which combined an effective crime story with the anti-utopian elements of population explosion and the use of a human-like robot as the detective's assistant. The same characters featured in *The Naked Sun* (US 1957), where they solved a mystery on one of Earth's colonial worlds.

In 1963 Asimov received a Hugo for 'Distinguished Contributions to the Field', among which his intriguing robot stories must certainly be classed. In collaboration with John W. Campbell he devised the robotics laws that have been accepted by other writers but never really improved upon. Basically they are intended as a safeguard to protect human beings from robots, and from each other when robots happen to be around—a kind of ethical code of machine conduct. The stories have been gathered into two collections: *I, Robot* (US 1950) and *The Rest of the Robots* (US 1964).

Asimov has also produced a memorable time-travel drama in *The End of Eternity* (US 1955), which chronicles the activities of an inter-temporal élite who guide man's progress but at the same time weaken his ability to exercise free will. He won a third Hugo, and also a Nebula, for his novel *The Gods Themselves* (US 1972), which tells of the potentially catastrophic exchange of energy between Earth and a parallel world. While not his original idea, his *Fantastic Voyage* (US 1966) was a highly successful retelling of the film story.

In recent years Asimov has produced a formidable list of popularizations of science to stand beside his science fiction and his many sf 'juveniles' written under the pen-name of 'Paul French'. While his dedication to science clearly contributes to the diversity and appeal of his short stories, they are equally notable for their humanity, warmth and frequent flashes of humour. Many collections have been published, among them: *The Martian Way and Other Stories* (US 1955), *Earth is Room Enough* (US 1957), *Nine Tomorrows* (US 1959), *Nightfall and Other Stories* (US 1969), *The Early Asimov* (US 1972) and *Buy Jupiter and Other Stories* (US 1975). He has also edited a variety of anthologies: *The Hugo Winners* (US 1962), *Fifty Short Science Fiction Tales* (US 1963—with Groff Conklin), *Tomorrow's Children* (US 1966), a compilation of sf and fantasy stories centred around children and the young, and the eighth in the *Nebula Award* series (US 1973). An interesting and unusual study of Asimov's work is Neil Goble's *Asimov Analyzed* (US 1972). *The Science Fiction of Isaac Asimov* (US 1974), by Joseph F. Patrouch Jr, is also worth reading, but not necessarily in agreement. *Isaac Asimov* (US 1976), edited by J. D. Olander and M. H. Greenberg, is the latest study.

Hilary Bailey

Hilary Bailey is a British writer and anthologist who was born in

1936. She was educated at Cambridge, where she graduated with an honours degree in English. In 1962 she married Michael Moorcock and subsequently became associated with *New Worlds* magazine. She was co-compiler with Charles Platt of the anthology *New Worlds Seven* (UK 1975) and sole compiler of its immediate successors. She has also written a few short stories, among the best known being 'The Dog Man of Islington'.

J. G. Ballard

An expert in slow choreographies of physical and mental disintegration, James Graham Ballard is a British writer who was born in Shanghai in 1930. As a boy he was interned in a Japanese POW camp. After the war he studied medicine at Cambridge and later worked on advertising copy and film scripts before turning to full-time writing. His first story, 'Prima Belladonna', appeared in *Science Fantasy* in 1956. He became a regular contributor to *New Worlds* and was subsequently associated with the 'New Wave' writers, particularly by virtue of the psychological content of his work. He is not regarded as an optimist; his reaction to the moon-plaque wording 'We Came in Peace for All Mankind' was—as reported by Michael Moorcock—'If I were a Martian I'd start running now'.

Ballard's novels are almost universally tales of disaster, on either global or individual human levels. *The Wind From Nowhere* (US 1962) tells of the crumbling of civilization against the assault of continuous 100mph gales. Worldwide floods and droughts are portrayed respectively in *The Drowned World* (US 1962) and *The Burning World* (US 1964; retitled *The Drought*, UK 1965). *The Crystal World* (UK 1966) is a haunting account of the slow crystallization of Earth's organic material, including Man.

More recently Ballard has concentrated on the aspects of alienation and violence in modern life. Assassination, automobile accidents and sexual imagery are also interwoven in elaborate textures in *The Atrocity Exhibition* (UK 1970), *Crash* (UK 1973), *Concrete Island* (UK 1974) and *High Rise* (UK 1975).

His short stories can be found in the collections: *The Voices of Time* (US 1962), *Billenium* (US 1962), *The Four-Dimensional Nightmare* (UK 1963), *Passport to Eternity* (US 1963), *Terminal Beach* (UK 1964), *The Impossible Man* (US 1966), *The Day of*

Forever (UK 1967), *The Overloaded Man* (UK 1967), *The Disaster Area* (UK 1967), *Chronopolis* (US 1971) and *Vermilion Sands* (UK 1973).

Raymond Banks

Raymond E. Banks is an American author and industrial marketing executive who began contributing regularly to the US magazines in the early 1950s. One of his earliest stories was 'The Happiness Effect' in *Astounding* in 1953. Much of his work can be found in later issues of *The Magazine of Fantasy and Science Fiction*.

René Barjavel

Born in France in 1911, René Barjavel has been a regular contributor to the French sf magazine *Anticipations*. His best-known work outside his native country is *The Ice People* (France 1968)—a post-catastrophe romance in which two humans from the remote past revive from their frozen state to find Earth in the aftermath of a nuclear war. In another, and earlier, post-catastrophe story, *Ashes, Ashes* (France 1943), he tells of a return of society to the rural life in a world where electricity no longer works!

Arthur K. Barnes

Arthur Kelvin Barnes (1911–69) was an American writer who directed a certain amount of his substantial literary output in the direction of *Thrilling Wonder Stories* during the 1930s and 1940s. He began with 'Lord of the Lightning' in 1931 and became popular with his series featuring 'Gerry Carlyle', two stories of which he wrote in collaboration with Henry Kuttner. Some of them were collected in *Interplanetary Hunter* (US 1956).

Harry Bates

American editor and writer, of the 'Old School', Harry Bates was born in 1900 and made a name for himself in the sf world by editing the pre-Campbell *Astounding* from 1930 until 1933 and *Strange Tales* (all seven issues) from 1931 to 1932. He also wrote some stories worth remembering—'Farewell to the Master' (1940) in *Astounding*, on which the film *The Day the Earth Stood Still* (1951) was based, and the 'Hawk Carse' series in the same magazine.

John Baxter
An Australian scriptwriter and journalist whose contributions to *New Worlds*, *Analog* and *Science Fantasy* date from the early 1960s. His novel, *The Off-Worlders* (US 1968), depicts a society socially evolved around agriculture where the study and application of science is prohibited. His anthology, *The Pacific Book of Science Fiction* (Australia 1968), helped to put Australian science fiction on the map and later introduced American and British readers to such talents as Kit Denton, Lee Harding and Jack Wodhams.

Barrington J. Bayley
UK-based entrant to the field in the 1950s. His work includes *Empire of Two Worlds* (US 1972), a story of space colonization in which some humans are more favoured than others, and *The Soul of a Robot* (US 1974)—an impressive advance on the robot theme, with investigations into the possibilities of robots having souls and self-awareness. He has also written under the pseudonym 'P. F. Woods'.

Peter Beagle
Peter Soyer Beagle is an American freelance writer born in New York in 1939. He has travelled widely in Europe. More a fantasy writer than a hard sf man, but his *A Fine and Private Place* (US 1960) is an interesting psychological tale. *The Last Unicorn* (US 1968) is a delight, but pure fantasy.

Charles Beaumont
A pseudonym of the American writer C. Nutt, whose sinister, some-times funny, frequently ghoulish, short stories range across the fantasy and sf spectrum and have appeared in three collections: *Shadow Play* (US 1957), *Hunger and other stories* (US 1957) and *Yonder* (US 1958). Definitely not for the squeamish, they rival the work of Roald Dahl in their masterly invocation of nastiness. He died, nastily, in 1967.

41

Gregory Benford

Gregory Benford is an American writer who was born in Alabama in 1941. He lived in both Europe and Japan while his father was serving in the US Army, and began editing a fan magazine during his teens. In 1965 he won a writing competition in *The Magazine of Fantasy and Science Fiction* and has since produced several dozen short stories. Among them are 'And the Sea Like Mirrors', which appears in Harlan Ellison's *Again, Dangerous Visions*, and 'If the Stars are Gods'—a story written with Gordon Eklund which won a Nebula in 1974. His novel *Deeper than the Darkness* (US 1970) tells of an alien invasion against a future Earth dominated by a Chinese empire.

Alfred Gordon Bennett

Has to be mentioned if only by virtue of the choice British colloquialism which has derived from his name. Born in 1901, this one-time journalist, publisher, champion of the arts and wartime training-film producer actually wrote some science fiction before his death—*The Demigods* (UK 1939), in which enormous ants rule the world, and *Whom the Gods Destroy* (UK 1946), an Eastern setting bordering on fantasy.

Earle Bergey

American illustrator who, more than any other, was responsible for many sf pulp enthusiasts covering their magazines in plain wrappings when they read them in public. Bergey was the grand master of the garish, of the BEM lurking menacingly behind the bikini-clad space adventuress, of the highest common excitator in visual space opera. His cover work ranged from *Startling Stories*, through *Thrilling Wonder Stories*, to *Fantastic Story Magazine* and *Future SF*. He died in 1952.

Bryan Berry

Born in 1930, Bryan Berry was a British author who was formerly a publisher's editor and agency staff writer. He was very active in the sf field in the early 1950s when he first became a freelance writer, but died tragically young in 1955. His novels include *The Venom Seekers* (UK 1953), *And the Stars Remain* (UK 1952), *Born in Captivity* (UK

1952) and *From What Far Star?* (UK 1953). His 'Venus Trilogy', written under the name of 'Rolf Garner', and consisting of *Resurgent Dust* (UK 1953), *The Immortals* (UK 1953) and *The Industructible* (UK 1954), chronicles the struggle of the remnants of mankind on Venus after the destruction of Earth.

Alfred Bester

Although his output has been relatively small, US author Alfred Bester's contributions to the sf field are highly prized. Born in 1913, he received a degree in science and fine arts at the University of Pennsylvania but took to professional writing after winning a competition in *Thrilling Wonder Stories* with 'The Broken Axiom' in 1939. His work appeared in various pulp magazines in the early 1940s and he has also authored comic storybooks and strips. Now he largely concentrates on TV scriptwriting.

His *The Demolished Man* (US 1953), which won a Hugo in the following year, is a brilliant treatment of a murder mystery set in a world where the emergent ruling class possesses telepathic powers. By the use of different typefaces and the skilful juxtaposing of normal and telepathic dialogue, Bester added to the book's psychological impact and set a standard for future stories of this type. Another notable novel, *Tiger! Tiger!* (UK 1956—retitled *The Stars My Destination* for US 1957), is a compelling tale of interplanetary war. After a gap of eighteen years, he made a welcome return to the scene with *Extro* (US 1974), in which one of the few immortals in the solar system attempts to take over the master computer which controls all technology on Earth. Unfortunately, the tale is not up to his former standard.

Many of Bester's short stories can be found in the two collections: *Starburst* (US 1958) and *The Dark Side of the Earth* (US 1964).

Ambrose Bierce

A towering figure among American fantasy writers and a renowned and acid journalist on both sides of the Atlantic, Ambrose Bierce was born in 1842 and fought in the Union Army during the Civil War. He disappeared in Mexico in 1914. Some of his work is claimed for the canon of science fiction, but in the main it is difficult to see much evidence of it among his many stories of fantasy and horror.

43

'Moxon's Master', in which he dealt with artificially created life, is a possible contender. He may have had some influence on later writers, such as Robert Bloch, who have combined both horror and fantasy elements in science fiction; but it would be difficult to prove.

Many of Bierce's stories have been republished in fairly recent collections, among them *The Collected Writings of Ambrose Bierce* (US 1946) and *Ghost and Horror Stories of Ambrose Bierce* (US 1964).

Lloyd Biggle Jr

An American writer, born in Iowa in 1923, who started out to be a musician, was interrupted by the Second World War, and then turned to English literature and writing before returning to musicology. His first sf story, entitled 'Gypped', was run by *Galaxy* in 1956, and music entered into its plot. His first novel, *The Angry Espers* (US 1961), centred on ESP, as its title denotes. *Watchers of the Dark* (US 1966) was also concerned with mental powers, but more appropriate to its author's interests was *The Still, Small Voice of Trumpets* (US 1968)—mainly a musically orientated tale. Other books include *All the Colours of Darkness* (US 1964), *The Fury Out of Time* (US 1965), plus the short-story collection *The Rule of the Door and Other Fanciful Regulations* (US 1967). He also edited the seventh *Nebula Award* anthology (US 1972).

Otto O. Binder

Born in Michigan in 1911, Otto Oscar Binder originally appeared in *Amazing* in 1932 with 'The First Martian', a story written in collaboration with his elder brother Earl under the pen-name 'Eando Binder'. The collaboration continued for a number of years and various of the stories have appeared in collected form: *Adam Link—Robot* (US 1965) and *Anton York—Immortal* (US 1965). The 'Adam Link' series is remarkable for being the first concerted attempt in science fiction to present robot stories in which the narrator is the robot itself.

The brothers also wrote under the pseudonym of 'Gordon A. Giles', the partnership ending around 1940. Otto went on to script the 'Captain Marvel' and 'Superman' comic strips—the former being illustrated by another brother, Jack—and to edit the magazine

44

Space World. Several of his novels have been published in book form after early printing in the magazines. *Lords of Creation* (US 1949) first appeared as a serial in *Argosy* in 1939 and *Enslaved Brains* (US 1965) was serialized in *Wonder Stories* under the 'Eando Binder' name. Both deal with a future Earth where man is held under various forms of domination. A further story, *The Avengers Battle the Earth Wreckers*, was published in the US in 1967. He died in 1975.

Jerome Bixby

Another musical sf enthusiast, Jerome Lewis Bixby was born in the US in 1923. A one-time concert pianist, he is also an immensely productive writer with at least a thousand stories to his name (not all that many are science fiction). He edited *Planet Stories* briefly at the beginning of the 1950s, and subsequently worked under Horace Gold on *Galaxy*. The collection *Space by the Tale* (US 1964) is representative of his sf work.

John Blackburn

John Fenwick Blackburn is a British writer, born in Northumberland in 1923. Educated at the University of Durham, he has been a lorry driver, seaman, teacher and book dealer in his time. Principally a crime writer, he has also written some science fiction stories, usually with a strong mystery slant. Among them are *The Sour Apple Tree* (US 1959), *Children of the Night* (UK 1966) and *Nothing But the Night* (UK 1968). His best-known novel in the genre is *A Scent of New-Mown Hay* (UK 1958), in which a plastic-consuming fungus is loosed upon the world by a former Nazi scientist.

E. F. Bleiler

Everett Franklin Bleiler is an industrious American anthologist whose monumental effort, *The Checklist of Fantastic Literature* (US 1948), listed more than 5000 books which had appeared in the science fiction, fantasy and weird stories categories up to its time of publication. It was the first such work of reference and remains an invaluable guide.

Bleiler, who was born in 1920, joined Dover Publications in 1955, becoming managing editor and, finally, Executive Vice President in 1967. In the 1950s, until he joined Dover, he produced anthologies with T. E. Dikty in *The Best Science Fiction Stories* and *The Year's Best Science Fiction Novels* series. His other anthologies include *Imagination Unlimited* (US 1952) and *Frontiers in Space* (US 1955).

James Blish

A noted expatriate American writer, James Benjamin Blish was born in 1921. He studied zoology at Rutgers University and served for two years in the US Army as a technician in medical laboratories. After the Second World War he wrote for a time for trade papers and also worked in public relations. He moved to England with his family during the last few years of his life and died there in 1975.

Blish's first story, 'Emergency Refuelling', appeared in *Super Science Stories* in 1940; he did not begin writing novels for a further decade. His earliest, *Jack of Eagles* (US 1952), dealt with the development of psychic powers, and soon afterwards he embarked on his renowned 'Cities in Flight' series: *Earthman, Come Home* (US 1955), *They Shall Have Stars* (UK 1957), *The Triumph of Time* (US 1958) and *A Life for the Stars* (US 1962) (this is the order of first publication, but not of consecutive reading). Basically the tales are superior space opera and depict entire cities taking to space, some peacefully and some as pirates. The series culminates in the end of our Universe as it collides with another consisting of anti-matter. Other novels of the same period include *VOR* (US 1958) and *Titan's Daughter* (US 1961).

In 1959 he won a Hugo for *A Case of Conscience* (US 1958), a memorable account of the discovery of a seeming alien paradise which the Jesuit member of an exploration team regards as a genuinely diabolic trap. Ten years later Blish pursued this pre-occupation with satanic powers in *Black Easter* (US 1968) and its sequel, *The Day After Judgment* (US 1971), which he considered as forming the second part of a notional trilogy entitled 'After Such Knowledge' (the third part being *A Case of Conscience* and the first *Doctor Mirabilis*, his historical novel—and not science fiction—set around the life of Roger Bacon).

Other moral problems were explored in . . . *And All the Stars a Stage* (US 1971) which is a 'travelling ark' variation. *Midsummer Century* (US 1972) is set in AD 25000, when Earth is passing through a tropical phase and Man, having reverted to savagery, comes into conflict with intelligent birds. *The Quincunx of Time* (UK 1975) is an extended version of 'Bleep', which was included in his collection *Galactic Cluster* (US 1959).

Blish also wrote several stories for the juvenile sf market and collaborated with R. W. Lowndes on the adult novel *The Duplicated Man* (US 1959), also with Norman L. Knight on the utopian tale, *A Torrent of Faces* (US 1967). On another level he wrote book adaptations of the original *Star Trek* TV scripts, beginning with *Star Trek* (US 1967) and continuing to *Star Trek 7* (US 1972). Within this series he also produced a new story, *Spock Must Die!* (US 1970).

Among his collections are *The Seedling Stars* (US 1956), which is an amalgamation of his 'pantropy' tales featuring genetic engineering to suit men for unEarthlike worlds, *So Close to Home* (US 1961), *Best Science Fiction Stories of James Blish* (UK 1965) and *Anywhen* (US 1970). He compiled the fifth *Nebula Award* anthology (US 1970) and produced two notable collections of critical writings originally done for the magazines under the pseudonym of 'William Atheling Jr': *The Issue at Hand* (US 1964) and *More Issues at Hand* (US 1970). He was not a kindly critic of his sf contemporaries, but a highly constructive commentator. In 1960 he was Guest of Honour at the 18th World Science Fiction Convention.

Robert Bloch

A renowned sf fan and winner of a Hugo in 1959 for his short story 'That Hell-Bound Train' (*The Magazine of Fantasy and Science Fiction* 1958), Robert Bloch was born in Chicago in 1917. He was something of a protégé of H. P. Lovecraft in his early writings and his first stories were accepted by *Weird Tales* when he was only seventeen. Later he began a career in advertising and continued writing in his spare time until Alfred Hitchcock propelled him into the limelight with his film adaptation of Bloch's novel *Psycho*. Since then he has concentrated on TV writing and screenplays, together with further novel-length thrillers.

Bloch's main pursuit has generally been in the horror and fantasy field, and many collections of his stories in that vein have been published. His work in the science fiction pulps is represented by the collection, *Atoms and Evil* (US 1962) and he has also produced a selection of fan-writing in *The Eighth Stage of Fandom* (US 1962), which was specially prepared for that year's World Science Fiction Convention.

Tom Boardman Jr

Well known in British sf circles as a critic, publisher and anthologist, Thomas Volney Boardman Jr was actually born in Bronxville, New York, in 1930, being taken to England as an infant. He has been a consultant on science fiction to several publishers and a regular reviewer of the genre for *Books and Bookmen*. His anthologies include *Connoisseur's Science Fiction* (UK 1964), *The Unfriendly Future* (UK 1965) and *An ABC of Science Fiction* (UK 1966). During 1964-65 he edited the only two issues of the critical magazine *Science Fiction Horizons*.

Hannes Bok

One of the most original American illustrators in the sf and weird magazines, Hannes Vajn Bok (1914-64) produced many notable covers for *Weird Tales* and *Stirring Science Stories* during the early 1940s. In the following decade his work appeared in *Other Worlds*, *Fantasy Fiction*, *Imagination* and *Fantastic Universe*. His illustrations are immediately recognizable by their characteristic style and, in monotone, by their heavy lines which sometimes gives them the appearance of woodcuts. Interest in Bok has grown since his death, and a Bokanalia Foundation has been formed to reprint selections of his work. Two of his own fantasy novels have also recently appeared in book form: *The Sorcerer's Ship* (US 1969) and *Beyond the Golden Stair* (US 1970).

John Boland

John Bertram Boland was born in Birmingham, England, in 1913. A thoroughly practised writer, with several hundred published stories to his name, he has written only a small amount of science fiction. He contributed briefly to *New Worlds* in the late 1950s and his novels *White August* (UK 1955) and *No Refuge* (UK 1956), both set in Arctic-type environments, were no doubt inspired by his experiences in Alaska and Canada where he worked as a lumberjack.

Nelson Bond

Nelson Slade Bond (born 1908) made his name in the US magazines of the 1940s with series featuring such characters as 'The Lobblies' and 'Lancelot Biggs', both of which were later incorporated in the respective collections *Mr Mergenthwirker's Lobblies and Other Fantastic Tales* (US 1946) and *Lancelot Biggs: Spaceman* (US 1950). He has also written the interesting *Götterdämmerung* variation, *Exiles of Time* (US 1949), and been further collected in *No Time Like the Future* (US 1954) and *Nightmares and Daydreams* (US 1968).

J. F. Bone

An American veterinary surgeon, Jesse Franklin Bone was born in Washington in 1916. He appeared on the sf horizon with a first story in *Galaxy*, 'Survival Type', in 1957. Since then he has written a number of stories and the novel *The Lani People* (US 1962), a tale with a suitably anthropological slant.

Kyril Bonfiglioli

Editor of the British magazine *Science Fantasy* for two years beginning 1964 (its name was changed to *Impulse* early in 1966), Kyril Bonfiglioli is more usually at home surrounded by antiques and fine paintings, in which he has dealt. He also believes in the strict discipline of dogs and has lately taken to the authorship of mystery stories with each chapter prefaced by quotations from Browning. An eccentric.

Anthony Boucher

'Anthony Boucher', who was born William Anthony Parker White in 1911, rose to become a renowned editor in the world of US science fiction magazines. Also a well-known writer and anthologist of detective tales, he started *The Magazine of Fantasy and Science Fiction* in 1949 with J. F. McComas as co-editor. In all he produced eight anthologies from the magazine, the first three jointly with McComas, under the series title *Best From Fantasy and Science Fiction*. He also reviewed science fiction and fantasy for several major US newspapers, among them the *San Francisco Chronicle*, the *Chicago Sun Times* and the *New York Herald Tribune*. His early death in 1968 robbed American fiction of a discerning and elegant professional.

Boucher's own writing in the sf field was fairly limited. He contributed occasionally to *Unknown* and *Astounding*. His stories have been collected in *Far and Away* (US 1955) and *The Compleat Werewolf* (US 1969); while his detective novel *Rocket to the Morgue* (US 1942, under the pen-name 'H. H. Holmes') features several sf authors in its plot. His two robot stories, 'Q.U.R.' (1942) and 'Robinc' (1943) (both included in *The Compleat Werewolf*) are of particular interest as examples of anti-robotics arguments—or at least anti-all-purpose robots. He showed that it would be far more sensible, both economically and ergonomically, to build a host of individual, relatively simple machines, each designed for one specific task, than to attempt to devise an immensely complicated automaton which would be expected to handle them all.

Pierre Boulle

The progenitor of *Planet of the Apes*, Pierre Boulle has led a life which itself borders close to the fantastic. Born at Avignon in France in 1912, he went to Malaya as a rubber planter in his early twenties and served with the Free French Mission in the Second World War. He was captured fighting as a guerrilla in Indochina but later succeeded in escaping. He subsequently put his wartime experience to good use in *The Bridge Over the River Kwai*. He now lives in Paris.

The plot of *Planet of the Apes* (US 1963) is probably too well known to require description. The original film of the title by Twentieth Century-Fox stuck reasonably close to the novel and its success generated two further screenplays, a television series, and a popular eruption in Marvel Comics.

Boulle's collection, *Time Out of Mind and Other Stories* (UK 1966), contains one or two sf offerings; and his *Garden on the Moon* (France 1964) is an interesting variation on the beginning of space-flight.

Ben Bova

The man who took on the daunting task of filling *Analog*'s editorial chair on John Campbell's death in 1971. The measure of his success can be judged by his winning a Hugo in 1973 as 'Professional Editor', and again with the same citation in 1974 and 1975.

Benjamin William Bova was born in the US in 1932. He has a background of journalism, technical writing, and work in the communications field. His own science fiction is usually firmly rooted in the technical—in such stories as *The Weather Makers* (US 1967), which relates an attempted takeover of weather control by the military, *Out of the Sun* (US 1968) and *The Duelling Machine* (US 1971), the last being a variation on 'the machine that can run the Universe' theme. He also edited the 1973 *Science Fiction Hall of Fame* anthology, a contribution to a series which began in 1963 and consists of novels and short stories chosen by members of the Science Fiction Writers of America association.

John Boyd

Born Boyd Bradfield Upchurch, of British extraction, in Georgia in 1919. 'John Boyd' served in the British Royal Navy before the Second World War and has since worked mainly for a photographic company in Los Angeles. A relative newcomer to science fiction, he was first persuaded to write when race riots in the Watts district of Los Angeles prompted his interest in racial problems. Consequently his first novel, *The Last Starship from Earth* (US 1968), explores this aspect of society in anti-utopian terms and tells of a near future where mathematicians head the social order and mating partners are dictated by genetics. Boyd's humour, inventiveness and narrative powers have drawn an enthusiastic critical response, and the quality of *The Pollinators of Eden* (US 1969) and *The Rakehells of Heaven* (US 1969) also indicates a sound ability to handle sexual themes.

Leigh Brackett

Mrs Edmond Hamilton—but well known in her own right as a creator of popular dramas set on other planets. Leigh Douglas Brackett was born in the US in 1915. Even as a child she felt the urge to write, and her first published sf story, 'Martian Quest', appeared in *Astounding* in 1940. Other stories followed, some of which can be found in the 'Martian' collection *The Coming of the Terrans* (US 1967). Further Martian settings include *The Sword of*

Rhiannon (US 1953), *The Secret of Sinharat* (US 1964) and *People of the Talisman* (US 1964). Similar swashbuckling adventures, but transferred to a Venusian setting, are told in *Enchantress of Venus* (US 1949, in *Giant Anthology of Science Fiction*). Her excursions into interstellar travel and space opera are well represented by *The Starmen* (US 1952), *The Big Jump* (US 1955) and *Alpha Centauri or Die!* (US 1963).

Leigh Brackett married Edmond Hamilton in 1946. (They were joint Guests of Honour at the 22nd World Science Fiction Convention in 1964.) Since the mid-1950s she has written little science fiction and has concentrated on other fields and Hollywood scripts. Her most serious sf novel is *The Long Tomorrow* (US 1955), a post-catastrophe story of an attempt to resurrect a free society after an atomic war has led to an oppressive and reactionary régime in the US.

Ray Bradbury

A highly gifted writer and a constant bone of contention in the science fiction arena, Raymond Douglas Bradbury was born in Illinois in 1920, the descendant of English settlers who landed in America in 1630. As a child he showed a gift for conjuring, and a penchant for fantasy and horror magazines. While studying, he divided his spare time between theatre groups, newspaper vending and his first efforts at professional writing. In 1939 he published a short-lived fan magazine which featured contributions from Heinlein and Kuttner, among others. Three years later he achieved his first sale to *Super Science Stories* with 'Pendulum', written in collaboration with Henry Hasse. Much of his subsequent magazine work concentrated on fantasy, but towards the close of the 1940s he had begun producing tales set on Mars for *Planet Stories* and *Thrilling Wonder*. These were subsequently collected into *The Martian Chronicles* (US 1950).

Publication of this collection brought Bradbury's work to the attention of critics outside the sf field who hailed him as a brilliant new discovery and the writer most likely to elevate science fiction to the heights of Parnassus. Sf commentators were on the whole less impressed, many choosing to regard the stories as emotional offerings which could as easily have been set on Earth. They doubted if they should be classed as science fiction. However, no such reservations could be held regarding the novel *Fahrenheit 451* (US 1953), an impressive anti-utopian account of a war-threatened future where firemen are employed to destroy books and burn down any houses in which they are found. Told with the full power of Bradbury's gift for visual imagery, it was filmed in 1966 by François Truffaut—a puzzlingly underrated production.

Bradbury's later work has been largely concentrated on fantasy novels, the theatre (his early love) and films (the 1953 Warner Bros production *The Beast From 20,000 Fathoms* was based on his short story 'The Foghorn'). Many of his stories have been adapted for television on both sides of the Atlantic. He has become a respected writer in the conventional literary establishment, particularly for his haunting evocations of childhood and his eerie fantasies. His various short-story collections are individual mixtures of sf, fantasy and purely conventional—but always striking—flights of imagination. They include *Dark Carnival* (US 1947), *The Illustrated Man* (US 1951), *The Golden Apples of The Sun* (US 1953), *A Medicine for Melancholy* (US 1959; also published simultaneously in the UK, with mainly the same contents, as *The Day It Rained Forever*), and *I Sing the Body Electric* (US 1969). Two basically sf collections designed for the younger market are *R is for Rocket* and *S is for Space* (both US 1966).

Marion Zimmer Bradley

A US authoress who can lay claim to once having been the target in a carnival knife-throwing act—and who seems equally at home with flashing blades in much of her fiction. Marion Eleanor Zimmer Bradley was born in Albany, New York, in 1930. She became an enthusiastic reader of the genre in her teens and began writing without much success until her stories 'Keyhole' and 'Women Only' appeared in *Vortex 2* in 1953, and 'Centaurus Changeling' was accepted by *The Magazine of Fantasy and Science Fiction* in 1954.

Some of her tales are reminiscent of Leigh Brackett's swash-buckling approach and she is particularly noted for the series of novels set around the planet 'Darkover'. Unlike many series, each book tells of a different epoch of Darkover's long history and of its human and non-human inhabitants. Among these novels are: *The Door Through Space* (US 1961), *The Sword of Aldones* (US 1962), *The Planet Savers* (US 1962), *The Bloody Sun* (US 1964), *Falcons of Narabedla* (US 1964), *Star of Danger* (US 1965), *The World Wreckers* (US 1971) and *The Heritage of Hastar* (US 1975).

Reginald C. Bretnor

Siberian-born, US author whose main contribution to the sf field is the symposium *Modern Science Fiction: Its Meaning and Its Future* (US 1953). Divided into three sections: 'Science Fiction Today', 'Science Fiction as Literature' and 'Science Fiction, Science and Modern Man', it contains contributions by Asimov, Boucher, J. W. Campbell Jr, Arthur C. Clarke, de Camp, Pratt, Wylie, and Bretnor himself in a concluding essay, 'The Future of Science Fiction'. As a review of where science fiction stood at that time, as seen by a number of leading writers, the book is important.

Further comparable compilations which he has edited are *Science Fiction: Today and Tomorrow* (US 1974) and *The Craft of Science Fiction. A Symposium on Writing Science Fiction and Science Fantasy* (US 1976). The latter features essays by fourteen noted writers, among them Anderson, Clement, Ellison and Pohl.

Bretnor has also written a few sf stories for *Galaxy* and *The Magazine of Fantasy and Science Fiction*.

Miles J. Breuer

A revered name from the early pulp magazines, Miles John Breuer is remembered for the medical slant he brought to many of his stories. He was in fact a doctor—born in Chicago in 1889 and educated at the University of Texas and Rush Medical College. He served in the US Medical Corps during the First World War, and his studies of tuberculosis received wide recognition. He died in California in 1947.

Unfortunately, no collections of Breuer's sf work seem to have been made, and enthusiasts must turn to the early copies of *Amazing* if they wish to sample the delights of 'The Man with the Strange Head' (Jan. 1927) and 'The Appendix and the Spectacles' (Dec. 1928), and to *Amazing Stories Quarterly* (Summer 1930) for his novel *Paradise and Iron*.

Fredric Brown

Credited by Sam Lundwall as having written one of the shortest sf stories ever (three sentences)*, Fredric William Brown is particularly cherished for the humour and superlative satire he brought to many of his tales. 'Placet is a Crazy Place' (1946) must rank supreme in the annals of comically improbable worlds and can be found in his collection *Angels and Starships* (US 1954).

He was born in Cincinnati in 1906, working first in an office, and then as a proofreader and journalist, before becoming a full-time writer in 1947. Much of his work was devoted to detective fiction, but he succeeded in securing himself a lasting place in the SF Hall of Fame by the time of his death in 1972. The novel *What Mad Universe* (US 1949) is considered his best and provides a memorable satire of an alternative Earth where science fiction happenings are a reality. His other books include *The Lights in the Sky are Stars* (US 1953), *Rogue in Space* (US 1957), *The Mind Thing* (US 1961) and *Martians, Go Home* (US 1955)—this last being a humorous chronicle of a Martian invasion in which the assailants turn out to be the very reverse of the Wellsian prototype in *The War of the Worlds*, but equally as devastating.

Many more of Brown's stories, some of them written in collaboration with Mack Reynolds, can be found in the following collections: *Space on My Hands* (US 1951) which includes the hilarious 'Star Mouse', *Honeymoon in Hell* (US 1958), *Nightmares and Geezenstacks* (US 1961) and *Daymares* (US 1968). A joint anthology with Mack Reynolds of 13 humorous sf stories, *Science Fiction Carnival*, appeared in the US in 1953.

Rosel George Brown

A student of ancient Greek historians, Rosel George Brown arrived on the US sf scene in 1958 with her short story 'From an Unseen Censor' in *Galaxy*. Her promising début was cut short by her early death in 1967 at the age of 41. However, she produced enough stories of merit a collection, *A Handful of Time* (US 1963), and

---

* Reputedly it runs: 'After the last atomic war, Earth was dead; nothing grew, nothing lived. The last man sat alone in a room. There was a knock on the door. . . .' An even shorter one (anon) is '. . . And the sun set slowly in the East.' The Compiler would be interested to hear of others.

wrote *Sybil Sue Blue* (US 1966) which featured a versatile police-woman heroine who might rank as a 'stainless steel she-rat' (*see under* Harry Harrison). She also collaborated with Keith Laumer on *Earthblood* (US 1966), telling of one man's quest through space for the answer to his mysterious origin.

John Brunner

One of the most prominent and prolific of British authors, John Kilian Houston Brunner was born in Oxfordshire in 1934. Converted to science fiction by early readings of Wells, he had written, *and sold*, his first novel by the age of 17, at the same time announcing that he was leaving Cheltenham College because its syllabus interfered with his education. His American début was made in 1953 with 'Thou Good and Faithful' in *Astounding*. There followed National Service in the Royal Air Force and a short period in industrial communications and editorial work before he became a full-time writer. In 1958 he became actively involved in the Campaign for Nuclear Disarmament and he subsequently toured many countries to further its cause. He has also travelled widely in support of his sf activities and taken part in conventions in places as far flung as Stockholm and Brazil.

If his early novels leaned in the direction of space opera, they were nevertheless sufficiently original to arouse attention. Among them were *The World Swappers* (US 1959), *The Skynappers* (US 1960), *Slavers of Space* (US 1960), *Sanctuary in the Sky* (US 1960), *The Super Barbarians* (US 1962) and *Secret Agent of Terra* (US 1962). *The 100th Millenium* (US 1959) was a notable setting of a remote future, later revised as *Catch a Falling Star* (US 1968). However, Brunner really began to come into his own with terrestrial settings in which he was able to exercise his concern for human society and direct his able imagination to extending the problems of the present day. In this context *Stand on Zanzibar* (US 1968) ranks as a supreme example, portraying an overpopulated future by a jigsaw pattern of individual destinies and disasters. The book won a Hugo in 1969 and has attracted more critical and academic attention than any other recent sf novel.

A similar treatment is employed in *The Jagged Orbit* (US 1969); while *The Sheep Look Up* (US 1972) marks another Brunner mile-stone in employing the same technique to depict the results of the ecological disasters which we can see beginning now. Among other notable stories are his various treatments of time in *Times Without Number* (US 1962), *Timescoop* (US 1969) and *The Wrong End of Time* (US 1971), also his distinctive psychological approach in *The Whole Man* (US 1964, retitled *Telepathist*, UK 1965).

Further recent novels include an account of the near future in which both the collapse of current civilization and the outbreak of World War III are imminent—*The Stone That Never Came Down* (US 1973)—and *The Shockwave Rider* (US 1975) telling of an individual's revolt against future computer information systems which are depriving most people of their privacy. Three more are *The Dramaturges of Yan* (US 1971), *Age of Miracles* (US 1973—a revision of the earlier *Day of the Star Cities* (US 1965)) and *Web of Everywhere* (US 1974).

Brunner's many collections of short stories include: *No Future in It* (UK 1962), *Now Then* (US 1965), *Out of My Mind* (US 1967), *Not Before Time* (UK 1968), *Entry to Elsewhen* (US 1972), *From This Day Forward* (US 1972) and *Time-Jump* (US 1973).

His work is appraised by various contributors in *The Happening Worlds of John Brunner* (US 1975), edited by Joseph W. de Bolt.

Algis Budrys

A considerable talent and a master craftsman in the short story form. Algirdas Jonas Budrys was born in Prussia in 1931, moving to the US in 1936 when his father became Representative of the Lithuanian Government-in-Exile. After a brief period with American Express he entered publishing and was Assistant Editor with Galaxy Publications in 1953. Later he joined Playboy Press as Editorial Director. He contributed regularly to Horace Gold's *Galaxy* and his stories can be read in the collections: *The Unexpected Dimension* (US 1960) and *Budrys' Inferno* (US 1963).

Almost all Budrys' work is a worthwhile source for study, not to say of entertainment, and if any one novel must be singled out for particular note it is *Rogue Moon* (US 1960), which ought to have won a Hugo but unfortunately ran in the same lists as Walter Miller's *A Canticle for Leibowitz*. It is an excellent example of the use of symbolism in the genre, exploring aspects of both death and resurrection, without any loss to an inventive and gripping narrative set around the investigation of an alien structure on the moon. On a comparable level is *Who?* (US 1958), which relates the attempts to verify that an American scientist handed back by the Russians is actually the man he claims to be.

Other novels include *Man of Earth* (US 1958), *The Falling Torch* (US 1959) and *The Amsirs and the Iron Thorn* (US 1967), all featuring planetary adventure; and a post-catastrophe story, *Some Will Not Die* (US 1961, originally appearing in a shorter version in 1954 as *False Night*).

Kenneth Bulmer

Henry Kenneth Bulmer is a prolific British sf writer who was born in London in 1921. He became a fan before the Second World War, in which he served with the Royal Corps of Signals in North Africa and Europe. He continued his fan activities after the war, at the same time becoming a regular contributor to Carnell's *New Worlds* and producing many other stories under a variety of pseudonyms e.g., 'Philip Stratford', 'Frank Brandon' and 'Nelson Sherwood'. He took over the editing of the *New Writings in SF* series of anthologies after Carnell's death in 1972.

Many of Bulmer's novels fall into the space opera and galactic adventure category, among them *Encounter in Space* (UK 1952), *Empire of Chaos* (UK 1953), *Galactic Intrigue* (UK 1953), *Space Salvage* (UK 1953), *The Changeling Worlds* (US 1959), *Defiance* (UK 1963), *The Wizard of Starship Poseidon* (US 1963), *Worlds for the Taking* (US 1966) and *Blazon* (US 1970). Underwater sagas feature in *City Under the Sea* (US 1957) and *Beyond the Silver Sky* (US 1961), while revolutions, intrigues and alien invasions, all in an Earth setting, can be found variously in *Cybernetic Controller* (UK 1952, written with A. V. Clarke), *World Aflame* (UK 1954), *The Secret of ZI* (US 1958), *The Fatal Fire* (UK 1962), *Cycle of Nemesis* (US 1967) and *The Doomsday Men* (US 1968). Both *The Key to Irunium* (US 1967) and *The Key to Venudine* (US 1968) show Bulmer in the realm of fantasy. Further recent novels include *On the Symb-Socket Circuit* (US 1972) and *Roller Coaster World* (US 1972).

David R. Bunch

US writer formerly employed in the aeronautics field. His first sf story, 'Routine Emergency' appeared in *If* in 1957. Since then he has produced a series of stories centred around a highly technological society in a world of robots, many of which can be found in his collection *Moderan* (US 1971). He has made several appearances in Judith Merril's *Year's Best SF* anthologies and is the only writer with *two* contributions in Harlan Ellison's *Dangerous Visions*.

Eugene L. Burdick

American political scientist and co-author with William Lederer of *The Ugly American*, a stinging criticism of US involvement in SE Asia. His only venture into science fiction, but a notable one, was *Fail-Safe* (US 1962) on which he collaborated with J. H. Wheeler. Burdick clearly brought his own professional experience to bear on this story of an accidental US nuclear attack on the USSR. It was later adapted to make a successful film, unfortunately somewhat eclipsed by Kubrick's *Dr Strangelove*. Also unhappily, the joint authors were sued in 1963 by Peter George, who claimed the story was a plagiarism of his own *Two Hours to Doom* (written under the name of 'Peter Bryant') from which the idea for *Dr Strangelove* was drawn. Burdick died in 1965, aged 47.

Anthony Burgess

British novelist, born in Manchester in 1917, who has spent part of his early career in education, in the UK, Malaya and Brunei. His anti-utopian novel *The Wanting Seed* (UK 1962), which tells of an oppressed and overpopulated future, paled beside his equally anti-utopian *A Clockwork Orange* which was published in Britain in the same year. The vicious philosophy and lifestyle of its 15-year-old narrator and his use of 'Nadsat', a slang language incorporating Russian words picked up from Soviet propaganda, were faithfully carried over into Kubrick's Hugo-winning film adaptation a decade later. Contrary to many representations, today's prototypes of the hooligans the story depicts were certainly not influenced by the book, and probably not by the film; those of them who had chosen to were already behaving like that.

John Burke

British writer and former public relations executive, John Frederick

Burke was born in Sussex in 1922. He specializes in adapting film scripts into book form for Twentieth Century-Fox, but has also written a number of science fiction novels. He enjoyed some success with his sf short stories in the British magazines during the 1950s, some of which are included in the collection *Alien Landscapes* (UK 1955), and he has compiled several horror anthologies.

Among his novels are two treatments of parallel universes: *Dark Gateway* (UK 1954) and *The Echoing Worlds* (UK 1954); while the rather overworked theme of time travel into the past to change the course of history is the basis of *Pursuit Through Time* (UK 1956). His novel-length adaptation of the film *Moon Zero Two* appeared in Britain in 1969.

Arthur J. Burks

A treasured name from the pulp days, Arthur J. Burks was born in 1898 and pursued a full-time career in the US Army until he was thirty. He joined the Marines during the Second World War, being particularly active in the training of recruits. A great many of his pre-war stories fall into the 'weird' category, but he also produced genuine science fiction tales for *Astounding*, among them the 'Josh McNab' series. His military background inspired others such as 'West Point of Tomorrow' (1940) in *Thrilling Wonder*. He died in 1974.

Edgar Rice Burroughs

Occupies a category of his own in the annals of all fiction (as Arthur C. Clarke has pointed out: who, among those who have never read a book of any kind, hasn't heard of Tarzan? His science fiction, however, mostly excludes the jungle hero who was best exemplified on film by Johnny Weissmuller—his earsplitting yell developed from the yodels he practised in his native Austrian Tyrol). 'ERB', as he is usually known to his worldwide following, was born in the US in 1875. As a young man he tried his hand at a number of occupations, including service in the US Cavalry, gold mining, storekeeping and law enforcement. His first published tale, 'Under the Moons of Mars', appeared in *All-Story Magazine* in 1912 (the earliest Tarzan epic followed soon afterwards). Long before his death in 1950 he had made himself a fortune; his sales remain undiminished today.

In the sf field his work is more competent than inspired. His narrative powers were strong, and his output offers a substantial body of reading for those seeking undemanding, action-packed adventure. The major part of it appeared as magazine serials, often well before book publication, and consists of three main series. The first includes the Martian stories featuring 'John Carter': *A Princess of Mars* (US 1917, being the retitled book version of the original 1912 tale), *The Gods of Mars* (US 1918), *The Warlord of Mars* (US 1919), *Thuvia, Maid of Mars* (US 1920), *The Chessmen of Mars* (US 1922), *The Mastermind of Mars* (US 1928), *A Fighting Man of Mars* (US 1931), *Swords of Mars* (US 1936), *Synthetic Men of Mars* (US 1940), *Llana of Gathol* (US 1948) and *John Carter of Mars* (US 1964), the last two being collections of tales originally published in *Amazing*.

The second series features the underground lost world of 'Pellucidar' and includes one Tarzan story. It runs as follows: *At the Earth's Core* (US 1922), *Pellucidar* (US 1923), *Tanar of Pellucidar* (US 1930), *Tarzan at the Earth's Core* (US 1930), *Back to the Stone Age* (US 1936), *Land of Terror* (US 1944) and *Savage Pellucidar* (US 1963).

Venus is the setting of the third and shortest series: *Pirates of Venus* (US 1934), *Lost on Venus* (US 1934), *Carson of Venus* (US 1939) and *Escape on Venus* (US 1946). In addition there are several novels unconnected with any particular series, among them: *The Land That Time Forgot* (US 1924) and *Beyond the Farthest Star* (US 1964), the former being a compilation of three original novelettes.

An entry almost as long again would be necessary to cover the bibliography of studies of ERB and his work. The most comprehensive to date is Hardy Henry Heins's *Golden Anniversary Bibliography of Edgar Rice Burroughs* (US 1962).

William Burroughs

To those for whom William Seward Burroughs' books read like bad nightmares there may be little consolation in learning that some of them have been classed as science fiction. He was born in the US in 1914, grandson of the founder of the Burroughs accounting machine empire. Elements of anti-utopianism *can* be found in Burroughs' work, and depressing and generally unlovely futures are presented in both *Nova Express* (US 1964) and *The Soft Machine* (US 1966).

Parts of the latter are incorporated with material from *The Naked Lunch* and *The Ticket That Exploded* (US 1967) to make up *Dead Fingers Talk* (UK 1963). To be read wearing blue-tinted glasses.

James Branch Cabell

A fantasy writer who is noted for his creation of Poictesme, a mythical country derived from medieval Provence. Cabell was born in Richmond, Virginia, in 1879 and lived there almost exclusively until his death in 1958. His *magnum opus*, *Biography of the Life of Manuel*, spans more than twenty volumes chronicling numerous adventures in the land of Poictesme. However, he is probably best remembered for *Jurgen* (US 1919), which was the subject of an unsuccessful obscenity lawsuit. As was to be expected, the book has remained in print ever since. Comparatively innocuous, it is a witty if rambling tale and a perfect example of Cabell's wryly sardonic view of human nature. Its flavour reappears in the work of later science fantasy writers and lingers on even in Farmer's *Maker of Universes* trilogy.

Martin Caidin

American aviation specialist Martin Caidin is founder of a TV and radio network covering aerospace matters. Born in 1927, he established himself in the field of aviation literature well before the age of twenty and has since written many popular books on the subject. In keeping with his background, his best science fiction has a solid technical basis, as illustrated in *Marooned* (US 1964), which tells of a rescue operation in space and was filmed in 1969. He has explored the world of submarine warfare in *The Last Fathom* (US 1967) and the use of cybernetic organisms in *Cyborg* (US 1972). His other novels include *The Long Night* (US 1956), *No Man's World* (US 1967), *The God Machine* (US 1968) and *The Mendelov Conspiracy* (US 1969).

Herbert J. Campbell

British research chemist and writer, Bert Campbell (born 1925) was editor of *Authentic Science Fiction* from the end of 1952 until early 1956. After which he more or less retired from the field to concentrate on his scientific pursuits. He has produced two anthologies, *Tomorrow's Universe* (UK 1953) and *Authentic Book of Space* (UK 1954), and a novel, *Beyond the Visible* (UK 1952), which deals with an unseen menace threatening man.

John W. Campbell Jr

A prodigious influence on magazine science fiction, John Wood Campbell was born in New Jersey in 1910. His real education began at the Massachusetts Institute of Technology. An early fan of *Amazing*, and particularly of 'Doc' Smith's interplanetary tales, he began writing stories in a similar vein but with a greater emphasis on scientific accuracy. The first was published in *Amazing* as 'When the Atoms Failed' in 1930, and thereafter he became a regular and popular contributor. In 1934 he partially shifted his allegiance to *Astounding* with 'Twilight', written under the pseudonym 'Don A. Stuart' (derived from his wife's maiden name, Dona Stuart). In this persona he moved away from the 'hard' science stories produced under his own name.

In 1936–37 he contributed an impressive series of articles on the sun's planets to *Astounding*; and in October 1937, having followed several occupations since leaving MIT, he was appointed that magazine's full-time editor. He held the position until his death in 1971, and during much of that time *Astounding* (or *Analog Science Fiction/Science Fact*, which it became in 1960) occupied a dominant place among its competitors. Campbell introduced many new writers who quickly gained notable reputations, among them Heinlein, Asimov, del Rey, van Vogt and Sturgeon—all within three or four years of his assuming editorship. His standards were demanding and he frequently insisted on rewrites, even from his star contributors. But he was also generous with guidance and help. It was he, for instance, who helped to originate the 'Three Laws of Robotics' which Asimov was to propound so imaginatively.

In the 1960s much of *Analog*'s contents reflected Campbell's growing preoccupation with psi-powers and other paranormal factors, a trend which distressed many earlier enthusiasts but which also introduced a further array of new writers. Regardless of its occasional periods in the doldrums, *Astounding/Analog* proved a powerful motive force under Campbell, winning the Hugo award for the best magazine no less than eight times (in 1953 jointly with *Galaxy*, in 1955, 1956, 1957, 1961, 1962, 1964 and 1965). Campbell was Guest of Honour at the World Science Fiction Conventions of 1947, 1954 and 1957.

His own short stories are collected in several volumes: *Who Goes There?* (US 1948), *Cloak of Aesir* (US 1952), *The Planeteers* (US 1966) and *The Best of John W. Campbell* (UK 1973). Among his novels are *The Mightiest Machine* (US 1947), a good example of his space opera period, and its sequel *The Incredible Planet* (US 1949). A dramatic account of a lunar rescue can be found in *The Moon is Hell* (US 1951), while *The Black Star Passes* (US 1953), *Islands of Space* (US 1956) and *Invaders from the Infinite* (US 1961) all feature the popular 'Arcot, Morey and Wade' series from the early *Amazing*. The 1951 RKO film production, *The Thing*, based on Campbell's story 'Who Goes There?', was acclaimed at the time but the basis of the tale had been changed substantially, for no very good reason and to little effect.

Campbell also edited many anthologies from *Astounding/Analog*, beginning with *The Astounding Science Fiction Anthology* (US 1952) and *Analog 1* (US 1962). *Analog Anthology* (UK 1965) contains twenty-six stories selected from *Prologue to Analog* (US 1962) and from the first two volumes of the *Analog* series.

Karel Čapek
The Czech philosopher and writer (born 1890) who introduced the world to the word 'Robot' in his play *R.U.R.* (US 1923). 'Rossum's Universal Robots', however, were not machines, but the chemically constructed beings which came to be known in the genre as 'Androids'. The word 'robot' in Czech means 'compulsory labour'; in Polish it means 'worker'; in science fiction it means the incredible collection of mechanical characters, both intended and otherwise, which have clanked through its pages to achieve a kind of immortality and to deposit frequent trails of rust, grease, and in Harry Harrison's *The Stainless Steel Rat*—soot!

In *R.U.R.*, Čapek's androids were persecuted by their human creators and subsequently rebelled, a familiar situation for this particular artificial lifeform in sf stories. He wrote of a comparable conflict in his novel *War With the Newts* (US 1939), in which the amphibians of the title aspire to the thinking condition. He explored the theme of longevity in the play *The Makropoulos Secret* (US

1925) and the world-destroying potential of atomic bombs in *Krakatit* (US 1925) and *The Absolute at Large* (US 1927).

As a humanitarian Čapek ranked with Stapledon and Wells. He died in 1938.

Paul Capon

Harry Paul Capon is a British film and television director who was born in Suffolk in 1912. His sf output has largely been aimed at the juvenile market, and his work in the adult field is mainly run-of-the-mill space opera. His novel *The Other Side of the Sun* (UK 1950) has been serialized on BBC radio.

E. J. Carnell

A renowned name among British editors, Edward John Carnell was born in 1912. An enthusiastic sf fan from an early age, he was to become Publicity Director and Editor of the British Interplanetary Society. Soon after seeing active service in the Second World War he made an abortive attempt to launch *New Worlds*, a former fan magazine, on to the professional market. Only three issues were produced before its publishers went out of business. Undeterred, Ted Carnell elicited the support of many fans and helped to form Nova Publications, the company which relaunched *New Worlds* in 1949 for a long and successful run. He edited it until 1964, although the publishing venture was taken over by Maclaren and Sons in 1953.

He also edited *New Worlds'* companion magazines, *Science Fantasy* and *Science Fiction Adventures,* and later compiled the *New Writings in SF* anthologies from 1964 until his death in 1972. His other anthologies were *No Place Like Earth* (UK 1952), *Gateway to Tomorrow* (UK 1954), *Best From New Worlds Science Fiction* (UK 1955), and *Gateway to the Stars* (UK 1955).

Carnell was instrumental in bringing many new British sf writers into print, John Brunner and J. G. Ballard among them. He was active behind the scenes in both the adjudicating of the International Fantasy Award and the selections for the Science Fiction Book Club. He took the Chair at the 15th World Science Fiction Convention held in London in 1957.

Terry Carr

Terry Gene Carr was born in Oregon in 1937. Formerly on the staff of the Scott Meredith literary agency, he became an editor for Ace Books, a leading US sf paperback publisher, in 1964. He has written some short stories and published various anthologies, including *Science Fiction for People Who Hate Science Fiction* (US 1966), *New Worlds of Fantasy* (US 1967), *Step Outside Your Mind* (UK 1967) and the annual series with Donald A. Wollheim: *World's Best Science Fiction* (beginning in the US in 1965). Of his novels, *Warlord of Kor* (US 1963) tells of an expedition to an alien world, and *Invasion From 2500* (US 1964, written in collaboration with Ted White) features an enemy which uses time travel to foresee all the defenders' ploys.

Carr is also well known for his activities within the Science Fiction Writers of America organization, both as an editor and as founder of their forum in 1967.

Lin Carter

Linwood Vrooman Carter is an American author, much of whose work can be classed in the same field as that of Robert E. Howard; in fact he has completed a number of Howard's unfinished drafts and produced new 'Conan' stories, such as *Conan the Buccaneer* (US 1971) in collaboration with L. Sprague de Camp. Born in 1930, he became a regular contributor to the fan magazines before taking up writing as a career. His science fiction stories include *The Man Without a Planet* (US 1966). Examples of his 'Sword and Sorcery' fantasies can be found in the 'Thongor' series, beginning with *The Wizard of Lemuria* (US 1965).

Recent stories in a similar vein are *Invisible Death* and *The Nemesis of Evil* (both US 1975). He has also compiled some anthologies of fantasy: *The Young Magicians* (US 1971), *Dragons, Elves and Heroes* (US 1971) and *Great Short Novels of Adult Fantasy I* (US 1972).

Edd Cartier

An American artist, Edd Cartier illustrated *Astounding* for John W. Campbell before joining the US Army during the Second World War and being wounded in the Battle of the Bulge. Later his illustrations appeared regularly in *Unknown*; but in 1954 he gave up freelance work to follow a career in flexographic art.

Cleve Cartmill

Deserves a mention as the writer who propelled the American secret service in the direction of *Astounding*'s offices with his short story 'Deadline' in 1944. The government bloodhounds had sniffed the suspicion that he might have acquired highly-classified data about the Manhattan Project (the code-name for the first atomic bomb). (Much the same reaction was experienced by Philip Wylie, and in the same context.) Cartmill was born in 1908 and followed various professions—from journalism to accountancy—before he died in 1964.

A. Bertram Chandler

Arthur Bertram Chandler is a British sf author and Merchant Navy officer who now lives in Australia. He was born in 1912 and served on tramp steamers around the coast of India before joining a passenger line on the Britain–Australia run. His first contribution to *Astounding* was 'This Means War' (1944) and he produced numerous short stories during the late 1940s and the 1950s. Many of these were written around his 'Mannschen Drive' method of space flight, which also featured in the novel *Bring Back Yesterday* (US 1961).

More recently Chandler has concentrated on novels set on the edge of the Milky Way—his 'Rim Worlds' series. Among these are *The Rim of Space* (US 1961), *Contraband From Otherspace* (US 1967), *The Road to the Rim* (US 1967), *False Fatherland* (US 1968) and *Catch the Star Winds* (US 1969). *The Deep Reaches of Space* (UK 1964) draws on his experience in the Merchant Navy, while *The Alternate Martians*, *Empress of Outer Space* and *Space Mercenaries* (all US 1965) illustrate a more fantastic approach.

Louis Charbonneau

Louis Charbonneau is an American author, born in Detroit in 1924. He served in the US Air Force in the Second World War and has been an advertising copywriter, journalist and author of radio plays. His first sf novel, *No Place on Earth* (US 1958) found favour as a gripping anti-utopian nightmare, an approach which he repeated in *The Sentinel Stars* (US 1963) and improvised on further in *Psychedilic-40* (US 1964). His *Corpus Earthling* (US 1960) recounts a psychological invasion of human heads by particularly repellent Martians.

Charles Chilton

British radio producer whose *Journey into Space* BBC serial achieved wide popularity, particularly among young listeners, in 1954. Charles Frederick William Chilton (born 1927) has also written the *Riders of the Range* Western series. The adventures of his radio space captain, Jet Morgan, are retold in three novels: *Journey into Space* (UK 1954), *The Red Planet* (UK 1956) and *The World in Peril* (UK 1960).

John Christopher

'John Christopher' is the pseudonym of British writer Christopher Sam Youd. Born in 1922, he was an sf addict before he reached his teens and later produced his own fan magazine. Having served in the British Army during the Second World War, he began writing short sf stories. Some of them can be found in the collection *The Twenty-Second Century* (UK 1954). His first novel, *The Year of the Comet* (UK 1955), told of future societies organized along the lines of business complexes.

He came to prominence in the sf field with the publication of *The Death of Grass* (UK 1956, retitled *No Blade of Grass* for subsequent serialization in the *Saturday Evening Post*). It depicts the rapid breakdown of society following a natural bacterial assault on grass and grain crops throughout the world.

Other novels of note are *The World in Winter* (UK 1962, retitled *The Long Winter* for the US in the same year), which presents the onset of a new Ice Age, *Cloud on Silver* (UK 1964), relating the discovery of an island of mutants in the South Pacific, and *A Wrinkle in the Skin* (UK 1965), a post-catastrophe earthquake story. Both *Pendulum* (UK 1968) and *The Guardians* (UK 1970) describe rebellious upheavals, the former following economic collapse, but the latter in an affluent age. He has also written a trilogy featuring the fight of Earth against alien invaders: *The White Mountains* (UK 1967), *The City of Gold and Lead* (UK 1967) and *The Pool of Fire* (UK 1968).

Arthur C. Clarke

Seer of *2001*, prophet of the space satellite, early star and later Chairman of the British Interplanetary Society, Arthur Charles Clarke has risen to a renowned position in the factual world of science which comes near to rivalling his importance as a giant of science fiction. He was born in Somerset in 1917 and became interested in astronomy during his early 'teens. At the same time he encountered the heady delights of the sf pulps and was soon an enthusiastic fan. He joined the Civil Service in 1936 and was a technical officer with the Royal Air Force during the Second World War. Afterwards he studied physics and mathematics at Kings' College, London.

Clarke's early interest in astronomy served him in good stead during his subsequent writing career. He began contributing factual articles to *Tales of Wonder* and short stories to the amateur publications of the British Science Fiction Association, of which he was a founder member in 1937. During the war he sent many articles to technical magazines and provided a remarkable forecast of communications satellites for the October 1945 issue of *Wireless World*. His short stories found their way to Walter Gillings' *Fantasy* in the UK and then to Campbell's *Astounding*. He became an enthusiastic and persuasive advocate of space flight in such books as *Interplanetary Flight* (UK 1950) and *The Exploration of Space* (UK 1951), the latter winning him the International Fantasy Award for non-fiction. Further popularizations followed, among them *The Exploration of the Moon* (UK 1954), *The Making of a Moon* (UK 1957), *The Challenge of the Space Ship* (US 1959), *The Coming of the Space Age* (US 1967), *Profiles of the Future* (UK 1962), *Man and Space* (US 1964), *Voices From the Sky* (US 1965) and *The Promise of Space* (US 1968).

In 1962 Clarke received the Unesco Kalinga Award in New Delhi for his efforts in popularizing science. Since 1956 he has lived in Ceylon, from where he has carried out many underwater photographic projects, the basis of several books with his partner Mike Wilson.

Clarke's science fiction stories frequently reflect his abiding and usually optimistic interest in space flight. Combined with a powerful sense of cosmic destiny which he admits inheriting from Stapledon, this quality makes his work memorable in a way quite different from his contemporaries. Rarely strong on characterization, his short stories are also noted for last-line twists which have been called contrived, but are no less effective for that. They can be found in his collections: *Expedition to Earth* (US 1953), *Reach for Tomorrow* (UK 1956), *Tales from the White Hart* (US 1957), *The Other Side of the Sky* (US 1958), *Tales of Ten Worlds* (US 1962), *The Nine Billion Names of God* (US 1967), *The Wind from the Sun* (UK 1972), *Of Time and Stars: the Worlds of Arthur C. Clarke* (UK 1972) and *The Best of Arthur C. Clarke 1937–1971* (UK 1973).

Among his novels are *The Sands of Mars* (UK 1951), *Prelude to Space* (US 1951) and *Islands in the Sky* (UK 1952), all accounts of early space exploration, and *Against the Fall of Night* (US 1953), a setting of the far future which was later revised as *The City and the Stars* (UK 1956). *Earthlight* (UK 1955) and *A Fall of Moondust* (UK 1961) tell respectively of conflict and rescue operations on the moon, while *The Deep Range* (UK 1957) draws on Clarke's undersea experience in an account of ocean farming. *Childhood's End* (US 1953) is a strikingly imaginative story of the translation of humanity into a united Overmind, following a century of supervision by advanced extraterrestrials; and *2001—A Space Odyssey* (UK 1968) is based on Kubrick's and Clarke's screenplay for the Hugo-winning film, which in turn was derived from Clarke's 1951 short story 'The Sentinel'. He has edited the anthology *Time Probe* (UK 1967) and introduced Silverberg's *Three for Tomorrow* (UK 1970). His most recent work, *Imperial Earth* (UK 1975), is subtitled 'A Fantasy of Love and Discord'.

Clarke won a Nebula for 'A Meeting with Medusa' in 1972, and another in the following year for *Rendezvous with Rama* (UK 1973) which also won a Hugo in 1974. He was Guest of Honour at the 14th World Science Fiction Convention in 1956. His work is assessed in *Arthur C. Clarke* (US 1976), edited by J. D. Olander and M. Greenberg.

I. F. Clarke

Ignatius Frederic Clarke (born 1918) is a lecturer in English whose checklist *The Tale of the Future* (UK 1961) is a useful guide to *futuristic* works published in Britain since 1644. However, its contents are limited to that category, and sf stories not actually set in the future are excluded. There are also some errors, as there are bound to be in any such work; but many have been carried over into a revised edition. The main value of the book is its listing of very early speculative writings.

Clarke's other contribution to the genre, *Voices Prophesying War 1763–1984* (UK 1966) is an interesting study of fictional wars and invasions, ranging from Chesney's *The Battle of Dorking* and Wells's *The War of the Worlds* to Orwell's *Nineteen Eighty-four* and Huxley's *Ape and Essence*.

Hal Clement

'Hal Clement' is the pseudonym of Harry Clement Stubbs, an American spare-time sf writer who was born in Massachusetts in 1922. Educated at Harvard and Boston Universities, he served as a pilot in the Second World War and later became a science teacher. His first story was 'Proof' in *Astounding* in 1942, followed by many others in the same magazine.

Clement is noted for a highly scientific approach in his tales. The best-known, *Mission of Gravity* (US 1954), deals with an expedition to the planet Mesklin where gravity ranges from 3g at the equator to 700g at the poles. Humans are trying with native help to retrieve a crashed rocket probe. Among his earlier novels are *From Outer Space* (US 1949), which describes an alien invasion via human bodies; *Needle* (US 1950), a variation on the symbiosis theme within the framework of a detective story; and *Iceworld* (US 1953), telling of a narcotics hunt on a frozen planet. Both *Cycle of Fire* (US 1957) and *Close to Critical* (US 1958) are further tales of crash landings on inhospitable worlds. Three of Clement's novelettes, 'Assumption Unjustified', 'Technical Error' and 'Impediment' are collected in *Natives of Space* (US 1965); and a number of his shorter stories can be found in *Space Lash* (US 1969).

Mark Clifton

Hugo winner in 1955, for the novel *They'd Rather Be Right* (US 1957, written in collaboration with Frank Riley), Mark Clifton was born in the US in 1906. He spent some twenty-five years in personnel work in industry and did not turn to writing until the last ten years of his life. He died in 1963. As a fairly regular contributor to *Astounding* he was noted for his stories in the 'Ralph Kennedy' and 'Bossy' (a master computer) series, and for other tales dealing with psi-powers.

They'd Rather Be Right is, in fact, a 'Bossy' novel, in which the computer runs into trouble by providing a means for human immortality. Ralph Kennedy also appears in Clifton's solo effort *When They Come From Space* (US 1962), an amusing satirical view of inefficient bureaucracy confronted by handsome and apparently agreeable extraterrestrials.

Mildred Clingerman

Only an occasional writer, Mildred McElroy Clingerman was born in Oklahoma in 1918. She first appeared in *The Magazine of Fantasy and Science Fiction* in 1952 with 'Minister Without Portfolio'. A collection of her stories from that magazine and others, noted for their blending of sf themes with elements of fantasy and the supernatural, has been published as *A Cupful of Space* (US 1961).

Stanton A. Coblentz

American poet and author, Stanton Arthur Coblentz (born 1896) was among the early popular contributors to *Amazing Stories* in the late 1920s. Heartily imbued with 'Sense of Wonder' and frequent satire, his novels can be found in the original copies of *Amazing Stories Quarterly* where his first, *The Sunken World*, appeared in 1928. More recent book reprints of his tales include *Under the Triple Suns* (US 1955), *The Runaway World* (US 1961) and *Moon People* (US 1964).

His satirical approach is well represented by *Hidden World* (US 1957), *Next Door to the Sun* (US 1960) and *Lord of Tranerica* (US 1966). He has made at least one excursion into prehistory, in *The Wonder Stick* (US 1929), and has produced a variety of verse collections and anthologies.

Theodore Cogswell

US author and Professor of English, Theodore Rose Cogswell was born in Pennsylvania in 1918. He shares with George Orwell the distinction of having been with the Republicans during the Spanish Civil War (in his case driving an ambulance), and he later served in the US Army Air Force during the Second World War. Since then he has taught in a number of universities and colleges. He began writing sf and fantasy short stories in the early 1950s, his first published being 'The Specter General' in *Astounding* in 1952. Two collections have appeared to date: *The Wall Around the World* (US 1962), the title story being one of his most memorable, and *The Third Eye* (US 1968).

Everett B. Cole

Former professional soldier at Fort Douglas, Utah, Everett B. Cole was born in 1910. His popular 'Philosophical Corps' series appeared in *Astounding* during the 1950s and formed the basis for a novel, *The Philosophical Corps* (US 1962), in which Commander A-Riman, the 'Fighting Philosopher', pursues a heady space-operatic career fighting alien 'degraders'.

D. G. Compton

David Guy Compton was born in London in 1930. After a decade of struggling to establish himself as a writer in the 1950s he achieved some success in radio playwriting and also has a number of sf novels to his name. His first, *The Quality of Mercy* (UK 1965), is a dramatic treatment of the population explosion theme, while its successor, *Farewell, Earth's Bliss* (UK 1966), tells of the early hardships of a colonial convict settlement on Mars.

In his later work Compton has become noted for his powers of characterization and the authentic presentation of backgrounds. His inventiveness and the wide range of his ideas are particularly evident in *Synthajoy* (UK 1968), *Chronocules* (US 1970), which is a nightmarish story of time research in a period of increasing chaos, and *The Electric Crocodile* (UK 1970). *The Missionaries* (UK 1972) and *The Unsleeping Eye* (US 1974), an account of a man whose eyes are linked to TV circuits for the vicarious pleasure of viewers, maintain the same high standard.

Groff Conklin

The most productive of American sf anthologists, Edward Groff Conklin was born in 1904. In the course of his career he was editor and scientific researcher in a variety of publishing and advertising fields, a reviewer for *Galaxy* and editorial consultant for the American Diabetes Association. He died in 1968. He first appeared on the sf scene with what is still one of the finest of all anthologies, appropriately titled *The Best of Science Fiction* (US 1946). At the time it was also one of the earliest such compilations. Together with Healey's and McComas's *Adventures in Time and Space* it helped to bring science fiction to a wider audience and to encourage new writers in the immediate post-war era. It was also graced with a preface by John W. Campbell.

Conklin's subsequent anthologies, all of which are valuable for their diversity and sureness of selection, run as follows: *A Treasury of Science Fiction* (US 1948), *The Big Book of Science Fiction* (US 1950), *The Science Fiction Galaxy* (US 1950), *In The Grip of Terror* (US 1951), *Possible Worlds of Science Fiction* (US & UK 1951), *The Omnibus of Science Fiction* (US 1952), *Crossroads in Time* (US 1953), *Science Fiction Adventures in Dimension* (US 1953), *Science Fiction Thinking Machines* (US 1954), *6 Great Short Novels of Science Fiction* (US 1954), *Science Fiction Adventures in Mutation* (US 1955), *Science Fiction Terror Tales* (US 1955), *Operation Future* (US 1955), *Four for the Future* (US 1959), *13 Great Stories of Science Fiction* (US 1960), *Six Great Short Science Fiction Novels* (US 1960), *Great Science Fiction by Scientists* (US 1962), *Worlds of When* (US 1962), *Great Science Fiction About Doctors* (US 1963, in collaboration with N. D. Fabricant), *Great Stories of Space Travel* (US 1963), *12 Great Classics of Science Fiction* (US 1963), *17 × Infinity* (US & UK 1963), *Dimension 4* (US 1964), *Five-Odd* (US 1964), *5 Unearthly Visions* (US 1965), *Giants Unleashed* (US 1965), *13 Above the Night* (US 1965), *Another Part of the Galaxy* (US 1966), *Seven Come Infinity* (US 1966), *Elsewhere and Elsewhen* (US 1968) and *Seven Trips Through Time and Space* (US 1968).

Robert Conquest

George Robert Ackworth Conquest was born at Malvern, England, in 1917. A distinguished scholar, poet and lecturer, he has published one sf novel, *A World of Difference* (UK 1955), but is chiefly

known in sf circles for his joint production of the *Spectrum* anthologies
with Kingsley Amis.

Edmund Cooper

Former teacher, merchant seaman and industrial writer, Edmund
Cooper (born 1926) has maintained a steady output of novels over
the past two decades which have brought him into the front rank of
British sf authors. He has also been the *Sunday Times* sf reviewer
for a number of years. There are few themes to which Cooper has
not given some attention in his stories—he is currently spinning out
a racy confection of space opera in the *Expendables* series under the
pen-name of 'Richard Avery'. His serious early work includes
Deadly Image (US 1958), a notable treatment of androids; *Seed of
Light* (UK 1959), based on the 'travelling ark' theme; and *Transit*
(UK 1964), in which humanity is judged against another galactic
species (and in which the central character happens to be called
Richard Avery).

Cooper's *forte* is his portrayal of suspiciously Heinlein-type
male heroes who are nevertheless interested in women as human
beings, and who act out their particular destinies (not always
gloriously) against unfamiliar backdrops. They may be found in
Five to Twelve (UK 1968) where women outnumber men by that
ratio, in *All Fools' Day* (UK 1966), a psychopaths' paradise after
the 'sane' members of society have committed suicide, and in *Sea-
Horse in the Sky* (UK 1969). A sympathetic treatment of an alien
society distinguishes *A Far Sunset* (UK 1967), while *The Overman
Culture* (UK 1973) relates the attempt of a master computer to
recreate human civilization in a post-catastrophe world. An allied
theme appears in *The Cloud Walker* (UK 1973), telling of the
struggle to re-attain heavier-than-air flight in a future Luddite
world.

Other novels of note are: *Son of Kronk* (UK 1970), *The Last
Continent* (UK 1970), *Prisoner of Fire* (UK 1974) and *The Slaves of
Heaven* (UK 1975). Cooper's short stories are available in several
collections, including *Tomorrow's Gift* (US 1958), *Tomorrow Came*
(UK 1963) and *News from Elsewhere* (UK 1968).

Alfred Coppel

Alfred Coppel was born in California in 1921. Before he had a chance to pursue any profession he was caught up in the throes of the Second World War, and served as a fighter pilot. While much of his subsequent writing has not been science fiction, he has produced a quantity of short stories in the genre and a convincing post-catastrophe novel, *Dark December* (US 1960), in which a young flier searches for his family in the aftermath of a nuclear war.

Juanita Coulson

American housewife and long-time fan. In 1965 she won a Hugo for the fan magazine *Yandro*, jointly edited with her husband. Juanita Coulson was born in Indiana in 1933. Originally intended for a career in teaching, she gave it up after a year. Her first published story was 'Another Rib', which she wrote as 'John Jay Wells' in collaboration with Marion Zimmer Bradley. It appeared in *The Magazine of Fantasy and Science Fiction* in 1963. Since then she has produced several novels, among them: *Crises on Cheiron* (US 1967), *The Singing Stones* (US 1968) and *War of the Wizards* (UK 1970).

Richard Cowper

'Richard Cowper' is the sf pseudonym of the British writer Colin Middleton Murry. He was born in Dorset in 1926 and is the son of the well-known critic and author, John Middleton Murry. A relative newcomer to the sf scene (he was teaching English until 1967), he has recently established a reputation as an imaginative and evocative writer. His first science fiction novel under his pen-name, *Breakthrough* (UK 1967), was a highly effective treatment of ESP. It was followed by *Phoenix* (UK 1968), and *Kuldesak* (UK 1972)—a post-catastrophe novel in which men emerge after 2,000 years underground. *The Twilight of Briareus* (US 1974) recounts the birth of a mutated race after Earth has been bathed in the cosmic particles of a supernova 130 light years distant. Other recent novels of note are *Clone* (UK 1974), which is an accomplished satire about a cloned man who can teleport and induce hallucinations in others, and *Worlds Apart* (UK 1974). Four of his shorter tales are collected in *The Custodians* (UK 1976).

Michael Crichton

American author, born in Chicago in 1942, who enjoyed an over-night success with his story *The Andromeda Strain* (US 1969). The novel was a Book-of-the-Month Club selection in the US and was subsequently filmed by Robert Wise. It tells compellingly of the race to find an antidote to a lethal alien organism brought to Earth by a returning space satellite.

Edmund Crispin

'Edmund Crispin' is the pen-name of Robert Bruce Montgomery, who was born in England in 1921. He is a writer and editor of mystery stories and a reviewer in that field for the *Sunday Times*. He also composes music under his real name. One-time Chairman of the British Science Fiction Association, Crispin's principal con-tribution to the genre has been the compilation of a number of anthologies, including the *Best SF* series, which began in the UK in 1955, *The Stars and Under* (UK 1968) and *Outwards From Earth* (UK 1974).

Kendall Foster Crossen

US author and newspaperman (born 1910) who has written much detective fiction and some sf stories under several pseudonyms. He produced a series of humorous 'Manning Draco' tales for *Thrilling Wonder Stories* in the early 1950s, some of which were later amalgamated to form *Once Upon a Star* (US 1953). Another short story of note is 'The Ambassadors from Venus' (1951), in which intelligent trees dismiss Man as a parasite.

Among Crossen's sf novels are *Year of Consent* (US 1954) and *The Rest Must Die* (US 1959, written under the pen-name 'Richard Foster'). He has also edited the anthologies: *Adventures in Tomor-row* (US 1951) and *Future Tense* (US 1952).

Ray Cummings

A cherished name among the pioneers, Raymond King Cummings enjoyed what today would be the dubious distinction of being born in Times Square, New York. (It has changed since his arrival in 1887.) As a young man he drifted into various adventurous occupations—gold prospecting, oil fields, orange plantations—before becoming editor to the rapacious patent collector Thomas Alva Edison. It was then that he took to writing. Probably his most famous story is also one of his earliest, 'The Girl in the Golden Atom' (1919), to which he wrote many sequels. Gernsback used him in the early *Amazing*, but he never really fulfilled the promise of his first sf stories, although he contributed to the genre for thirty years before his death in 1957.

Among his 'Atom' variations (set in sub-atomic worlds) are *Beyond the Stars* (US 1942), *The Princess of the Atom* (US 1950), *Beyond the Vanishing Point* (US 1958) and *Explorers Into Infinity* (US 1965). Examples of his space opera include *Brigands of the Moon* (US 1931) and *Wandl the Invader* (US 1961).

Roald Dahl
Roald Dahl is best known as a purveyor of chillingly well-written vignettes, some of which qualify as science fiction, and most of which bear his individual stamp of macabre and sometimes emetic nastiness. Born in Wales in 1916, of Norwegian parentage, he served in the Royal Air Force during the Second World War. Injured and subsequently posted to the US, he began writing flying tales before finding his true *métier*. His stories can be read in two collections: *Someone Like You* (US 1953) and *Kiss, Kiss* (US 1960).

Basil Davenport
US anthologist (born 1905) who concentrated more on horror and ghost collections than on science fiction. However, at least one of his compilations contains the genuine article: *Invisible Men* (US 1960), which includes stories by Bradbury, Gold, Sturgeon and Wells. He also wrote a useful study of the genre, *Inquiry Into Science Fiction* (US 1955), and provided an introduction for *The Science Fiction Novel* (US 1964) which is a valuable collection of analyses of the form by Heinlein, Kornbluth, Bester and Bloch. Basil Davenport died in 1966.

Leonard Daventry

Born in London in 1915, Leonard John Daventry followed his father into the British Army in 1932. A polished writer in other fields—he won the Atlantic Literary Award in 1946—he has only recently arrived on the sf scene. His first sf novel, *A Man of Double Deed* (UK 1965), is an account of telepaths attempting to maintain order in a world recovering from a nuclear war, but facing growing delinquency amongst its young. Further novels are *Degree XII* and *Twenty-One Billionth Paradox* (both UK 1972).

Avram Davidson

American author, editor and anthologist, Avram Davidson was born in Yonkers in 1923. He saw service with the US Navy in the Second World War and later with the Israeli Army in the Middle East. He began writing science fiction short stories during the 1950s, the first published being 'My Boy Friend's Name Is Jello' (1954) in *The Magazine of Fantasy and Science Fiction*. He became Executive Editor of that publication in 1962, leaving in 1964 to devote himself fully to his own writing. His tales can also be found in the collections *Or All the Seas With Oysters* (US 1962), the title story of which won him a Hugo in 1958, and *What Strange Stars and Skies* (US 1965).

Among Davidson's novels, an unusual treatment of parallel worlds and universes can be found in *Masters of the Maze* (US 1965). Space and planetary adventures are related in *Mutiny in Space* (US 1964), *Rork!* (US 1965) and *Enemy of My Enemy* (US 1966). His other books include the novels *Rogue Dragon* (US 1965) and *The Kar-Chee Reign* (US 1966), and the anthologies *Best From Fantasy and Science Fiction*, series 12–14 (US 1963, 1964 and 1965). His collaboration with Ward Moore, *Joyleg* (US 1962), tells of a survivor of the American Civil War in a 'lost world' situated in the US.

Julie Davis

Julie Davis became editor of the British magazine *Science Fiction Monthly* on its launch by New English Library in 1974. Hands other than hers helped to shape the basic format and contents mix, decreeing that it should combine the two categories of fandom and actual sf writing. It did work reasonably well, though perhaps satisfying no one entirely. The magazine ran regular art competitions which were well supported, and it featured some noted interviews with J. G. Ballard, Edmund Cooper, Harlan Ellison, and others. A futher high point was a long series on 'Modern Masters of Science Fiction' contributed by Walter Gillings, who also handled the query column. The magazine ceased publication in mid-1976.

Bradford M. Day

Bradford Marshall Day (born 1916) is an American sf fan whose main published contribution to the field is *The Complete Checklist of Science-Fiction Magazines* (US 1961). A valuable guide for its time, it lists not only all the sf magazines which had appeared before its publication, including many foreign-language items, but also a good number of magazines which only occasionally ran sf stories. Further compilations are *The Supplemental Checklist of Fantastic Literature* (US 1963) and *The Checklist of Fantastic Literature in Paperbound Books* (US 1965).

Donald B. Day

Science fiction fan, publisher and compiler, Donald Bryne Day was born in Syracuse, New York, in 1909. In 1935 he began collecting material for what was to be the first full-scale bibliography of the modern sf short story, *Index to the Science-Fiction Magazines, 1926–1950* (US 1952). It includes the authors and titles of all the stories published in 58 different magazines during the period mentioned and is also an enlightening guide through the undergrowth of pseudonyms with which the genre abounds.

Day was Chairman of the 8th World Science Fiction Convention, held in Portland, Oregon in 1950. His pioneering work in the indexing field has been followed by further authoritative compilations: *Index to the Science Fiction Magazines, 1951–1965* (US 1966) compiled by Erwin S. Strauss for the MIT Science Fiction Society, *The Index of Science Fiction Magazines, 1951–1965*, compiled by Norm Metcalf (US 1968) and *Index to the Science-Fiction Magazines, 1966–1970* (US 1971) compiled by the New England Science Fiction Association.

L. Sprague de Camp

A highly gifted all-rounder, Lyon Sprague de Camp (born 1907) is as well known for his fantasies, his science popularizations and his historical novels, as he is for his work in the sf field. Originally a graduate in aeronautical engineering, he was a patents engineer and editor before turning to freelance writing when he was thirty. His work appeared in many of the science fiction magazines from the late 1930s and included the thinking bear series 'Johnny Black' in *Astounding*, and the 'Gavagan's Bar' fantasy stories (written with Fletcher Pratt) in *The Magazine of Fantasy and Science Fiction*.

Wearing his fantasy mantle, de Camp has edited and refurbished various of Robert E. Howard's 'Conan' stories and produced new ones in collaboration with Lin Carter. Much of his science fiction also contains elements of 'romantic barbarism'. This can be found in *Lest Darkness Fall* (US 1941), in which a time traveller attempts to revive the Roman Empire, and in *The Search for Zei* (US 1962) and its sequel *The Hand of Zei* (US 1963). His long series of 'Viagens Interplanetarias' stories gave rise to the collection *The Continent Makers and Other Tales of the Viagens* (US 1953), and the novel *Rogue Queen* (US 1951). The tales are mainly built around interstellar traders in the 21st and 22nd centuries. Other novels include *The Carnelian Cube* (US 1948, again written with Fletcher Pratt) and a zany account of Man ruled by kangaroo-like aliens, *Divide and Rule* (US 1948); also *Genus Homo* (US 1950) in collaboration with P. Schuyler Miller.

Further collections of de Camp's stories are *Sprague de Camp's New Anthology* (UK 1953) and *A Gun for Dinosaur* (US 1963). He has compiled a number of fantasy anthologies and also produced *Science-Fiction Handbook* (US 1953), a genuinely useful guide to would-be sf writers with sound advice on plotting, construction and how to attempt to sell the finished product. A revised edition, which actually said nothing new, ran in the US in 1975.

Miriam Allen de Ford

A notable woman on the American literary scene, Miriam Allen de Ford was born in Philadelphia in 1888. Her career included some forty years of prolific journalism, public relations work, contributing editorship of *The Humanist*, and much freelance writing. Her science fiction and fantasy stories have appeared in such magazines as *Amazing* and *Galaxy*, and her interest in crime cases is reflected in an anthology of science fiction stories with a criminal slant: *Space, Time and Crime* (US 1968). *Xenogenesis* (US 1969) is a collection of her own tales in which sexual fantasy often plays a part, and 'The Malley System' appears in Harlan Ellison's anthology *Dangerous Visions*. She died in 1976.

Samuel R. Delany

A recent starshell on the science fiction horizon, Samuel Ray Delany has already collected more awards for his stories than many older and as notable writers have amassed during their entire careers. A negro, he was born in Harlem in 1942 and took an early interest in poetry and writing. *The Jewels of Aptor* (US 1962), his first novel, was written when he was nineteen. There followed the 'Toromon' trilogy, *Captives of the Flame* (US 1963), *The Towers of Toron* (US 1964) and *City of a Thousand Suns* (US 1965), which chronicled the machinations of a future Earth society supported by planetary colonies.

'Chip' Delany's work commands attention by its quality of style and poetic symbolism, products of both erudition and a keen imagination. These can be seen in *The Ballad of Beta-2* (US 1965), a travelling ark variation; in *Empire Star* (US 1966), and in *Babel-17* (US 1966) which won a Nebula Award as the best novel of the year and tells of the attempt of a poetess to decipher an alien language.

With *The Einstein Intersection* (US 1967), an allegorical quest into the myths and motivations of Man, Delany carried off his second Nebula and capped it with a third, also in 1967, for his short story 'Aye, and Gomorrah . . .' written for Harlan Ellison's mammoth anthology, *Dangerous Visions*. Almost as if by habit, he collected a fourth in 1969 for 'Time Considered as a Helix of Semi-Precious Stones' which *also* won a Hugo in 1970. His long novel *Nova* (UK 1968) tells of the rivalry between two leading families in a galactic empire setting. Among his other recent novels is *Dhalgren* (US 1974), a notable post-catastrophe vision. To date, Delany has written few short stories, but has at least one collection: *Driftglass* (US 1971).

Lester del Rey

A man whose supposed forenames have defeated more than one

compiler, Ramón Alvarez del Rey (born US 1915) is a well-known author and editor. Not much is known of his early career before he turned to writing. His first story, 'The Faithful', was published in *Astounding* in 1938. More followed and he also contributed to *Unknown*, wrote 'juveniles', and briefly edited *Fantasy Fiction*, *Science Fiction Adventures* and *Space Science Fiction* at the beginning of the 1950s. He became Managing Editor of *Galaxy* and *If* in 1968.

Del Rey is noted for his often vivid writing and for his imaginative treatment of a number of themes. His memorable robot story 'Helen O'Loy', included in the collection . . . *And Some Were Human* (US 1948), tells sympathetically of the problems of a man married to a robot who continues to appear physically young while he ages. More of his stories can be found in other collections: *Robots and Changelings* (US 1957) and *Mortals and Monsters* (US 1965).

While the majority of del Rey's novels have been written for the juvenile market, he has produced some impressive work in the adult field—none more so than *The Eleventh Commandment* (US 1962), a post-catastrophe story in which a new Catholic Church appears actively to be encouraging the gross overpopulation of an already starving world. The plot revolves around the gradual enlightenment to the realities on Earth of a scientist deported from Mars for genetic reasons. *Nerves* (US 1956) is a tightly-narrated account of a nuclear power station accident, and *The Sky is Falling* (originally published in the US with *Badge of Infamy*, 1963) is a subtle blending of science and fantasy in a parallel world where the heavens really are a solid bowl and the stars mere points of light.

Among del Rey's other adult novels are *Police Your Planet* (US 1957, under the pseudonym of 'Erik Van Lhin'), *The Scheme of Things* (US 1966) and the full-blown fantasy *Day of the Giants* (US 1959). He has also written a number of factual books on space flight and geophysical subjects. His compilation *Fantastic Science-Fiction Art* (US 1975) is one of many such illustrated potpourris now available.

August Derleth

August William Derleth was an American writer, editor and anthologist who became noted for his championship of H. P. Lovecraft. He was born in Wisconsin in 1909 and took to writing while in his early 'teens. His main interests lay in the mystery and supernatural fields and many of his stories appeared in *Weird Tales*. In 1939 he founded the Arkham House publishing venture with Donald Wandrei specifically to republish Lovecraft's work. The company continued with the publication of other writers' stories in the weird category and was still in operation at the time of Derleth's death in 1971.

Among his anthologies, many concerned with horror and the macabre, the following are devoted to science fiction: *Strange Ports of Call* (US 1948), *The Other Side of the Moon* (US 1949), *Beyond Time and Space* (US 1950), *Far Boundaries* (US 1951), *The Outer Reaches* (US 1951), *Beachheads in Space* (US 1952), *Worlds of Tomorrow* (US 1953) and *Time to Come* (US 1954).

Philip K. Dick

A versatile and prolific American writer, Philip Kendred Dick was born in Chicago in 1928. He entered the sf field in the 1950s and has since written many novels. Noted for the variety of themes he has tackled, he is particularly adept at 'awareness of reality' stories— *Time Out of Joint* (US 1959) being a good example. It tells of a man's gradual realization that he is not in fact living in what he had thought was mid-twentieth-century America.

His other novels of the 1950s include *Solar Lottery* (US 1955), in which future politics are run along quiz-show lines, and *Eye in the Sky*, *Vulcan's Hammer* and *The Man Who Japed* (all US 1956), also *The Cosmic Puppets* (US 1957).

Among his time stories are *The World Jones Made* (US 1956), a post-catastrophe tale featuring a leader who can see one year ahead in the future, *Dr Futurity* (US 1960), in which a physician is abducted from present times, and *Now Wait for Last Year* (US 1967), where time travel is achieved by means of a hallucinogen.

His notable alternative history, *The Man in the High Castle* (US 1962), a Hugo winner of 1963, depicts the US following its conquest by the Axis powers in the Second World War. What may one day be regarded as the definitive story on androids can be read in *Do Androids Dream of Electric Sheep?* (US 1968), another post-catastrophe treatment in which a person's most treasured possession is a live animal, or, failing that, an android surrogate. *Galactic*

84

Pot-Healer (US 1969) is a witty account of a ceramics repairer invited on a chancy enterprise to another world.

Further books are *The Game Players of Titan* (US 1963), *Clans of the Alphane Moon* (US 1964), *The Penultimate Truth* (US 1964), *The Simulacra* (US 1964), *Martian Time-Slip* (US 1964), *The Three Stigmata of Palmer Eldritch* (US 1965), *Dr Bloodmoney, or How We Got Along After the Bomb* (US 1965), *The Unteleported Man* (US 1966), *The Zap Gun* (US 1967), *Counter Clock World* (US 1967), *Ganymede Takeover* (US 1967, written in collaboration with R. Nelson), *A Maze of Death* (US 1970), *Ubik* (US 1970) and *Our Friends from Frolix 8* (US 1970). His short stories can be found in a number of collections: *A Handful of Darkness* (US 1955), *The Variable Man* (US 1956), *The Preserving Machine and other stories* (US 1969) and *The Book of Philip K. Dick* (US 1973).

A study of his work, *Philip K. Dick: Electric Shepherd* (Australia 1975), edited by Bruce Gillespie with an introduction by Roger Zelazny, includes a contribution by Stanislaw Lem.

Gordon R. Dickson

Born in Alberta in 1923, Gordon Rupert Dickson moved to the US at the age of 13. After three years' service in the Second World War he returned to his studies at the University of Minnesota and then took to writing. He has had a great many stories published in the science fiction magazines, his 'Soldier, Ask Not' winning a Hugo in 1965 and 'Call Him Lord' a Nebula in 1966. He has collaborated with both Poul Anderson and Keith Laumer, and has produced a number of 'juveniles' in the 'Robby Hoenig' series and in *Space Winners* (US 1965).

Dickson's adult science fiction novels began with *Alien From Arcturus* (US 1956) and *Mankind on the Run* (US 1956). *The Genetic General* (US 1960) is a superior treatment of a future galactic civilization as a background to the progress of a young soldier. Its sequel, *Soldier, Ask Not* (US 1967), is a novel-length expansion of his Hugo-winning story. The mutant theme is explored in *Time to Teleport* (US 1960), and a man's intrusion into an alien's brain in *The Alien Way* (US 1965). *Delusion World* (US 1961) is an unusual treatment of two co-existing societies incapable of perceiving each other's presence.

Planetary adventures and exploration feature in *Naked to the*

Stars (US 1961) and *Spatial Delivery* (US 1961). Among his more recent books are *Hour of the Horde* (US 1970), *The Outposter* (US 1972) and *Sleepwalkers' World* (US 1971), in which populations undergo enforced sleep while energy is drawn from the Earth's core. *The Lifeship* (US 1976) is a collaboration with Harry Harrison.

Dickson's respective collaborations with Anderson and Laumer are *Earthman's Burden* (US 1957) and *Planet Run* (US 1967).

His *Dorsai* trilogy (an epic space opera based on serials appearing in *Astounding* from 1959 onwards) consists of *Soldier, Ask Not, Tactics of Mistake* and *Dorsai!* (all republished as paperbacks in the UK in 1975). Some of his stories are collected in *The Star Road* (US 1973), and he has also edited *Combat SF* (US 1975), an anthology devoted to accounts of armed conflict.

T. E. Dikty

American anthologist born in 1920, Thaddeus Eugene Dikty collaborated with E. F. Bleiler on the early *Best Science Fiction Stories and Novels* series and continued it singlehanded from 1955 until 1958. His other anthologies include *Great Science Fiction Stories About Mars* (US 1966), *Great Science Fiction Stories About the Moon* (US 1967) and the 'juvenile', *Every Boy's Book of Outer Space Stories* (US 1960).

Thomas M. Disch

A noted arrival in the sf field of the 1960s, Thomas Michael Disch became a freelance writer in 1964 after working for a year in advertising. He was born in Iowa in 1940 and educated at New York University. His first published sf story, 'The Double Timer' appeared in *Fantastic* in 1962.

Disch has been regarded in some quarters as part of the 'New Wave', perhaps by virtue of his one-time association with Moorcock's *New Worlds*, but the label seems inappropriate. His first novel, *The Genocides* (US 1965), is a vivid account of Man going ineffectually to his doom while Earth is used as nothing more than a vast vegetable plot by unseen extraterrestrials. A comparable presentation of the relative unimportance of humans to an alien culture can be found in *Mankind Under the Leash* (US 1966).

Echo Round His Bones (US 1966) tells of an unexpected 'echo effect' produced by matter transmission, while in *Camp Concentration* (UK 1967) intelligence in selected prisoners is temporarily enhanced at the eventual cost of their lives. *334* (UK 1972) is an oppressive view of a dying culture in a future over-populated world.

If Disch's outlook appears essentially gloomy, there is also humour to be found in his story collections: *One Hundred and Two H-Bombs* (UK 1966), *Under Compulsion* (UK 1968), *White Fang Goes Dingo* (UK 1971) and *Getting Into Death: The Best Short Stories of Thomas M. Disch* (UK 1973). He has also written *The Prisoner* (US 1969), based on British ITV's stories starring Patrick McGoohan (who actually initiated the idea for the series), and has compiled the anthologies *The Ruins of Earth* (UK 1973) and *Bad Moon Rising* (UK 1974). *Black Alice* (US 1968) was written in collaboration with John T. Sladek.

G. D. Doherty

Geoffrey Donald Doherty (born 1927) is a senior English teacher in Manchester. He has produced the following anthologies specifically for reading in schools: *Aspects of Science Fiction* (UK 1959), *Second Orbit* (UK 1965) and *Stories From Science Fiction* (UK 1966). An excellent selection of modern writers, together with examples of Wells, is included—plus questions, exercises and further reading lists.

Elliott Dold

American illustrator whose work in *Astounding* during the 1930s maintained a consistently high standard. Earlier he had done scenic painting, and visuals for commercial advertising. He was *Astounding*'s chief artist from 1934 to 1938, mostly in the magazine's pre-Campbell era, and he also edited the short-lived *Miracle Science & Fantasy Stories* in 1931.

Sonya Dorman

American authoress whose various forms of employment have included cook, receptionist, flamenco dancer and breeder of

Japanese Akitas. In the past few years Sonya Dorman has contributed to a number of popular magazines and her work in the science fiction field has appeared in *Galaxy* and *The Magazine of Fantasy and Science Fiction*. Good examples of her narrative power are the stories, 'Splice of Life' in Damon Knight's anthology *Orbit I* (US 1966) and 'Go, Go, Go, Said the Bird' in Harlan Ellison's *Dangerous Visions* (US 1967). She is also a noted poetess.

A. Conan Doyle

The creator of Sherlock Holmes, Sir Arthur Conan Doyle might possibly have enjoyed a reputation approaching Edgar Rice Burroughs', had he written more scientific romances and devoted less time to his enigmatic detective. He was born in Edinburgh in 1859 and trained originally as a doctor, a practice which he actually followed during the 1880s and early 1890s. However, public enthusiasm for Holmes and the proceeds of his other popular writings persuaded him to abandon medicine for a literary career. He died in 1930.

Doyle wrote only a small amount of science fiction, but nearly all of it was good, and his story of the discovery of a prehistoric plateau in South America, *The Lost World* (UK 1912), has twice been filmed and is rarely out of print. Its main 'scientific' character, Professor George Edward Challenger, also features in *The Poison Belt* (UK 1913) and in a number of short stories which were included in the collection *The Professor Challenger Stories* (UK 1952). Another collection containing science fiction is *The Maracot Deep and Other Stories* (US 1929), while two of Doyle's most notable sf tales, 'The Horror of the Heights' and 'The Great Keinplatz Experiment' can be found in *The Conan Doyle Stories* (UK 1929).

Gardner R. Dozois

An American writer, born in the 1940s, who sold his first sf story when he was seventeen. He has since produced some distinguished work for the *Orbit* and *New Dimensions* anthologies; his 'Strangers' was short-listed for a Hugo in 1975 (it can be read in Silverberg's *New Dimensions 4*). He has also compiled the anthology *A Day in the Life* (US 1972).

David Duncan

David Duncan was born in Montana in 1913. Formerly an economist, he has been writing full-time since the 1940s and is the author of many books, screenplays and television scripts. His work in science fiction has been limited, but of note. His first sf novel was *The Shade of Time* (US 1946), followed nearly a decade later by *Dark Dominion* (US 1954), a dramatic account of the first satellite launch. *Beyond Eden* (US 1955) relates the accidental formulation of a miraculous by-product in a saline distillation process, while *Occam's Razor* (US 1957) tells of the discovery of a parallel world which, in a roundabout way, prevents the outbreak of nuclear war on Earth.

G. C. Edmondson

An American born in Guatemala in 1922, and a former US Navy man —real name José Mario Garry Ordonez Edmondson y Cotton. He began contributing short stories to *The Magazine of Fantasy and Science Fiction* at the end of the 1950s, and a good representation of these appears in his collection *Stranger Than You Think* (US 1965). His novel, *The Ship That Sailed the Time Stream* (US 1965), draws on nautical experience while depicting the excursions through time of a US Navy craft.

Geo Alec Effinger

A newcomer to the scene, Effinger is an American writer who attended the Clarion Writers' Workshop in 1970. He has had a number of short stories published in sf magazines and anthologies, and his *What Entropy Means to Me* (US 1972) is described as 'Sword and Sorcery' with a refreshing difference—an accolade equivalent in sf terms to the sound of one hand clapping. It might be added that the description comes from the jacket blurb, and is a good example of how not to sell the product.

Larry Eisenberg

US writer noted for his humorous approach, Eisenberg has contributed to *Harpers* and other American magazines. His story 'The Pirokin Effect' appears in Judith Merril's anthology *The Year's*

Best SF (10th in the series), and 'What Happened to August Clarot?' seems to have driven even Harlan Ellison into a microsecond of speechlessness when he included it in *Dangerous Visions* in 1967.

Gordon Eklund
A Californian who has seen service in the US Air Force and has earned himself a growing reputation in the sf field in the 1970s. His first novel, *The Eclipse of Dawn* (US 1971) pointed the way to the success he achieved three years later by winning a Nebula jointly with Gregory Benford for 'If the Stars are Gods', and securing a place in Wollheim's *The 1974 Annual World's Best SF* (US 1974) with his short story 'Moby, Too'. Another novel, *All Times Possible* (US 1974), is a parallel worlds variation set in the US of a different 20th century.

Harlan Ellison
Purveyor of *Dangerous Visions* and a true product of the science fiction age, it has been suggested that if Harlan Jay Ellison didn't exist it would be necessary for John Brunner to invent him. He was born in 1934 in Cleveland, Ohio, and spent a youth of avid fandom, including publishing his own fan magazine. He passed a number of years pursuing unlikely occupations, ranging from store detective to bookie's runner. He ran with young hoodlums in New York to see what made them tick, and took to writing science fiction, by no means his only literary pursuit, in the early 1950s. In the following decade his talent became widely recognized, and he has assembled an astonishing array of awards in recent years.

Ellison's stories reflect his own live-wire and quirky personality; they are filled with movement, colour, zest, and fierce energy. They can be read in several collections: *Touch of Infinity* (US 1959); *Ellison Wonderland* (US 1964); *Paingod and Other Delusions* (US 1965) which contains his Hugo- *and* Nebula-winning ' "Repent, Harlequin!" said the Ticktockman'; *I Have No Mouth and I Must Scream* (US 1967), the title story of which won a Hugo in 1968; *From the Land of Fear* (US 1967); *Love Ain't Nothing But Sex Misspelled* (US 1968); *Partners in Wonder* (*see below*); *Over the Edge* (US 1970); *The Time of the Eye* (US 1971) and *Alone Against*

90

Tomorrow (US 1971). In 1969 he won a Hugo for his short story 'The Beast that Shouted Love at the Heart of the World' (a collection with the same title, and containing the winning story, was published in the US in 1969), another in 1974 for his novelette 'The Deathbird' and yet another for 'Adrift Just Off The Islets of Langerhans' in 1975. A further Nebula came his way in 1969 for 'A Boy and His Dog', and he also scripted the 1968 Hugo-winning episode of *Star Trek*: 'City on the Edge of Forever'.

As an anthologist Ellison has achieved acclaim, and not a little notoriety, with his three gargantuan compilations, *Dangerous Visions* (US 1967), *Again, Dangerous Visions* (US 1972) and *The Last Dangerous Visions* (US 1976). Each consists of new stories, specially written for the undertaking, not only by old-established writers but also by some of the very latest arrivals. The anthologies have aroused some controversy by dint of the sexual themes many of the stories contain, but overall they are refreshing in their diversity and give an important indication of the state of the genre today. As such, they are mentioned in various entries in this 'Who's Who?'. The original *Dangerous Visions* won Ellison his umpteenth Hugo in 1968 as editor of 'the most significant and controversial sf book published in 1967'.

Ellison's output of sf novels is relatively small, but includes: *The Man With Nine Lives* (US 1959), a complicated fast-moving story of revenge, and *Doomsman* (US 1967). There is also the unusual collection, *Partners in Wonder* (US 1971), consisting of stories written by Ellison in collaboration with various writers, including Sheckley, Bova, Bloch, Davidson, Sturgeon, Slesar, van Vogt, Delany, Silverberg, Budrys, Laumer and Zelazny.

Roger Elwood
An up-and-coming US anthologist who gives many indications of one day inhabiting the mantle of Groff Conklin. His compilations include *Alien Worlds* (US 1964), *Invasion of the Robots* (US 1965), and *Children of Infinity* (US 1973), a selection of original stories for younger readers. He has also collaborated with Sam Moskowitz on: *Strange Signposts* (US 1966), *The Human Zero and Other Science Fiction Masterpieces* (US 1967), *The Time Curve* (US 1968), *Alien Earth and Other Stories* (US 1969) and *Other Worlds, Other Times* (US 1969). A more unusual compilation is the four-volume anthology *Continuum* (concluding US 1975), each book containing

one part of eight four-part stories by Anderson, Farmer, McCaffrey, Malzberg, Oliver, Pangborn, Scortia and Gene Wolfe.

Carol Emshwiller

Wife of the artist Ed (*see below*), Carol Emshwiller has contributed a number of stories to *The Magazine of Fantasy and Science Fiction*. Her 'Sex and/or Mr Morrison' appears in Ellison's *Dangerous Visions*.

Ed Emshwiller

Noted illustrator, particularly for *Galaxy*, Edmund Alexander Emshwiller was born in Michigan in 1925. After serving in the US Army during the Second World War, he graduated from the University of Michigan and studied art in Paris. His first work for *Galaxy* dates from 1950 and he has since produced many covers and illustrations for various sf magazines, usually under the signature 'Emsh'. He is particularly interested in experimental films and has won awards in that field.

George Allan England

A largely forgotten writer, undeservedly so—his work in the early magazines ranks with that of Edgar Rice Burroughs. George Allan England was born in 1877, the son of an American army officer. He was educated at Harvard but was laid low by tuberculosis after graduating. Thereafter he followed a literary career. He first gained popularity with his story 'Elixir of Hate' (1911) and confirmed his reputation in the following year with the beginning of his 'Darkness and Dawn' trilogy. Later he became obsessed with treasure hunting and far-flung expeditions. How he met his death in 1936 still appears to be a mystery.

The Flying Legion (US 1930) was one of England's most popular novels, telling of an attempted conquest of the world by aviators. The 'Darkness and Dawn' trilogy has recently been republished by Avalon in, paradoxically, five volumes: *Darkness and Dawn* (US 1964), *Beyond the Great Oblivion* (US 1965), *The People of the Abyss* (US 1966), *Out of the Abyss* (US 1967) and *The Afterglow* (US 1967).

Paul Ernst

Not to be confused with his better-known namesake, American writer Paul Frederick Ernst (born 1902) contributed regularly to the sf magazines during the 1930s. He is probably best remembered for his 'Doctor Satan' series in *Weird Tales* and for such stories as 'Nothing Happens on the Moon' (*Astounding*, 1939) and 'The Way Home' (*Weird Tales*, 1935), the latter written under the pseudonym of 'Paul Frederick Stern'.

Walter Ernsting

West German writer who, under the pseudonym 'Clark Darlton', collaborated with K. H. Scheer to produce some of the first of the 'Perry Rhodan' stories—the latest, but probably not the last, of the 'BEM and Blaster' space operas which have thundered through the genre since the early pulp days. The series is now the work of a team of writers and has acquired an international following —with films, clubs and other memorabilia all devoted to the cult of the galactic super-hero.

Ernsting, who was born in Koblenz in 1920, served in the Luftwaffe during the Second World War and was captured in Russia. He survived five years in a Siberian POW camp before being repatriated in 1950. Later, working as a translator for the British Army of Occupation, he began to write sf stories and to translate others. He has also been active in the German sf magazine field as both editor and publisher.

Lloyd Arthur Eshbach

A writer whose first appearance in *Amazing* with 'The Voice From the Ether' (1931) is still cherished by ageing fans. He later went into publishing and founded Fantasy Press, taking over full ownership in 1950 for some eight years. His collection of stories, *The Tyrant of Time* (US 1955), not unnaturally appeared bearing the Fantasy imprint, but probably more enduring is the compendium of essays which he edited under the title *Of Worlds Beyond: The Science of Science-Fiction Writing* (US 1947). It includes advice on how to succeed in the genre by Heinlein, Taine, Williamson, van Vogt, de Camp, 'Doc' Smith and John W. Campbell. An engrossing guide at the time, and still a very useful book for aspirants with starry eyes.

E. Everett Evans
Edward Everett Evans was an American writer who was known during the greater part of his life for his activities in the fan field. Late in the day he began to write science fiction himself and produced some forty short stories before his death in 1958 just after his sixty-fifth birthday. His 'juvenile' novel, *The Planet Mappers* (US 1955), won the annual award of the Boys' Clubs of America; while *Man of Many Minds* (US 1953) and its sequel, *Alien Minds* (US 1955) deal with the missions of a spy gifted with the powers of extrasensory perception. A memorial volume of his stories, *Food for Demons*, was published in the US in 1971.

I. O. Evans
Born in South Africa in 1894, Idrisyn Oliver Evans is a British writer and retired Ministry of Works official. Much of his contribution to science fiction is related to Jules Verne, whose works he translated and edited for the 'Fitzroy Edition' (1958 onwards). He is also the author of *Jules Verne and His Work* (US 1967). In the more general area he has produced two anthologies, *Science Fiction through the Ages 1* and *2* (both UK 1966), the first book being extracts from the writings of the forerunners—from Lucian, via Kepler, to Poe—while the second is devoted to current practitioners.

Paul W. Fairman
US writer, born 1916, Paul W. Fairman has spent many years editing popular magazines. His sf stories began appearing in *Amazing* in the early 1950s and fifteen have been collected in *The Forgetful Robot* (US 1968). His 'Deadly City', written under the pen-name of 'Ivar Jorgensen', was filmed by Allied Artists in 1954 as *Target—Earth*, and another of his stories, 'The Cosmic Frame' found its way to the screen as *Invasion of the Saucer Men* (American International, 1955). Two of his books are derived from television series: *City Under the Sea* (US 1963) from *Voyage to the Bottom of the Sea*, and *The World Grabbers* (US 1964) from *One Step Beyond*. Among his other novels are *Rest in Agony* (US 1963, under the 'Jorgensen' pseudonym) and *I, The Machine* (US 1968).

R. L. Fanthorpe

Robert Lionel Fanthorpe is a British writer who has turned out a considerable number of stories for Badger Books under equally as many pseudonyms. He was born in Norfolk in 1935 and has pursued a career as a school teacher with a brief spell in the field of industrial training. His output for Badger can best be described as 'at the drop of a hat' productions, and should be accepted as such. It includes *Time Echo* (UK 1959, under the pen-name 'Lionel Roberts'), *Exit Humanity* (UK 1960, as 'Leo Brett'), *Crimson Planet* (UK 1961, as 'J. E. Muller'), *Galaxy 666* (UK 1963, as 'Pel Torro'), *Somewhere Out There* (UK 1963, as 'Bron Fane'), *No Way Back* (UK 1964, as 'Karl Zeigfreid') and *Lightning World* (UK 1964, as 'Trebor Thorpe').

Ralph Milne Farley

A popular contributor to the pre-war US magazines whose real name was Roger Sherman Hoar. Born in 1887, he graduated from Harvard and taught engineering and mathematics before taking charge of a company legal and patents department. For a time he was a Wisconsin senator. He wrote for most of the magazines during the 1930s and 1940s, producing many stories in his 'Radio Man' series which also led to three novels: *The Radio Planet* (US 1942), *The Radio Man* (US 1948) and *The Radio Beasts* (US 1964), all first appearing as magazine serializations between 1924 and 1926. Other books are *The Immortals* (US 1946), *The Hidden Universe* (US 1950) and the collection *The Omnibus of Time* (US 1950). Hoar died in 1963.

Philip José Farmer

Generally hailed as the man who brought real sex into science fiction, Philip José Farmer was born in Indiana in 1918. His early career was studded with a variety of jobs—in a steel mill, a dairy, a brewery and electronics—until he began writing sf tales early in the 1950s. He was awarded a Hugo in 1953 as the best new writer in the field, a reputation which owed much to a single story.

The Lovers (US 1961), which chronicles the romance between a human and an alien parasitic insect that has assumed the shape of a woman, met with strong reactions when it first appeared in *Startling Stories* in 1952. For some it represented bestiality of the worst sort; for others, the idea of sexual relations between Man and extraterrestrials on an affectionate basis was the kind of imaginative jump they felt science fiction needed. Further examples of Farmer's progress in this direction can be found in the collection of short stories *Strange Relations* (US 1960) and in his novels *Flesh* (US 1960) and *A Feast Unknown* (US 1969), the latter being a well-deserved send-up of the grotesque sexual symbolism in much 'Sword and Sorcery' fantasy.

Farmer's trilogy, *Maker of Universes, The Gates of Creation* and *A Private Cosmos* (US 1965–68), marks something of a departure from his other work. It tells of an alternative continuum where many of the cultures and myths of human history exist simultaneously on ascending levels in a multi-tiered, flat-bottomed world—the creation of a number of men who have assumed god-like powers but have retained many of the least desirable human failings. *Dare* (US 1965) has a similar flavour.

The Gate of Time (US 1966) is another variation on the parallel universe theme, while *Tongues of the Moon* (US 1964) is a post-catastrophe drama set on the satellite of an uninhabitable Earth. *A Woman a Day* (US 1960) actually has very little to do with sex, other than a purely gratuitous opening chapter, but is set in post-catastrophe France where an African underground and other factions help a dissenting surgeon to escape from a dictatorial system.

In 1968 Farmer won his second Hugo for the story 'Riders of the Purple Wage', written for Ellison's *Dangerous Visions*. He received a third for his novel *To Your Scattered Bodies Go* (US 1971), the first of the 'Riverworld' series in which Mark Twain is the leading character in an alternate world where all the humans in history have been resurrected. Also among his recent novels are: *Night of Light* (US 1966), *The Wind Whales of Ishmael* (US 1971), *The Fabulous Riverboat* (US 1971), *Traitor to the Living* (US 1973), and *The Other Log of Phileas Fogg* (US 1973), an interstellar updating of Verne's *Around the World in Eighty Days*. Further examples of his short stories can be found in the collections *The Celestial Blueprint* (US 1962) and *The Alley God* (US 1962).

Venus on the Half-Shell by 'Kilgore Trout' (US 1975) is also his work, lifting the name of Vonnegut's invented writer.

John Russell Fearn

One of the most productive of all science fiction writers in terms of sheer volume, John Russell Fearn enjoyed a double career in the field, vying at one time with the noted writers in the American magazines and later disgorging a flood of hastily written stories for his native British market. He was born in Manchester in 1908 and began writing at an early age. He contributed to many of the US pulps during the 1930s, beginning with 'The Intelligence Gigantic' in *Amazing* in 1933. Many of his stories, such as *Liners of Time* (UK 1947), can be classified as space opera at its most flamboyant. The numerous short stories in his 'Golden Amazon' series, originally written under the pseudonym of 'Thorton Ayre', are further examples. He also produced a host of other stories, some containing original and seminal ideas.

He wrote under many pseudonyms and 'house-names', from 'Laurence F. Rose' to the tongue-twisting 'Volsted Gridban', but his best-known alias was 'Vargo Statten', under which he wrote more than fifty paperbacks for the Scion Press in Britain. The rapidity with which he delivered these and other books in the early 1950s almost evokes 'Sense of Wonder' in its own right. In 1953, for example, the following titles were published under the 'Statten' name: *Black Avengers*, *Black-wing of Mars*, *Black Bargain*, *The Dust Destroyer*, *The Interloper*, *Man in Duplicate*, *Man of Two Worlds*, *Odyssey of Nine*, *Pioneer 1990*, *To the Ultimate* and *Zero Hour*. Complementing these came ten titles under the 'Gridban' pseudonym, some of which were definitely not written by Fearn, plus the following which certainly were: *The Amazon's Diamond Quest* and *The Golden Amazon's Triumph*, under his real name. One or two further books appeared in 1954, but then the flood was over; Fearn died in 1960. A comprehensive study of Fearn's extraordinary output can be found in Philip Harbottle's *The Multi-Man* (UK 1968).

Edward L. Ferman

Ed Ferman (born 1937) is an American editor who took over the editorial chair of *The Magazine of Fantasy and Science Fiction* in 1966. As such he continued the annual anthologies, *Best From Fantasy and Science Fiction*, beginning with the fifteenth of the series in the same year. A further anthology, *Once and Future Tales*

97

From the Magazine of Fantasy and Science Fiction (US 1968), contains an introduction by Judith Merril.

Virgil Finlay

Noted American illustrator who won a Hugo in 1953 for his work in the sf and fantasy magazines. Virgil Warden Finlay was born in 1914. Although he received no tuition in art he was a professional painter by the time he was twenty. By 1935 his work was appearing in *Weird Tales* and he was employed for several years by Abraham Merritt as a staff artist on *American Weekly*. He served in the Army Corps of Engineers during the Second World War and resumed his contributions to the sf field after its end. Finlay's illustrations and magazine covers are characterized by his fine attention to detail and by his delicate draughtsmanship. Of the many illustrators in the genre he was certainly one of the most gifted. His paintings executed outside the science fiction idiom had been hung in many galleries and exhibitions by the time of his death in 1971.

Jack Finney

American writer and freelance journalist, who was born Walter Braden Finney in Milwaukee in 1911. Jack Finney found success in writing during the 1940s, particularly in detective fiction. Many of his sf short stories first saw print in *Collier's* and were subsequently republished in *The Magazine of Fantasy and Science Fiction*. A good selection of them can be found in *The Third Level* (US 1956) and *I Love Galesburg in the Springtime* (US 1963). His novel, *The Body Snatchers* (US 1955), which elaborated on the by then familiar theme of alien entities invading the bodies of human beings, was filmed by Allied Artists as *The Invasion of The Body Snatchers* (1956). Another novel, *The Woodrow Wilson Dime* (1968), extends the eternal triangle theme into a parallel worlds dimension.

Francis Flagg

'Francis Flagg' was the pen-name of Henry George Weiss, an early contributor to *Amazing* and, more particularly, to *Weird Tales*. His first story in *Amazing*, 'The Machine Man of Ardathia', appeared in 1927, and he soon came to be known as a writer more interested in the social rather than the technical aspects of science fiction. One of his last stories—and also one of his best—'The Distortion Out of Space' featured in *Weird Tales* in 1934; and his only novel, *The Night People* (US 1947), was published a year after his death at the age of of 48.

Homer Eon Flint

An American writer whose name might still strike sparks for some enthusiasts and whose life and achievements could be regarded as equally odd. He was found dead at the foot of a canyon in 1924 while still in his youngish thirties. Certain wags have since suggested that no more appropriate fate could overtake the joint perpetrator, with Austin Hall, of *The Blind Spot* (US 1951) which was first serialized in *Argosy* in 1921. It has the reputation of being the worst science fiction story ever published—an achievement of sorts—and, in terms of construction, characterization and a profligacy of loose ends, it undoubtedly lives up to its title. But opinions differ; Donald Tuck in his *Encyclopaedia* describes it as 'a noted classic'—so the reader had better decide for himself.

Flint contributed a great many stories to *Argosy* and *All-Story Weekly* around the beginning of the 1920s; and his novels, *The Devolutionist and The Emancipatrix* and *The Lord of Death and The Queen of Life* (both US 1966) were derived from stories originating in those magazines.

Charles Fort

Charles Hoy Fort wrote no science fiction, but he was the originator of ideas which later served as the plot bases of various distinguished stories. Born in the US in 1874, he began a career in journalism before embarking on the series of compilations of inexplicable phenomena which were to occupy him for the remainder of his life. For anything which defied scientific explanation, Fort had his own inimitable theory; and he proffered his conclusions to an unready public in four extraordinary books, *The Book of the Damned, New Lands, Lo!* and *Wild Talents*, which were collected together in *The Books of Charles Fort* (US 1941).

Many sf writers have gone to Fort's theories for inspiration, among the most notable being Eric Frank Russell, whose *Sinister*

Barrier is a classic dramatization of a Fortean idea. Fort died in 1932, two years before *Lo!* was serialized in *Astounding*. Interest in his work continues, and a sane look at his theories can be found in Damon Knight's recent study, *Charles Fort: Prophet of the Unexplained* (US 1970).

Pat Frank

'Pat Frank' is the pseudonym of the American writer Harry Hart, who was born in 1907. His professional career has been conducted in US Government service and he worked with the UN Mission in Korea at the time of the armistice in 1952–53. Science fiction represents only a part of his literary output, and what he has written in the genre concerns the immediate future and clearly draws on his personal experience. *Mr Adam* (US 1946) is a satirical observation of the American governmental system, while *Forbidden Area* (US 1956) depicts a post-catastrophe struggle for survival. In *Alas Babylon* (US 1959) the threat, rather than the aftermath, of nuclear war is the main preoccupation.

Herbert Franke

A Viennese physicist, who ranks among the better original writers in the German language, Herbert W. Franke is noted for his grim predictions regarding the future terrors of technology, which his scientific profession has enabled him to relate authoritatively. An expert in anti-utopias utterly devoid of *gemütlichkeit*, he has laid out his warnings in an authentic but plodding fashion in *The Thought Net* (1961), *Cage of Orchids* (1961), *The Desert of Steel* (1962), *The Glass Trap* (1962) and *Zone Null* (1970). A collection of his stories can be found in *The Green Comet* (1960). The dates given are for German first editions.

H. Bruce Franklin

Howard Bruce Franklin (born 1934) is an American Professor of English among whose scholarly studies can be found *Future Perfect: American Science Fiction of the Nineteenth Century* (US 1966). As an anthology it is valuable for the examples it gives of stories by many notable writers which could now be classed as science fiction—Hawthorne, Poe, Melville, Mark Twain, Edward Bellamy and Ambrose Bierce among them. It also contains one of the better short definitions of science fiction: '. . . the literature which, growing with science, relates it meaningfully to the rest of existence'.

Frank Kelly Freas
An American illustrator whose covers for *Astounding* and others have won Hugos in 1955, 1956, 1958, 1959, 1970, 1972, 1973, 1974 and 1975. Freas is noted for his dominant foregrounds and his individual use of colour. A slim, but deserved testimonial to his work, *Frank Kelly Freas: A Portfolio*, was published by Advent, Chicago, in 1957.

Oscar J. Friend
US writer Oscar Jerome Friend (born 1897) was sf editor of *Thrilling Wonder Stories*, *Startling Stories* and *Captain Future* in the early 1940s, later becoming head of the Otis Kilne literary agency. He contributed a number of stories to the magazines he edited; but his best-known work, which has been much translated, is *The Kid From Mars* (US 1949), a superb send-up of the 'alien envoy' theme, roughly written but mostly very funny and a wicked jibe at the US publicity and promotions scene. A further novel, *The Star Men* (US 1963), appeared in the year he died. Friend also collaborated with Leo Margulies on several anthologies.

H. B. Fyfe
American professional writer who succeeded in getting just one story, 'Locked Out', published in *Astounding* in 1940 before becoming otherwise employed in Europe during the Second World War. Horace Brown Fyfe was born in Jersey City in 1918. His earlier jobs included laboratory work and draughtsmanship before he turned to full-time writing. He has contributed many individual stories to the US magazines and a series eulogizing the 'Bureau of Slick Tricks' to *Astounding*. His novel *D-99* (US 1962) tells of rescue operations to liberate humans from alien captivity on various worlds.

Raymond Z. Gallun

Born in Wisconsin in 1911, Raymond Zinke Gallun was among the early pre-war contributors to *Amazing* and *Astounding* and achieved some popularity with his 'Old Faithful' series featuring a self-sacrificing Martian. Since the war he has produced some novels: *People Minus X* (US 1957) telling of the physical duplication and reconstruction of men, and *The Planet Strappers* (US 1961), an account of the first manned expedition beyond the moon, also *The Eden Cycle* (US 1973).

Dan Galouye

Daniel Francis Galouye is a talented American writer who can rightly claim to be one of the first rocket pilots in history—he served as a Navy test pilot in the Second World War. He was born in Louisiana in 1920, did a brief spell of newspaper work before the war and resumed the profession for some while afterwards. His first published science fiction story, 'Rebirth', appeared in *Imagination* in 1952. He later contributed to *Galaxy* and other magazines and some of his stories are collected in *The Last Leap and Other Stories of the Super-Mind* (UK 1964) and *Project Barrier* (UK 1968).

Galouye's first novel, *Dark Universe* (US 1961), is a striking and evocative treatment of life underground, and in darkness, several generations after a nuclear war. His *Lords of the Psychon* (US 1963) and *The Lost Perception* (UK 1966) both deal with alien invasions against a weakened Earth. His *Simulacron—3* (US 1964) is a clever variation on the 'dawning of reality' theme.

Randall Garrett

An American writer who has contributed regularly to the US magazines, particularly to *Astounding/Analog* since the early 1950s. Randall Garrett is by no means the only writer to be slated critically by James Blish under the guise of 'William Atheling, Jr', but in his case the assault was a devastating piece of hatchet work. To this, however, Blish granted one exception—'The Hunting Lodge' (*Astounding*, 1954)—which he described as 'superb'.

A number of Garrett's short stories have been collaborations, with such writers as Lin Carter, Avram Davidson and Robert Silverberg, and the same holds for the majority of his novels: *Shrouded Planet* (US 1958) and *Dawning Light* (US 1959) both with Silverberg;

Pagan Passions (US 1960), *Brain Twister* (US 1962), *The Impossibles* (US 1963) and *Supermind* (US 1963) all with Larry M. Harris. His solo novels include *Unwise Child* (US 1962), an imaginative treatment of a robot programmed with free will, and *Too Many Magicians* (US 1966).

Richard E. Geis

Richard Erwin Geis (born in Portland, Oregon in 1927) is an American freelance writer known in the field of sf fandom for his editing of *Science Fiction Review* (formerly *Psychotic* and for a time *The Alien Critic*), a notable amateur magazine. It was given Hugos in 1969 and 1975, and Geis himself won the award as a fan writer in 1971 and 1975. Among his novels are *The Sex Machine* (US 1967) and *The Endless Orgy* (US 1968). Their titles are a good guide to their contents.

Peter George

Peter George was born in Wales in 1924 and spent most of his career in the Royal Air Force. His novel *Two Hours to Doom* (UK 1958, also titled *Red Alert* and written under the pseudonym of 'Peter Bryant') is a serious account of the outbreak of a nuclear war. He later used it as the basis for the satirical *Dr Strangelove, or How I Learned to Stop Worrying and Love the Bomb* (UK 1963) which was filmed by Kubrick in 1963. His *Commander—1* (UK 1965) is a further treatment of nuclear warfare, a subject he dealt with in other books and which evidently worried him greatly. He shot himself in 1966.

Hugo Gernsback

For many years described as 'The Father of the Science Fiction Magazine', and presented with a Hugo as such at the 18th World Science Fiction Convention in 1960, Gernsback has been described in retrospect as a mixed blessing to the genre. He has been hailed by some as its actual inventor; in fact it is doubtful if he was even the first to coin the expression 'science fiction' although he received credit for its origin. (The first *modern* appearance of the term occurred in Swedish, in the magazine *Hugin* which was devoted entirely to science fiction and began publication in 1916, ten years before the advent of Gernsback's *Amazing Stories*.*) What he *did* invent was a battery, bringing it with him from his native Luxembourg in 1904 in the hope of marketing it in America.

He also designed the first home radio set in history and gradually developed the catalogue he used for its promotion into the magazine *Modern Electrics*. As page fillers in this publication he ran occasional serializations of scientific romances, beginning in 1911 with his own *Ralph 124C41+* (US 1925), a poorly-written space opera which nevertheless contained some astonishingly accurate technical predictions. The popularity of this type of material prompted him a decade later to fill a complete issue of his *Science and Invention* with what he called 'scientifiction' stories, and three years later in 1926 he launched *Amazing Stories* as a magazine exclusively designed for enthusiasts of the genre. Relying to some extent on reprints of Wells, Verne and Poe, he also assembled a team of scientists gifted in the kind of technical extrapolation to which he was dedicated, but hardly noted for their literary ability. Initially his magazines also published stories by such sf writers as E. E. Smith, Harl Vincent, Jack Williamson, Ray Cummings, Murray Leinster and Edmond Hamilton.

It is currently being argued that Gernsback's failure to see much of value in science fiction other than the technical mastery of the future held back more imaginative writers and established constricting guide-lines which many later editors accepted uncritically. Although his business empire, which included a local radio station, went into liquidation at the end of 1928 and he lost control of *Amazing*, he was back within a year with *Science Wonder Stories* and *Air Wonder Stories* (both later merged in *Wonder Stories*). His supporters argue that his magazines were too early to include the flights of imagination and psychological treatments which later editors were able to exploit.

Born in 1884, two years before the publication of Stevenson's *Dr Jekyll and Mr Hyde*, Gernsback lived long enough to see his own limited concept of science fiction first submerged in the wider vistas of Campbell's *Astounding* and then lost altogether in the turbulent psychological eddies of the New Wave. He died in 1967, the year in which Harlan Ellison's huge anthology *Dangerous Visions* gave pride of place to a new generation of writers who metaphorically were as far from Gernsback as *he* was from Godwin's *The Man in the*

*See Sam Lundwall's *Science Fiction: What It's All About*.

Moone. Nevertheless, he deserves his respected place in the annals of the genre, and the Hugo awards are so-named in his honour.

David Gerrold

David Gerrold is an American newcomer whose story of a computer becoming a god-like entity, *When Harlie Was One* (UK 1969), attracted favourable attention. He has since collaborated with Larry Niven on *The Flying Sorcerers* (US 1971) and showed himself adept at characterization in *Yesterday's Children* (US 1972), a dramatic spaceship setting complete with near-mutinous crew and other distractions. *The Man Who Folded Himself* (UK 1973) is a time paradox variation with a distinct sexual slant, the central character eventually achieving what has been considered a biological impossibility but has been wished upon enough people, past and present. He has also compiled the anthology *Alternities* (US 1974).

Mark S. Geston

A newcomer of promise. Mark Symington Geston was born in Atlantic City in 1946 and has studied law at New York University. His first novel, *Lords of the Starship*, met with acclaim when it was published in the US in 1967. *Out of the Mouth of the Dragon* (US 1969), his second book, was also completed while he was still a student.

Walter Gillings

Born in 1912, Walter Gillings is a British fan, editor, writer, and the man who furnished Arthur C. Clarke with his first typewriter. By profession a journalist, he launched *Tales of Wonder*, Britain's first sf magazine, in 1937. Many of his editorial ventures in the genre have been unhappily short-lived, but *Fantasy Review*, which he edited from 1947 to 1950, achieved renown in the critical field. It was largely with his help that Ted Carnell was able to set up Nova Publications in 1949, leading to the reappearance of *New Worlds*, and the launch of *Science Fantasy* which Gillings initiated. In 1974–75 he contributed a notable series of articles to *Science Fiction Monthly* on 'Modern Masters of Science Fiction'.

Tom Godwin

American author, born in 1915, who first appeared in *Astounding* in 1953 with 'The Gulf Between'. Since then he has written *The Survivors* (US 1958) and its sequel, *The Space Barbarians* (US 1964), involving captivity and warfare on the planet Ragnarok. His short story 'The Cold Equations', originally published in *Astounding* in 1954, has been included in several anthologies. It is a sympathetic variation on the universal dilemma of the sacrifice of one for the good of many.

H. L. Gold

American editor and writer, Horace Leonard Gold was born in Montreal in 1914 and moved with his family to New York two years later. His first published sf story, 'Inflexure', appeared in *Astounding* under the pseudonym of 'Clyde Crane Campbell' in 1934. He followed a number of occupations before the Second World War and contributed several more stories to *Astounding* and *Unknown*. He came into prominence in 1950 when World Editions appointed him to edit their new publication *Galaxy*. The magazine began well and was soon considered an important rival to *Astounding* and *The Magazine of Fantasy and Science Fiction*. However, ill-health forced Gold to relinquish the editorial chair in 1961 and *Galaxy*'s reputation is now less than it was.

A dozen of Gold's short stories have been collected in *The Old Die Rich* (US 1955) and he has compiled various anthologies, including the *Galaxy Reader* series (beginning in 1952); *Five Galaxy Short Novels* (UK 1958) featuring the work of Gunn, Knight, McIntosh, Sturgeon and F. L. Wallace; *The World That Couldn't Be and Eight Other Novelets From Galaxy* (US 1959) and *The Weird Ones* (US 1962).

Rex Gordon

'Rex Gordon' is a pseudonym of Stanley Bennett Hough, a British writer who was born in Lancashire in 1917. His first sf novel, *Utopia 239* (UK 1955), describes a post-catastrophe Britain in which an anarchic society holds sway. Other variations on the outbreak of World War III are explored in *Extinction Bomber* (UK 1956, written under his own name) and *Beyond the Eleventh Hour* (UK

1961). Adventures in space and time can be found in *No Man Friday* (UK 1956), *First to the Stars* (US 1959) and *First Through Time* (US 1962). Later novels are *The Yellow Fraction* (US 1969) and *Utopia Minus X* (US 1966), the latter telling of an ideal Earth disrupted by the return of a long-departed space expedition.

Ron Goulart
An American freelance writer. Ron Goulart's stories have become popular in the last few years, chiefly for their delicately zany humour. He is particularly good at inventing incompetent robots, several of which can be found in *After Things Fell Apart* (US 1970), set in a near future US where society is fractionated and a private detective is hired to track down a lesbian underground organization bent on murdering men. Another novel is *The Hellhound Project* (US 1975), a variation on the theme of 'the ultimate weapon' which involves the impersonation of a man long dead in an attempt to discover the weapon's secret. He has also written *An Informal History of the Pulp Magazines* (US 1972).

Joseph L. Green
Joseph Lee Green is a freelance American writer, born in Florida in 1931, whose stories began appearing in *New Worlds* in 1962. Dealing with the meeting of aliens on a distant world, some were later incorporated in *The Loafers of Refuge* (US 1965). Among his novels is *Gold the Man* (US 1971), a dazzling flight of imagination involving the re-animation of a dead alien's giant body by a mentally advanced human introduced into its brain. The story is enhanced by touches of insight and compassion to make it a genuine *tour de force*.

Conscience Interplanetary (UK 1972) is a rewriting of several short stories to form a novel on Man's relationship with, and responsibility to, aliens.

Martin Greenberg
American anthologist, born in 1918, Martin Greenberg started the Gnome Press in 1948 with co-founder David Kyle. The publishing house was formed specifically to produce science fiction and fantasy books, and many of its anthologies have been edited by Greenberg

himself, among them: *Men Against the Stars* (US 1950), *Travellers of Space* and *Journey to Infinity* (both US 1951), *The Robot and the Man* (US 1953), *All About the Future* (US 1955) and *Five Science Fiction Novels* (US 1952). The last includes stories by Fritz Leiber, van Vogt and Jack Williamson.

George Griffith

A Victorian adventurer of some repute, 'George Griffith' was born G. C. G. Jones, the son of a British clergyman. A real-life Phileas Fogg, he travelled round the world several times and located the source of the Amazon River before his death in 1906. He is chiefly remembered now for *A Honeymoon in Space* (UK 1901) in which the interiors of spacecraft were reminiscent more of English tea-rooms than the multi-dialled control panels of his successors. A collection of his short stories, *Gambles With Destiny*, appeared in Britain in 1899.

James Gunn

James Edwin Gunn is an American writer, editor and teacher who was born in Kansas City in 1923. He served in the US Navy during the Second World War and began writing shortly afterwards. His M.A. English thesis for North-western University was devoted to an analysis of science fiction and later published in *Dynamic SF* during 1953 and '54. He now teaches at the University of Kansas. His sf novels deal frequently with future civilizations and their cultures, e.g. *This Fortress World* (US 1955) in which the church has become omnipotent, and *The Joy Makers* (US 1961), an imaginative setting of a society based on a pursuit of artificial pleasure comparable with Huxley's *Brave New World*. His collaboration with Jack Williamson, *Star Bridge* (US 1955), is a venture into space opera, and *The Immortals* (US 1962), as its title denotes, is an account of a new species of Man pursued by wealthy 'normals' who are literally after its blood—transfusions pass on the gift of immortality.

A number of Gunn's short stories are incorporated in his novels, while others have appeared in the collections *Station in Space* (US 1958) and *Future Imperfect* (US 1964). He compiled the tenth *Nebula Award* anthology (US 1975) and has also written *Alternate Worlds:*

The Illustrated History of Science Fiction (US 1975), a useful and relatively straightforward survey of the development of the modern genre. Obviously written from the American viewpoint, it is a required companion piece to Aldiss's *Billion Year Spree*. Unfortunately its illustrations are only poorly reproduced (and a myopic caption-writer has succeeded in identifying Maxim Gorky as Molotov on page 101).

Peter Haining
Born in 1940, Peter Haining is a British writer and editor whose many anthologies are devoted mainly to the supernatural and macabre. However, *The Future Makers* (UK 1968) is a useful collection of sf stories by eight notables: Aldiss, Asimov, Bradbury, Clarke, Heinlein, Leinster, Sheckley and Sturgeon; and *The Fantastic Pulps* (UK 1975) includes some early delights by George Allan England, Victor Rousseau and David H. Keller.

Austin Hall
Joint perpetrator of *The Blind Spot* with Homer Eon Flint, Austin Hall was an American writer who concentrated on Westerns. His individual sequel to the Flint collaboration was *The Spot of Life* (US 1964) which first appeared in *Argosy* in 1921. His other sf novels were *Into The Infinite* (serialized in *All-Story Weekly* in 1919) and *People of the Comet* (US 1948), an early treatment of the 'solar system as an atom' theme which originally ran in *Weird Tales* as 'Hop O' My Thumb' in 1923. Hall died in 1933 aged about fifty.

Edmond Hamilton
Affectionately known as 'The World Wrecker', and joint Guest of Honour, with his wife, at the 22nd World Science Fiction Convention in 1964, Hamilton ranks alongside 'Doc' Smith and Jack Williamson as an early and fertile pioneer of space opera. He was born in Ohio in 1904 and spent some years as a railroad clerk after being expelled from school for the admirable pastime of skipping chapel. His first story in *Amazing*, 'The Comet Doom' (1928), found him hailed as 'a major new talent', and Farnsworth Wright,

editor of *Weird Tales*, who never turned down a Hamilton offering, called him 'the supreme master of the weird scientific story'. His prolific output flowed over into other stalls in the Gernsback stable, from *Air Wonder Stories* to *Scientific Detective Monthly*; and he began travelling America, frequently with Jack Williamson, in search of ideas material. His creation of the 'Captain Future' series is epitomized in *The Comet Kings* (US 1942), one of the galactic high points in space opera. The series was originally commissioned by Standard Magazines as the basis of their *Captain Future* quarterly, some of the stories being written under the pseudonym of 'Brett Sterling', a house name also shared by J. Samachson. Two further series consist of the 'Interstellar Patrol' and 'Starwolf' stories.

Probably Hamilton's grandest foray into space opera is *The Star Kings* (US 1949), although it is closely rivalled by *The Haunted Stars* (US 1960), the 'Interstellar Patrol' compilation *Crashing Suns* (US 1965), *Outside the Universe* (US 1964) and *Fugitive of the Stars* (US 1965). The idea of an all-powerful weapon is the central issue in both *The Sun Smasher* (US 1959) and *Doomstar* (US 1966); while *City at the World's End* (US 1951) employs a device similar to Heinlein's *Farnham's Freehold* to precipitate the central characters into the future by dint of a nuclear explosion. Other novels include *Battle for the Stars* (US 1961) and *The Valley of Creation* (US 1964); the three 'Starwolf' paperbacks: *The Weapon From Beyond* (US 1967), *The Closed Worlds* (US 1968) and *The World of the Starwolves* (US 1968); also *A Yank at Valhalla* (first published in *Startling Stories* in 1941) which could be described as a Nordic complement to Mark Twain's Arthurian prototype.

Hamilton was married in 1946 to sf writer Leigh Brackett. They now live on a farm in Ohio, where they are writing still.

Charles L. Harness

A small producer, but one of merit, Charles Leonard Harness (born 1915) is by profession an American patent attorney. His first sf stories date from the end of the 1940s, but his reputation is based on three novels. *Flight Into Yesterday* (US 1953) is an intricate story of the decline of civilization; while *The Ring of Ritornel* (UK 1968) is an equally complex interweaving of several themes, ranging from a man's individual investigation into the fate of his father in an anti-utopian society to religious symbolism and eternal recurrence. Most impressive, however, is *The Rose* (UK 1966), a parable of the relationship between Art and Science which is as rich in visual imagery as it is imaginative in its handling of the future evolution of man. Also included in the book are two notable short stories: 'The Chessplayers'—a satirical account of a remarkable rat —and 'The New Reality', which ends in the creation of a post-Einsteinian universe and contains some lighthearted play on the names of high-ranking Nazis (for those who enjoy such literary games). After some years of inactivity on the sf front, Harness has recently produced several further intriguing stories for *Analog*.

Clare Winger Harris
The first American female writer to invade the masculine domain of Gernsback's *Amazing*, Clare Winger Harris achieved popular recognition with 'Miracle of the Lily' (1928) and 'A Baby on Neptune' (1929, in collaboration with Miles J. Breuer). Both can be found in her collection *Away From the Here and Now* (US 1947). She was born in 1891 and may yet be going strong.

Harry Harrison
Peripatetic inventor of 'The Stainless Steel Rat', and about as energetic as his creation, Harry Harrison was born in Connecticut in 1925. He studied art in New York before serving in the US Army during the Second World War as a machine-gun instructor. He continued his art studies afterwards and began a career as a commercial illustrator, progressing to art director and editor for various picture, news and fiction magazines based in New York. He subsequently changed to freelance writing, uprooting his family to, in turn, Mexico, England, Italy, Denmark, Spain and California. He now lives in Ireland. He was briefly editor of *Amazing* and *Fantastic* during 1967–68.

His first sf short story, 'Rock Diver', appeared in *Worlds Beyond* in 1951, and he became a regular contributor in the magazine field, particularly with his 'Jason dinAlt' series in *Astounding*, which he also extended into three novels: *Deathworld* (US 1960), *Deathworld 2* (US 1964) and *Deathworld 3* (US 1968), each chronicling the adventures of dinAlt on hostile planets.

The Stainless Steel Rat (US 1961) introduced 'Slippery Jim di-

Griz', the space-hopping master criminal who was finally clobbered and bent to the service of the forces of law and order, but not without occasional lapses. His exploits were further compounded in *The Stainless Steel Rat's Revenge* (UK 1970) and *The Stainless Steel Rat Saves the World* (UK 1973).

Other humorous excursions followed: *Bill, the Galactic Hero* (US 1965) is a lighthearted account of future military bunglings, while *The Technicolor Time Machine* (US 1967) tells of a movie company which travels back to Viking times to save the cost of hiring extras. However, Harrison demonstrated his serious side in a powerful anti-utopian novel, *Make Room! Make Room!* (US 1966), set in a hideously over-populated New York of 1999. It was filmed as *Soylent Green* by M-G-M in 1973 and the production, directed by Richard Fleischer, won a Nebula in the same year, but it strayed unnecessarily far from the original story.

More recently, the moods have alternated. *Star Smashers of the Galaxy Rangers* (US 1973) was deliberately written as a space opera to 'out-space opera' all space operas. It succeeds. On the other hand, *The California Iceberg* (UK 1975) involves the towing of icebergs from Antarctica to provide water for drought-stricken areas (written as a 'juvenile' book). *The Lifeship* (US 1976) recounts the conflicts between an alien crew and human passengers aboard an escape craft following a spaceship explosion. It was written in collaboration with Gordon R. Dickson.

Other books include *Planet of the Damned* (US 1962), *Plague from Space* (US 1964), *The Man from P.I.G.* (US 1968), *Captive Universe* (UK 1970), *In Our Hands, The Stars* (UK 1970), *Spaceship Medic* (UK 1970), *Transatlantic Tunnel, Hurrah!* (UK 1972) and *One Step From Earth* (UK 1972). Some of Harrison's short sf stories can be read in the collections: *War With the Robots* (US 1962) and *Two Tales and Eight Tomorrows* (UK 1965).

He has also compiled a number of anthologies, among them: *Backdrop of Stars* (UK 1968), *Blast Off* (UK 1969), *The Light Fantastic* (US 1971), *The John W. Campbell Memorial Anthology* (US 1973) and *Nova* (series commencing US 1970). He was co-compiler with Leon Stover of *Apeman, Spaceman* (US 1968) and has enjoyed a partnership with Brian W. Aldiss on the second in the *Nebula Award* series (US 1967) and the annual anthologies, *The Year's Best Science Fiction* (UK from 1968), as well as *The Astounding-Analog Reader No. 1* (US 1972) and *No. 2* (US 1973).

Jon Hartridge

A British writer and Oxford Don who has worked for the *Oxford Mail* and occasionally deputized for Brian Aldiss when the latter was literary editor. His first sf novel, *Binary Divine* (UK 1969) tells of the failure of a world-wide computer in which everyone has come to confide—the future counterpart of today's advice column. Another novel is *Earthjacket* (UK 1970), telling of a deprived future where even air supply is rationed.

Henry Hasse

US short-story writer, fan, and the man who helped Ray Bradbury with his first published tale. He contributed to the magazines mainly during the 1930s and 1940s but was still producing the occasional piece in the 1960s and has continued the practice into the 1970s. His novel *The Stars Will Wait* was published in the US in 1968.

George Hay

The archetypal British sf enthusiast, George Hay has pterodactyls on his letter-heading and almost as many ideas flying off in different directions as Leonardo. He was born in Chelsea, London, in 1922, and was pronounced ineducable at the age of fourteen because he wasted his time reading *Amazing* and *Astounding*. His was the original concept which led to the establishment of the Science Fiction Foundation in London, and he is now its vice-president.

He has promoted the work of various sf writers, including John Brunner, and has compiled several anthologies including *The Disappearing Future* (UK 1970) and *Stopwatch* (UK 1974). He also edited the collection *The Best of John W. Campbell* (UK 1973). In the past he has been connected with Hubbard's Dianetics and Scientology; he is now communications officer for Spectrum—which he calls 'Britain's only upbeat futures-oriented society'—and also co-founder of the Applied Science Fiction Association.

As chairman of the H. G. Wells Society, he has been instrumental in the recent republication of several of Wells's long out-of-print works.

Raymond J. Healey

Born in Brooklyn in 1907, Raymond John Healey has spent a career in book publishing. His claim to fame in the sf world is as an anthologist, beginning with his collaboration with J. Francis McComas, *Adventures in Time and Space* (US 1946). It was one of the first major anthologies after the Second World War and a guide for future collections. Since then he has compiled *New Tales of Space and Time* (US 1951) and *9 Tales of Space and Time* (US 1954).

H. F. Heard

Henry Fitzgerald Heard (1889–1971) was a British author, philosopher and pre-war science commentator for the BBC who moved to the US in 1937. His sf stories include *The Doppelgangers* (US 1947), a late 20th-century setting of a psychological power struggle, and *Gabriel and the Creatures* (US 1952), which is predominantly fantasy but with some interesting twists on Darwinian evolutionary theory. He wrote several other fantasies and fantasy collections, also the factual *Riddle of the Flying Saucers: Is Another World Watching?* (UK 1950).

Robert A. Heinlein

A major and continuing influence, and progressively controversial, Robert Anson Heinlein has more than once come close to dominating the sf scene since he first entered it in 1939 with 'Life-Line' in *Astounding*. He was born in Missouri in 1907 and as a youth was an avid reader of Senarens' 'Frank Reade' stories, later graduating to Verne and Wells. He served for six years in the US Navy before being invalided out from the post of gunnery officer at the age of twenty-seven. Ill-health also dogged his studies in maths and physics, and he tried several jobs before turning to writing full-time. His early reputation was quickly established with a number of effective stories in *Astounding*, among them 'Requiem', which later served as a tail-piece for the collection *The Man Who Sold The Moon* (US 1950), and 'If This Goes On . . .', subsequently incorporated into *Revolt in 2100* (US 1953).

Heinlein's *forte* in his first stories (for which he sometimes used the pseudonyms 'Anson MacDonald' and 'Lyle Monroe') was his ability to create totally convincing backgrounds—a Wellsian device for encouraging 'willing suspension of disbelief'. The themes he explored were universal, reflecting his interest in politics, religion, science and sociology. Nevertheless, when he devoted himself to basically technical subjects he was equally imaginative. His short story 'Blowups Happen' (1940) foretold the dangers of an atomic pile going critical, and 'The Roads Must Roll' (1940) was a striking projection of the travelator principle applied to major highways. 'Solution Unsatisfactory' (1941) proved a far-sighted realization of the futility of a nuclear arms-race. His two paradoxical time-travel tales, 'By His Bootstraps' (1941) and 'All You Zombies' (1959) have yet to be surpassed.

In all these stories were inherent the qualities of what came to be identified as the 'Heinlein ethos'—a pronounced respect for 'law and order', patriotism, self-discipline, and above all an upholding of individual freedom *earned* and not granted as of right. In such novels as *Starship Troopers* (US 1959), which won a Hugo in 1960 but also aroused fierce controversy, Heinlein finally spelt out with undisguised clarity many of the things he stood for (those who disapproved of the authoritarian slant were still held spellbound by the sureness of his technique). In *Farnham's Freehold* (US 1965), portraying a future in which the blacks have the upper hand and even eat their white slaves, the fight for individual rights was further emphasized; it was reinforced yet again in *The Moon is a Harsh Mistress* (US 1966), where a lunar penal colony rebels against Earth with the aid of a sentient computer. It won a Hugo in 1967.

An earlier novel, *Stranger in a Strange Land* (US 1961) had resulted in Heinlein's unexpected elevation to the position of guru for the 'Flower Power' generation of the mid-1960s, by dint of the invented religion it propounded and the gentle ideas of shared sex and emotional experience emanating from its central character (who was as ingenuous as Oscar J. Friend's 'Kid from Mars' and arrived from the same direction). The book brought its author another Hugo in 1962, and can now be seen as the first major novel of Heinlein's third period. Whatever the perceived merits for its younger readers, the work is dominated by the thoughts and interminable verbosity of the ageing lawyer who takes the boy messiah into his charge. Heinlein had fallen into the same trap which had caught the successful Wells (who thankfully only succumbed when most of his science fiction was already in print), the fatal flaw of a best-selling author using story plots as platforms from which to deliver harangues. He has mostly stayed in it since, with the long diatribes of *I Will Fear No Evil* (US 1971), involving the transplant of an old man's brain into the corpse of his girl secretary, and with the repeatedly-aired Oedipus complexes of *Time Enough for Love* (US 1973). However, it did not prevent his receiving a Nebula in 1974 as a 'Grand Master' of the genre, which in his time he has certainly been.

Other books of note include *Beyond This Horizon* (US 1948); *Waldo & Magic Incorporated* (US 1950); *The Puppet Masters* (US 1951), a fast-moving account of an invasion by alien symbiotes; *Double Star* (US 1956), which won him his first Hugo; and *Methuselah's Children* (US 1958), the precursor of *Time Enough for Love* and originally serialized in *Astounding* in 1941. He has also produced the fantasy *Glory Road* (US 1963) and several popular novels for the juvenile market, among them *Rocket Ship Galileo* (US 1947), on which George Pal's competent film, *Destination Moon* (1950), was based.

Encouraged by John W. Campbell during his *Astounding* period, Heinlein embarked on a 'Future History' series into which many of his tales could be conveniently slotted. It incorporated all his moon stories and others found in his collections, *The Worlds of Robert Heinlein* (US 1966) and *The Past Through Tomorrow* (US 1967), and also included complete novels such as *Orphans of the Sky* (US 1963)—a 'travelling ark' story in which later generations begin to believe that their spaceship is the entire cosmos.

Other short story collections are: *The Green Hills of Earth* (US 1951), *Assignment in Eternity* (US 1953), *The Menace From Earth* (US 1959) and *The Unpleasant Profession of Jonathan Hoag* (US 1959). He has also compiled the anthology *Tomorrow the Stars* (US 1951). Heinlein was Guest of Honour at the 3rd World Science Fiction Convention in 1941, and again at the 19th Convention in 1961. A contemporary study of his work is *Robert A. Heinlein* (US 1976), edited by J. D. Olander and M. H. Greenberg. (*See also under* Alexei Panshin.)

Zenna Henderson
A US schoolteacher born in Arizona in 1917. She is well known for her 'People' series in *The Magazine of Fantasy and Science Fiction*, beginning in 1952, which tells of extraterrestrials of human appear-

ance inhabiting Earth in the present day. They can be found in novel form in *Pilgrimage: the Book of the People* (US 1961) and in the collection *The People: No Different Flesh* (UK 1966). Collections of her other stories include *The Anything Box* (US 1965) and *Holding Wonder* (US 1971).

Joe L. Hensley

Joe L. Hensley was born in Indiana in 1926. He studied at the State University, served in the US forces in the South Pacific during the Second World War and again for some sixteen months during the Korean War. He has since followed a legal profession, recently being a prosecuting attorney in the State of Indiana. He began writing sf stories in 1951 and has contributed to a number of the magazines, including *Planet Stories* and *Amazing*. His first novel was *The Colour of Hate* (US 1960). He has often collaborated with Harlan Ellison, and his 'Lord Randy, My Son' appears in the latter's *Dangerous Visions* anthology.

Frank Herbert

US author, born 1920, he has been a professional photographer, TV cameraman, oyster diver, lay analyst and West Coast newspaperman. His first sf novel, *The Dragon in the Sea* (US 1956), described a psychological hunt for a saboteur in an underwater craft.

During the next decade he wrote short stories for the magazines, and it was a combination of two contributions to *Astounding* which produced *Dune* (US 1965). Depicting in great detail the ecology and inhabitants of a water-starved planet, it won a Nebula in 1965 and a Hugo in 1966. *Dune Messiah* (US 1969) is a sequel.

The Eyes of Heisenberg (US 1966) is a story of genetic engineering and the achievement of immortality, for *some* people. *The Green Brain* (US 1966) tells of a mutant conquest of Earth. A means of intergalactic travel through 'jump-doors', and the dangers of using them, form the basis of *Whipping Star* (US 1970).

Other novels include *The Heaven Makers* (US 1968), *The Santaroga Barrier* (US 1968) and *Hellstrom's Hive* (US 1973). His short stories have been collected in *The Worlds of Frank Herbert* (UK 1970) and *The Book of Frank Herbert* (US 1973).

Philip E. High

Philip Empson High, born in Biggleswade, UK in 1914, has been a bus driver, salesman, newspaper reporter and insurance agent. A contributor to *New Worlds*, he began writing sf novels in the 1960s, the earliest being *No Truce with Terra* and *The Prodigal Sun* (both US 1964).

The Mad Metropolis (US 1966) is set around a computer-run city of the future, while *These Savage Futurians* (US 1967) is a post-catastrophe variation. *Reality Forbidden* (US 1967) features a machine which makes daydreams appear real, and *The Time Mercenaries* (US 1968) tells of submarine experts sent on a mission into the future.

Other books include *Twin Planets* (US 1967), *Invader on My Back* (UK 1968), *Double Illusion* (UK 1970), *Come Hunt an Earthman* (UK 1973) and *Sold—For a Spaceship* (UK 1973).

Mark Hillegas

Mark Hillegas is a professor of English at the University of Southern Illinois, at Carbondale, who has also been running courses in science fiction for a number of years. His major contribution to the field is the critical study, *The Future as Nightmare: H. G. Wells and the Anti-Utopians* (US 1967), a gifted appraisal of Wells's utopian and anti-utopian writings, and of his enduring influence on other writers in the same major area of the genre.

Christopher Hodder-Williams

A British author and composer who was born in 1926. He has served with the Royal Corps of Signals in the Middle East and written music for television. His first sf novel, *Chain Reaction* (UK 1959), told of the dangers of eating food exposed to atomic radiation. It was followed by *The Main Experiment* (UK 1964), a story featuring psi-powers in a research station setting; *The Egg-Shaped Thing* (UK 1967); *A Fistful of Digits* (UK 1972); *Panic O'Clock* (UK 1973) and the *Prayer Machine* (UK 1976).

W. H. Hodgson

William Hope Hodgson (1877–1918) was the son of a British clergyman. His nightmarish visions rival those of Lovecraft; they are also considered by many initiates to be the more convincing. They are certainly much fewer, Hodgson's work being cut short by his death in France while serving as an officer in the First World War. Among his output of supernatural and macabre stories only two have much relation to science fiction: *The House on the Borderland* (UK 1908) and *The Night Land* (UK 1912). The former includes an imaginative account of the physical death of the solar system, while the latter is set on Earth in the far future when vast mythological beasts keep a constant watch on the last representatives of Man.

J. Hunter Holly

'J. Hunter Holly', whose real name is Joan Holly, is a US psychologist born in Michigan in 1932. Many of her stories have a psychological slant, among them *Encounter* (US 1959), in which future men fight against a mind-destroying alien. Her accounts of extraterrestrial invasions can also be found in *The Dark Planet* (US 1962), *The Running Man* (US 1963) and *The Time Twisters* (US 1964). *The Dark Enemy* (US 1965) is another psychological tale, recounting the attempts to treat psychopaths with the use of telepathy. More of her novels are *The Green Planet* (US 1960), *The Flying Eyes* (US 1962) and *The Grey Aliens* (US 1963).

Charles D. Hornig

US editor, born in Jersey City in 1916, Charles D. Hornig is a noted early enthusiast and one-time producer of the amateur magazine *The Fantasy Fan*. He was made managing editor of *Wonder Stories* by Hugo Gernsback in 1933 and also helped Gernsback to form the Science Fiction League, the prototype of many subsequent fan and writer organizations.

Hornig was also active as a professional editor during the germinal period 1939–41, when he was responsible for the magazines *Science Fiction, Future Fiction* and *Science Fiction Quarterly*.

Robert E. Howard

An American progenitor of heroic fantasy, Robert Ervin Howard was born in Texas in 1906 and shot himself in 1936 when he learned of his mother's fatal illness. Howard's regular contributions to *Weird Tales* over a relatively short period secured him a wide readership which still persists today. His best-known creation is the barbarian 'Conan', closely pursued by 'Almuric' and 'Bran Mak Morn'. Many of his 'Conan' stories have been collected, come-pleted, and even continued by L. Sprague de Camp and Lin Carter. None of them can really be considered as science fiction, but they have clearly influenced some later sf writers during their occasional forays into 'Sword and Sorcery' territory.

Fred Hoyle

A distinguished British astronomer, who also writes science fiction, Sir Fred Hoyle, F.R.S., was born in 1915 and educated at St John's College, Cambridge. In addition to his appointments in the UK he has worked at the Mt Wilson and Palomar observatories in the US. His first novel, *The Black Cloud* (UK 1957), received widespread attention and was praised for its scientific authenticity. It tells of the approach of an extraordinary alien entity towards Earth, and of the efforts of a handful of scientists to communicate with it. It was followed by *Ossian's Ride* (US 1959).

His next novels, *A for Andromeda* (UK 1962) and *Andromeda Breakthrough* (UK 1964)—both written in collaboration with John Elliot—depict the threat to Man from a giant computer operating from the nebula of the title. *Fifth Planet* (US 1963, written with his son Geoffrey) is another tale of an interstellar body passing close to Earth, and of the joint East–West expedition which goes out to meet it. *October the First is Too Late* (UK 1966) is an account of the reconstitution of earlier parts of the Earth by way of experimentation.

Further collaborations with Geoffrey Hoyle are *Rockets in Ursa Major* (UK 1969), *Seven Steps to the Sun* (UK 1970) and *The Molecule Men and The Monster from Loch Ness* (UK 1971). Shorter stories can be found in his collection *Element 79* (US 1967).

L. Ron Hubbard

The Prophet of Dianetics and Founder of the 'Church of Scien-tology', Lafayette Ronald Hubbard was born in the US in 1911.

His science fiction writing began after reasonable success in other literary fields and he first appeared in *Astounding* with 'The Dangerous Dimension' in 1938. He served as an officer in the US Navy during the Second World War and spent only a few years afterwards as a writer of fantasy and sf stories before devoting himself fully to the 'religion' of psychotherapy which he founded and continues to head.

His stories were run under such pseudonyms as 'René Lafayette' and 'Kurt Von Rachen', in addition to his own name, and were popular in their time.

Final Blackout (US 1948), his best-known novel, originally serialized in *Astounding* in 1940, tells of the rise of a dictatorship in a post-world-war Britain. *Fear & Typewriter in the Sky* (US 1951) are two notable tales, the latter being the experience of a man who finds himself actually incorporated into the events of a science fiction story written by a friend. *The Kingslayer* (US 1949) and *Return to Tomorrow* (US 1954) are examples of Hubbard beneath a space-opera hat.

E. Mayne Hull

Guest of Honour at the 4th World Science Fiction Convention in 1946, Edna Mayne Hull was an American writer who became Mrs A. E. van Vogt in 1939. Daughter of a Canadian newspaper editor, she wrote both fantasy stories and a little science fiction. Her 'Arthur Blord' series, featuring a star-roving business entrepreneur, was published in *Astounding* during the 1940s and partially formed the basis of her collection *Planets for Sale* (US 1954). She was also collaborator with van Vogt on a number of ventures, including *The Winged Man* (US 1968). She died in 1975.

Mel Hunter

US illustrator, born 1929, who began producing covers for various magazines in the 1950s. Originally an advertising copywriter, he established a reputation with his work for *Galaxy*, *The Magazine of Fantasy and Science Fiction* and *If* which has placed him securely among the ranks of the better sf artists.

Aldous Huxley

Decrier of the Brave New World and posthumous guru of *some* latter-day hippies, Aldous Leonard Huxley was born in 1894. Grandson of Darwin's fiercest champion, T. H. Huxley, and brother of Nobel-prize-winning zoologist, Julian, he was educated at Eton but left prematurely because of serious eye trouble. Later he studied at Balliol College, Oxford, and embarked from there on a journalistic career. He soon became known as a brilliant but essentially cynical writer, and continued as such while living in Italy and France before moving to the US in 1937. In California he began experimenting with hallucinogenic drugs in the pursuit of mystical experiences; he died there in 1963.

At least three of his novels were written in the sf idiom, the first as a reaction against the utopian vision of Wells's *Men Like Gods*. When it appeared, *Brave New World* (UK 1932) made a deep impression with its portrayal of a future in which humanity descended into drug-induced sexual frivolity once technology had relieved it of every other care. It was followed by *Ape and Essence* (US 1948), a post-catastrophe story in which religious intolerance and the persecution of mutants were given free rein.

In *Island* (US and UK 1962) Huxley paradoxically tried to depict a positive utopia based on the same kind of drugs he had employed to the detriment of Man in *Brave New World*. He also envisaged it being ultimately destroyed by teenage hooligans. His non-fictional *Brave New World Revisited* (US 1958) reviewed prevailing world developments as compared with the hedonistic and purposeless culture he had envisaged in the original story.

Carl Jacobi

An early contributor to the US pulps (he was born in Minneapolis in 1908), Carl Jacobi has spent a career in writing and journalism. He won a competition in *Weird Tales* in 1932 with his story 'Mive' and subsequently wrote many sf, fantasy and macabre tales. Some three dozen of them can be found in the collections *Revelations in Black* (US 1947) and *Portraits in Moonlight* (US 1964).

Laurence M. Janifer

The true name of Larry Mark Harris, an American writer and

editor who was born in 1933. He worked with the Scott Meredith Literary Agency in the 1950s before going freelance. He has also used the pen-name 'Mark Phillips', particularly in several collaborations with Randall Garrett.

His solo novels include the space operas *Slave Planet* (US 1963) and *The Wonder War* (US 1964). A more psychological approach is evident in *You Sane Men* (US 1965) and *A Piece of Martin Cann* (US 1968). Another collaboration, with J. Treibich, produced *Target: Terra* (US 1968), an amusing account of orbiting astronauts who are uncertain whether World War III has erupted in their absence. He has also compiled a highly readable anthology, *Master's Choice* (US 1966).

D. F. Jones
Dennis Feltham Jones is a British writer and former naval officer who has produced at least two novels in the sf category. *Colussus* (UK 1966) relates the takeover of mankind by the joint efforts of American and Russian computers; and *Implosion* (US 1968) tells of the efforts made in Britain to overcome growing sterility in the female population.

Neil R. Jones
Another early US pulp stalwart, Neil Ronald Jones was born in New York State in 1909 and began writing stories and essays while still very young. He arrived in the sf arena with 'The Death's Head Meteor' (1930) in *Air Wonder Stories*, and then embarked on his 'Professor Jameson' series which ran for two decades in *Amazing*, *Astonishing* and *Super Science Stories*. This long-staying series is amply represented in the collections *Planet of the Double Sun*, *The Sunless World*, *Space War*, *Twin Worlds* (all US 1967) and *Doomsday on Ajiat* (US 1968), which between them incorporated sixteen of the longer tales.

Raymond F. Jones
Born in Salt Lake City in 1915, Raymond F. Jones began contributing short stories to Campbell's *Astounding* during the 1940s. Among

his novels are *The Alien* and *Renaissance* (both US 1951), and *This Island Earth* (US 1952), in which aliens visit Earth in an attempt to enlist human help in their fight against an extraterrestrial enemy. The story was filmed by Universal-International in 1955, a well-handled production with some impressive special effects on the alien planet—but the screenplay strayed from the original text.

Other tales are *The Secret People* (US 1956), telling of mutants populating a post-nuclear-catastrophe world, and *The Cybernetic Brains* (US 1962) which incorporates human brains into computer circuits. Some of Jones's short stories are collected in *The Toymaker* (US 1951) and *The Non-Statistical Man* (US 1964). He has also written several 'juvenile' novels.

Colin Kapp

Colin Kapp is a British writer, now in his late forties, who works as a technician in electronics research. He began contributing to *New Worlds* during the 1950s, and his novel *Transfinite Man* (US 1964) was originally serialized in that publication. It is a dramatic account of the escapades of a man who cannot be killed by any normal means. A more recent novel is *The Patterns of Chaos* (UK 1972). His noted series 'The Unorthodox Engineers' appeared mostly in *New Writings in SF* over the last decade.

Frigyes Karinthy

A leading Hungarian writer of his day, Karinthy (1888–1938) produced a number of utopian works. Paul Tabori has translated his *Voyage to Faremido and Capillaria* (US 1966) which consists of two novelettes describing an alternate world.

Anna Kavan

'Anna Kavan' was the pseudonym of Helen Woods Edwards, who was born in France in 1901 and whose restless life was marked by compulsive travelling in the US, Europe, the East and Australasia before her death by suicide in 1968. The haunting and dreamlike quality of her small but notable output clearly owes much to her experiences as a heroin addict. It is particularly evident in her novel, *House of Sleep* (US 1947). Better known, however, is her last book, *Ice* (UK 1967), a moving allegorical tale set against an oncoming Ice

Age in a post-catastrophe world. Anna Kavan's short stories were collected in *Asylum Piece and Other Stories* (UK 1940).

David H. Keller
Another revered name from the early pages of *Amazing Stories*, David Henry Keller was important in his time as a pioneer explorer into the psychological aspects of science fiction. Born in 1880, he was at first a country doctor in New Jersey; he became interested in psychiatry and carried out original work in the treatment of 'shell shock' during the First World War. Although he had been a prolific spare-time writer since his youth, he rarely submitted anything for publication until he was nearly fifty. The enthusiastic reception for his 'The Revolt of Pedestrians' in 1928 prompted Gernsback to contract him for a further dozen stories; and he continued for a number of years as a regular contributor, concentrating on stories such as 'A Twentieth Century Homunculus' (1930), which emphasized his humanitarian outlook and his concern for future human welfare. His 'Taine' series of stories, which appeared in several other magazines besides *Amazing*, was also popular. He died in 1966, well into his eighties.

Keller's short stories have been published in several collections, including *Life Everlasting and Other Tales of Science Fantasy and Horror* (US 1949) and *Tales From Underwood* (US 1952). Among his novels, most of which have a strong psychological approach, are *The Devil and the Doctor* (US 1940) and, in very limited editions, *The Sign of the Burning Hart* (France 1938) and *The Eternal Conflict* (US 1949).

Frank K. Kelly
US journalist, cartoonist and writer, Frank K. Kelly was born in Kansas City in 1914. He wrote a number of stories for the sf pulps in the 1930s, all of which were highly prized. Among them: 'Exiles of Mars' in *Wonder Stories Quarterly* (1932) and 'Crater 17, Near Tycho' in *Astounding* (1934).

Gerald Kersh
A very productive British writer who was born in Russia in 1911.

Among his various colourful occupations he listed guardsman, baker, wrestler and club bouncer. He wrote a prodigious quantity of short stories, a few of which were science fiction. They can be found in his collections *The Horrible Dummy and Other Stories* (UK 1944), *The Brighton Monster* (UK 1953), which includes his noted 'Whatever Happened to Corporal Cuckoo?', *Men Without Bones* (UK 1955) and *Nightshade and Damnation* (US 1968). His novel *The Secret Masters* (US 1953) is a mystery story incorporating an 'end of the world' theme. Kersh died in 1968.

Daniel Keyes
American author Daniel Keyes was born in Brooklyn in 1927. He became assistant editor on *Marvel Stories* in 1950, but is chiefly known for his Hugo-winning 'Flowers for Algernon' which was published by *The Magazine of Fantasy and Science Fiction* in 1959. The story tells how an idiot's intelligence is scientifically raised to that of a genius and of its equally rapid relapse; it is a notable parable on man's inhumanity to man. It served as the basis for the novel of the same name (US 1966) and for the film, *Charly*, directed and produced by Ralph Nelson in 1968. Another novel is *The Touch* (US 1968).

Otis Adelbert Kline
Early US writer and celebrated authors' agent. He was born in Chicago in 1891 and wrote songs and published music before turning to film scripts and writing in the 1920s. He was a stalwart of *Argosy* and *Weird Tales*, and many of his stories are fantasies in the Rice Burroughs vein, such as *The Call of the Savage* (US 1937) and *The Swordsman of Mars* (US 1960), which were first serialized in *Argosy* respectively in 1931 and 1933. A selection of his oriental 'Dragoman' tales can be found in *The Man Who Limped and Other Stories* (US 1946), published in the year he died.

Nigel Kneale
TV playwright whose 'Quatermass' productions have been among the better science fiction offerings on British television. All three plays—*The Quatermass Experiment* (1953), *Quatermass II* (1955) and *Quatermass and the Pit* (1958) (each a six-part serial)—

were subsequently filmed for the cinema, but without any significant improvement. While there is a strong element of horror in the storylines, it rarely detracts from the essential science fiction basis of the stories which is both intelligent and socially critical. A further play, *The Stone Tapes*, which at one level is a chillingly effective ghost story, attempts to explain psychic apparitions in terms of the possible recording properties of such inorganic materials as the stone walls in a reputedly haunted house.

Damon Knight

A noted US editor and writer whose critical work in the sf field won him a Hugo in 1956. He was born in 1922 and followed various occupations before becoming editor of *Worlds Beyond* in 1950 (it ceased publication after only three issues). Later he edited *If* during the winter of 1958–59, continuing the book reviews which he had already been contributing to several magazines. He also provided some illustrations for the pulps.

His own stories include a number of novels, among them *Hell's Pavement* (US 1955), which tells of an oppressed, mind-controlled society in the twenty-first century, and *The People Maker* (US 1959), featuring a matter duplicator which makes living copies of people. *The Sun Saboteurs* (US 1961) tells of humans attempting to live on a very unEarthlike world, and *Mind Switch* (US 1965) depicts a man's mental transfer to an alien body. Other books are *Beyond the Barrier* (US 1963) and *The Rithian Terror* (US 1965). *Three Novels* (US 1967) consists of 'Rule Golden', 'Natural State' and 'The Dying Man'.

Knight's short stories have been collected in *Far Out* (US 1961), *In Deep* (US 1963), *Off Centre* (US 1965) and *Turning On* (US 1966). He is also a noted anthologist, having compiled: *A Century of Science Fiction* (US 1962); *First Flight* (US 1963), which contains the first stories of ten leading writers; *Tomorrow X 4* (US 1964), which includes Heinlein's 'The Roads Must Roll'; *A Century of Great Science Fiction Novels* (US 1964); *The Shape of Things* (US 1965); *13 French Science Fiction Stories* (US 1965); *Beyond Tomorrow* (US 1965); *The Dark Side* (US 1965); *Orbit 1* (US 1966, the first in a continuing series); *Nebula Award Stories 1965* (US 1966); *Cities of Wonder* (US 1966); *Worlds to Come* (US 1967); *Science Fiction Inventions* (US 1967); *Toward Infinity* (US 1968);

One Hundred Years of Science Fiction (US 1968) and *The Metal Smile* (US 1968).

Although basically a collection of book reviews, his *In Search of Wonder* (US 1956) is presented in such a way as to read as a critical and constructive study of the genre.

Norman L. Knight

Norman Lewis Knight was born in Missouri in 1895. He worked for a while in a weather bureau in Iowa, then graduated as a chemist and joined the US Insecticide and Fungicide Board in Maryland. He is noted in the sf field for his stories in *Astounding* at the beginning of John W. Campbell's editorship, and for his collaboration with James Blish on *A Torrent of Faces* (US 1967), a story of a utopian Earth in the 28th century.

Sakyo Komatsu

One of the most successful and productive of Japanese writers, Sakyo Komatsu was born in 1931. His bestselling cataclysmic story, *Nihon Chimbutsu (Sinking Japan)*, has sold more than a million copies in his home country. As yet no English version exists; but the US translation rights have recently been sold, so the wait may be nearly over.

Dean R. Koontz

An American arrival of the last few years. He was born in Pennsylvania some thirty years ago and taught there for a while before becoming a full-time writer in 1969. He has contributed to *The Magazine of Fantasy and Science Fiction* and his 'A Mouse in the Walls of the Global Village' appears in Ellison's *Again, Dangerous Visions*. However, he concentrates mainly on novels.

Among them are *Star Quest* (US 1968), *Fear That Man* and *The Fall of the Dream Machine* (both US 1969), *Dark of the Woods* and *Anti-Man* (both US 1970). *Beastchild* (US 1970) tells of an alien conquest of Earth during which one of the despised invaders befriends a human boy. *Nightmare Journey* (US 1975) depicts Earth a hundred millennia hence where Man has deliberately mutated into countless grotesque forms.

C. M. Kornbluth

Cyril M. Kornbluth is perhaps chiefly remembered for his collaborations with Frederik Pohl, of which *The Space Merchants* is the most renowned; however, many of his individual efforts were similarly noted. He was born in the US in 1923 and began writing professionally at an early age. He served as an infantryman in the Second World War and fought in the Battle of the Bulge (the last German offensive in Europe). Later he worked for Trans-Radio Press and contributed regularly to the sf magazines under a number of pseudonyms, particularly 'Cyril Judd' which he used in collaborations with both Pohl and Judith Merril. He died aged thirty-five in 1958.

Of his solo novels *Takeoff* (US 1952) is a detective story set around the construction of Earth's first spaceship, and *The Syndic* (US 1953) tells of a future in which society is ruled according to the ethics of mobsters. *Not This August* (US 1955) depicts the US occupied by a Russian–Chinese alliance, together with the inevitable Resistance uprising. (For his collaborations with Pohl, see the latter's entry.)

Kornbluth's short stories can be read in several collections: *The Mindworm and Other Stories* (US 1955), *A Mile Beyond the Moon* (US 1958), *The Marching Morons* (US 1959), *Best Science Fiction Stories of C. M. Kornbluth* (US 1968) and *Thirteen O'clock and Other Zero Hours* (UK 1972, edited by James Blish). In 1973 he was posthumously awarded a Hugo for 'The Meeting', written with Fred Pohl.

Roy G. Krenkel

US artist who has illustrated a number of magazines, such as *Astounding*, and has produced covers for sf novels and collections. Among them have been Ace Books publications and the amateur magazine *Amra*. His work earned him a Hugo as the best artist of the year in 1963.

Stanley Kubrick

Stanley Kubrick was born in the Bronx, New York, in 1928. Educated at Taft High School, he became a photo-journalist for *Look* magazine and shot his first documentary movie, which was later bought by RKO, when he was twenty-one. During the next dozen years he made his reputation with such films as *Paths of Glory* and *Lolita* before directing his talents towards science fiction with *Dr Strangelove, or How I Learned to Stop Worrying and Love the Bomb* (a Hawk Films production, 1963). Based on Peter George's original story, it won a Hugo in 1965.

With *2001—A Space Odyssey* (M-G-M 1968), which he scripted jointly with Arthur C. Clarke, Kubrick directed what is certainly the most impressively-filmed science fiction to date, even if many of its concepts were considered rather 'old hat' among part of the sf fraternity. It was awarded a Hugo in 1969, and another was given for *A Clockwork Orange* (Warner Brothers/Hawk Films, 1971) adapted from the novel by Anthony Burgess.

Henry Kuttner

One of the most prolific of all sf short story writers, Henry Kuttner was born in Los Angeles in 1915. His first job was in a literary agency where he learned some of the art of writing, at the same time becoming an ardent reader of *Amazing* and *Weird Tales*. He began corresponding with contributors to the latter, particularly H. P. Lovecraft whose influence is evident in Kuttner's first story in *Weird Tales*, 'The Graveyard Rats' (1936). It was Lovecraft who suggested he write to C. L. Moore with a view to collaboration, unaware of that writer's gender (the chauvinistic aura of the pulps prompted several women contributors to disguise their identities). Their first collaboration followed in 1937 with 'Quest of the Star Stone' and continued until Kuttner's early death in 1958. They married in 1940.

Kuttner's solo stories during his early career ranged all the way from horror and 'Sword and Sorcery' in *Weird Tales* to humorous science fiction like 'Hollywood on the Moon' in *Thrilling Wonder*. In that magazine he began using the pseudonym 'Kelvin Kent', the first of many which he employed either individually or jointly with C. L. Moore, and which included 'Keith Hammond', 'Lewis Padgett', 'Lawrence O'Donnell' and more than a dozen others.*

*When Jack Vance began writing in the 1950s a misunderstanding led to the assumption that he was one more *alter ego* of Kuttner. Two decades later he was still being described as such by I. F. Clarke in *The Tale of the Future*.

The majority of his novels first appeared as magazine serials and only later were produced in book form, several after his death. They include *Fury* (US 1950, written as 'Lawrence O'Donnell'), *Well of the Worlds* (US 1952, as 'Lewis Padgett') telling of an alternate universe, and *Beyond Earth's Gates* (US 1954, with C. L. Moore), a tale of a religiously harsh other world where the inhabitants regard Earth as their promised heaven. *Valley of the Flame* (US 1964, as 'Keith Hammond') is a 'Lost World' story set in the Amazon jungle, and *Earth's Last Citadel* (US 1964, with C. L. Moore) recounts a long struggle between men and aliens. Among other novels are a fantasy, *The Dark World* (US 1965), *Time Axis* (US 1965) and *The Creature From Beyond Infinity* (US 1968).

From Kuttner's multitude of short stories, both his individual work and his collaborations with C. L. Moore under the 'Padgett' pseudonym, many collections have been made, among them: *A Gnome There Was* (US 1950, as 'Padgett'), *Tomorrow and Tomorrow & the Fairy Chessmen* (US 1951, as 'Padgett'—consisting of two stories from *Astounding* of the mid-1940s), *Robots Have No Tails* (US 1952, as 'Padgett'), *Ahead of Time* (US 1953), *Mutant* (US 1953, as 'Padgett'), *Line to Tomorrow* (US 1954, as 'Padgett'), *No Boundaries* (US 1955, with C. L. Moore), *Bypass to Otherness* (US 1961), *Return to Otherness* (US 1962), *Best of Kuttner 1* (UK 1965) and *Best of Kuttner 2* (UK 1966).

R. A. Lafferty

Raphael Aloysius Lafferty is a tutor in electrical engineering who was born in Iowa in 1914. He began contributing to the US magazines when he was about fifty and has written a number of novels in the last few years. Among them are *Past Master* (US 1968), in which Sir Thomas More is resurrected by the citizens of a utopia with problems, *The Reefs of Earth* (US 1968), telling of an alien threat to humanity, and *Space Chantey* (US 1968), a future allegory of Homer's *Odyssey*. Others include *Nine Hundred Grandmothers* (US 1970), *Arrive at Easterwine*, *The Devil is Dead* and *The Flame is Green* (all US 1971), and *Strange Doings* (US 1972). In 1973 he won a Hugo for his short story 'Eurem's Dam'.

Kurd Lasswitz

The man who should rightfully be classed with Wells as one of the progenitors of modern science fiction, Lasswitz was born in Germany in 1848 and died there in 1910, having followed a career in the study of philosophy and physics at the Gymnasium Ernestinum at Gotha. It is astonishing that although his work was translated into almost every European language in his heyday, none of it appeared in English until Willy Ley undertook a handful of translations for *The Magazine of Fantasy and Science Fiction* in the 1950s. Among these was 'Aladdin's Lamp', a neat satire of Kant's argument that natural laws become reality only when man discovers them. In satirical stories of this kind, Lasswitz came very close to modern writers. He also developed many ingenious scientific speculations, some of them drawn from a compatriot, Gustav Theodor Fechner, of whom he wrote a biography. 'Against the Law of the World: A Story of the Year 3877' (1878) is a notable example, and tells of the electrical manipulation of children's brain patterns to encourage them in particular areas of thought. In 'Apoikis' he envisaged an intellectual utopia set on an Atlantic island which anticipated Aldous Huxley's own treatment of the theme in *Island* seventy years later.

Lasswitz's best-known work is the novel *Auf Zwei Planeten* (On Two Planets) (Germany 1897). It chronicles a successful invasion of Earth by Martians who, unlike Wells's, enjoy a highly utopian pluralistic society based on the Kantian dream of individual moral improvement (needless to say it was banned by the Nazis). It is also the first example of the use of artificial satellites as space stations and launching and stopping-off points for interplanetary flight. On another level it is a powerful criticism of European, particularly British, imperialism in the nineteenth century.

Keith Laumer

Keith Laumer is a prolific US writer who entered the sf field in 1959. He was born in Syracuse, New York, in 1925 and served with the US Army in the European theatre during the Second World War and after. From 1953 until 1956 he was with the US Air Force; he joined again in 1960. He has written many sf novels since the start of the 1960s, among the earlier being a parallel worlds story, *The Worlds of the Imperium* (US 1962), and its sequel *The Other*

Side of Time (US 1965); *A Trace of Memory* (US 1963) and *The Great Time Machine Hoax* (US 1964).

A Plague of Demons (US 1965) tells of humans forced to fight as mercenaries for alien captors, while *The Invaders* and *Enemies From Beyond* (both US 1967) are novelizations of the *Invaders* TV series. More recently, *The House in November* (US 1970) is another alternate worlds treatment, with a human awaking on a far more oppressive Earth than the one where he went to sleep.

Other tales include *The Time Bender* (US 1966), *Earthblood* (US 1966, in collaboration with Rosel George Brown), *Planet Run* (US 1967, written with Gordon R. Dickson), the space opera *Galactic Odyssey* (US 1967), *Assignment in Nowhere* (US 1968) and *The Star Treasure* (US 1971). His short stories can be read in the collections *Envoy to New Worlds* (US 1963) and *Galactic Diplomat* (US 1965), both of which chronicle the adventures of the interplanetary agent 'Retief'; also *Greylorn* (US 1968) and *It's a Mad, Mad, Mad Galaxy* (US 1968).

Stan Lee

A peripheral character as far as today's science fiction is concerned, but Stanley Leiber—to give him his full name—will probably be recalled with affection by the sf enthusiasts of tomorrow. As 'Stan the Man' he is the guiding light behind the extraordinary collection of flawed superheroes who pursue their various destinies across the sometimes brilliantly illustrated pages of Marvel Comics. 'Spider-Man', 'The Incredible Hulk', 'The Fantastic Four', 'The Silver Surfer' and others of that ilk will surely one day attract as many theses as the Disney culture, 'Tom and Jerry' and 'Charlie Brown'. At least they present their young devotees with a simplified but heightened view of the aspirations, self-dramatizations, frustrations and picturesque failings incorporated in the human personality—and above all they entertain. The story of the beginnings of the phenomenon is told by Lee himself in *Origins of Marvel Comics* (US 1974).

Walter W. Lee

Walter W. Lee is an American film man, a vice president of Technical Communications Inc, and the compiler of the most detailed checklist available of sf and fantasy films: *Reference Guide to Fantastic Films: Science Fiction, Fantasy & Horror*. The work has been published in three volumes: 'A–F' (US 1972), 'G–O' (US 1973) and 'P–Z' (US 1974). It is well illustrated with many familiar and some lesser-known stills.

Ursula K. Le Guin

Ursula Kroeber Le Guin was born in California in 1929. Her contributions to the sf field have all been made during the last ten years, but in that time she has assembled an impressive array of awards. She began fairly conventionally with a superior space opera in *Rocannon's World* (US 1966) and with accounts of conflicts with aliens in *Planet of Exile* (US 1966) and *City of Illusions* (US 1967). The breakthrough came with *The Left Hand of Darkness* (US 1969), a richly imaginative story of an extraterrestrial world called 'Winter' and of the lifestyle and sexual cycle of its inhabitants. The novel won a Nebula in 1969 and a Hugo in 1970.

There followed *The Lathe of Heaven* (US 1971) and *The Dispossessed* (UK 1974), the latter a beautifully-conceived allegorical portrayal of an Earthlike planet. Both stories fit into the 'Hainish' concept in Le Guin's work which postulates that an ancient race 'seeded' the galaxy, including Earth. *The Dispossessed* won a Nebula in its year of publication and a Hugo in 1975.

Other awards are a Hugo in 1973 for 'The Word for World is Forest', another in 1974 for 'The Ones Who Walk Away from Omelas', and a Nebula in 1974 for 'The Day Before the Revolution'. She has also written a trilogy of fantasies.

Fritz Leiber

Former actor, and son of a noted stage and movie performer, Fritz Reuter Leiber Jr was born in the US in 1910. He has written many fantasy stories, and contributed to *Weird Tales* before the Second World War, but he has also achieved much success with his science fiction. He won a Nebula and a Hugo in 1967–68 for 'Gonna Roll the Bones' (a very macabre gambling tale) and completed the double again with 'Ill Met in Lankhmar' in 1970–71. His story 'Ship of Shadows' also won a Hugo in 1970.

Among his award-winning novels are *The Big Time* (US 1958), a rollicking account of a relief station catering for the combatants in a time war ranging through several millennia (it was first serialized in *Galaxy* and won a Hugo in 1958), and *The Wanderer* (US 1964), a Hugo winner of 1965 which tells of the havoc caused on Earth by a planet straying close to the moon. His other sf stories include *Gather, Darkness!* (US 1950), depicting a future where religious leaders produce miracles with the surreptitious use of science, *The Green Millennium* (US 1953), *Destiny Times Three* (US 1957) and *A Spectre is Haunting Texas* (US 1969).

Many of his short stories can be found in the collections: *The Mind Spider and Other Stories* (US 1961), *A Pail of Air* (US 1964), *The Night of the Wolf* (US 1966) and *The Best of Fritz Leiber (1944–1970)* (UK 1974).

Murray Leinster

Until his death in 1975 the longest-staying of all sf writers. 'Murray Leinster' was the pseudonym of William Fitzgerald Jenkins, who was born in the US in 1896. He began writing in his teens and his first sf story 'The Runaway Skyscraper' appeared in the American *Argosy* in 1919. It was a notable account of a New York office building suddenly travelling back through time. He followed it in *Argosy* during the next year with 'The Mad Planet', telling of the world overrun by giant insects. Thereafter he wrote many stories and novels, also many crime mysteries which occasionally incorporated elements of science fiction. Much of his book fiction is drawn from earlier magazine serializations.

The Last Space Ship (US 1949), *Space Captain* (US 1966) and *Space Gypsies* (US 1967) are examples of his numerous space operas. *The Forgotten Planet* (US 1954) is a rewriting of many short stories to make a continuous account of the survivors of a crash struggling to exist on an alien world. *Outerspace* (US 1954) tells of the first exploration beyond the solar system, and *War with the Gizmos* (US 1958) depicts an alien invasion. Other tales include: *Creatures of the Abyss* (US 1961) *This World Is Taboo* (US 1961) and *The Duplicators* (US 1964). *Land of the Giants* (US 1968) is a novel-length adaptation of the US TV series (he also produced several other books of TV series).

Many of his short stories can be found in the collections: *Sidewise in Time* (US 1950), *The Aliens* (US 1960), *Twists in Time* (US

1960) and *SOS From Three Worlds* (US 1967). *A Murray Leinster Omnibus* (UK 1968) consists of three novels.

Leinster won a Hugo in 1956 for his novelette 'Exploration Team', which originally appeared in *Astounding* in the same year.

Stanislaw Lem

The Titan of East European science fiction, Stanislaw Lem was born in Lemberg in 1921. Originally intended for a career in medicine, he settled in Cracow at the end of the Second World War and began writing a year later. Also a screenwriter, he has seen his work translated into some thirty languages. He is co-founder of the Polish Astronautical Society and a member of the Polish Cybernetics Association.

Enviably versatile in his themes and treatments, Lem has been compared not unfavourably with both Wells and Stapledon. His real strength lies in the power and scope of his speculative ability, which covers a wide range of human sciences and includes philosophy. He is also noted for the depth of analysis he brings to the portrayal of extraterrestrial societies. His best-known work, *Solaris* (Poland 1961, UK translation 1971), which was filmed in the USSR in 1972, is a psychological drama dealing with attempts to assess, and even communicate with, an oceanic and possibly godlike entity on the planet of the title.

His other stories include *The Astronauts* (Poland 1951), *Guest in Space* (Poland 1952), *The Magellan Nebula* (Poland 1955) and *The Cyberiad* (Poland 1967). Among his English language editions are the utopian farce *Memoirs Found in a Bathtub* (Poland 1971, US translation 1973), and *The Invincible* (Poland 1963, US translation 1973), an effective mystery concerning the fate of an Earth spaceship when it landed on another world.

Milton Lesser

US writer who saw service with the UN Forces during the Korean War, Milton Lesser (born 1928) has written a number of sf 'juveniles' and some stories for the adult market. Among the latter are *Recruit for Andromeda* (US 1953), which develops the 'test to find the best galactic species' theme, and the two stories of space adventure in *Secret of the Black Planet* (US 1965). He has also compiled the anthology *Looking Forward* (US 1963).

Brian Lewis

Brian Lewis is a British illustrator who worked for a while as an engineering draughtsman after serving seven years in the Royal Air Force. He is noted for his cover work for the British magazines, *New Worlds* and *Science Fantasy*, where his engineering background proved valuable in the detail he applied to spacecraft and other futuristic hardware. He has free-lanced for over a decade.

C. S. Lewis

Clive Staples Lewis was a British academic and Professor of Medieval and Renaissance English at Magdalen College, Oxford. He was born in Belfast in 1898. Much of his fiction qualifies for the fantasy field and he also wrote many popular books on religion. His principal effort in science fiction was a trilogy designed to propagate Christian theology through the sf idiom—not, to many minds, particularly successful. It consists of *Out of the Silent Planet* (UK 1938), *Perelandra* (UK 1943) and *That Hideous Strength* (UK 1945), the last 'noted'—if such is the word—for a malicious portrayal of H. G. Wells (who was dying of cancer at the time) under the guise of the character 'Horace Jules'.

Lewis also produced two collections of essays and lectures, *World's Last Night* (US 1960) and *Of Other Worlds* (UK 1966) which have some bearing on sf ideas. He died in 1963.

Willy Ley

Willy Ley was for many years the principal contributor of factual science pieces to the American sf magazines, and won a Hugo for his work in 1956. He was born in Berlin in 1906 and was a founder member of the German Rocket Society (subsequently banned by the Nazis—the Fuehrer put little faith in rockets that went up but didn't come down to hit something on Earth). He emigrated to the US in 1935 and began writing for *Astounding* a few years later. He continued with similar factual pieces in *Galaxy* from 1952 until his death in 1969. His book-length popularizations include *Rockets,*

Missiles and Space Travel (US 1944), *The Conquest of Space* (US 1949), *Engineers' Dreams* (US 1954), *Satellites, Rockets and Outer Space* (US 1958), *Watchers of the Skies* (US 1963) and *Beyond the Solar System* (US 1964).

Frank Belnap Long

US writer who has contributed more to the weird category than to authentic science fiction, Frank Belnap Long was born in 1903, the grandson of the man who built the pedestal for the Statue of Liberty. He studied at the New York School of Journalism and became one of the stalwarts of *Weird Tales*, beginning in 1924 with 'Death Waters'. He has also published several books of verse. Many of his sf magazine serials have since been published as books, among them: *Space Station No. 1* (US 1957), *Woman From Another Planet* (US 1960), *Mars Is My Destination* (US 1962), *It Was the Day of the Robot* (US 1963), *The Martian Visitors* (US 1964), *This Strange Tomorrow* (US 1966) and *Survival World* (US 1971). Alien threats to Earth can also be found in *Let Earth Be Conquered* (US 1966), *Journey Into Darkness* (US 1967) and in . . . *And Others Shall Be Born* (US 1968).

H. P. Lovecraft

More a purveyor of horror and fantasy than science fiction, Howard Phillips Lovecraft produced just enough genuine contributions to the genre to warrant his inclusion here. Almost a recluse from the time of his birth in 1890 in Providence, Rhode Island, he maintained a tenuous contact with civilization through a prodigious output of letters. Many find his work turgid, repetitive and frequently well-nigh unreadable; but for others the compelling nightmarish quality of his tales elevates him to the rank of psychological grand master. He created his own mythology in the demonic lore of Cthulhu and peopled it with ghastly entities whose sole purpose seemed to be the destruction of Man. Among his better sf stories are 'The Colour out of Space' (*Amazing* 1927) and 'Herbert West—Reanimator' (the latter originally illustrated by Damon Knight), and such novels as *At the Mountains of Madness* (*Astounding* 1936) where some grasp of the evolutionary rise and fall of civilizations is evident. Two years after Lovecraft's death in 1937 August Derleth and Donald

138

Wandrei began republishing his work in more permanent form under the imprint of 'Arkham House'. But perhaps a more enduring memorial is the influence Lovecraft's fantasies exerted on writers of the standing of Kuttner, Fritz Leiber, Ray Bradbury and Robert Bloch during their formative years.

A full account of his life can be found in *Lovecraft: A Biography* (US 1975) by L. Sprague de Camp.

A. M. Low

Archibald Montgomery Low was a British inventor and writer, born in 1888, who laid rightful claim among his many inventions to the first radio-controlled rocket. A popularizer of science—and also, like Arthur C. Clarke, a President of the British Interplanetary Society—he wrote many factual pieces in addition to occasional science fiction before his death in 1956. His novel *Satellite in Space* (UK 1956) is an account of warfare between orbiting Earth stations, while *It's Bound to Happen* (UK 1950) is a good example of his non-fiction forays into futurology.

R. W. Lowndes

An industrious writer, editor and active fan, Robert Augustine Ward Lowndes was born in Connecticut in 1916. His work ranges across the whole spectrum of popular magazine fiction, and he is probably best known in the sf field for his editing of *Future Science Fiction* and *Science Fiction Quarterly* in the early 1940s and again when they reappeared after the Second World War. He was Managing Editor for all Columbia's pulp magazines for two decades up to 1960 when he moved to Health Knowledge Inc. He also edited the Avalon series of sf novels.

Lowndes' chief virtue as an sf editor has been his consistent ability to produce interesting publications on virtually minimal budgets, so that one can only speculate what he might have achieved had he been allowed larger appropriations. His own writings in the genre include stories under many pseudonyms and the novels *The Duplicated Man* (US 1959, jointly with James Blish), *Believers' World* (US 1961) and *The Puzzle Planet* (US 1961). His short study of the genre, *Three Faces of Science Fiction* (US 1973, limited edition) is a thoughtful and sensible appraisal.

Sam J. Lundwall

Author of probably the best popular study of science fiction to date, Sam J. Lundwall is a Swedish 'jack of all trades' who takes sf bibliography, editing, TV production, disc-jockeying and folk-music composition as part of a normal day's work. He became an sf enthusiast in his 'teens and published the fan magazine *Science Fiction Nytt*.

His bibliography of science fiction and fantasy was first published in 1964 in Sweden and was followed in 1969 by a broad review of the entire genre which he later enlarged and translated into English as *Science Fiction: What It's All About* (US 1970). While his approach is anecdotal, Lundwall has succeeded in this highly readable book in capturing the spirit of science fiction as effectively as any of the supposedly more heavyweight studies. At the same time his insights are penetrating and always to the point, making the work an exhilarating experience for newcomers and a refreshing reprise for the old gang.

Richard A. Lupoff

US writer who was born in Brooklyn, New York, in 1935. His magazine *Xero* won a Hugo in 1963 as the 'Best Amateur Publication of the Year', and his contribution to ERBdom, *Edgar Rice Burroughs: Master of Adventure* (US 1965), is a sound study of a literary phenomenon. His other books include *One Million Centuries* (US 1967), chronicling adventures in the remote future, and *Sacred Locomotive Flies* (US 1971).

John Lymington

John Lymington is a British writer who prefers to keep his personal details to himself. His *Night of the Big Heat* (UK 1959), which describes an alien invasion of Earth, was later adapted for BBC Television. *The Giant Stumbles* (UK 1960), *The Grey Ones* (UK 1960), *The Screaming Face* (UK 1963), *The Green Drift* (UK 1965), *Give Daddy the Knife, Darling* (UK 1969) and *The Sleep Eaters* (UK 1973) are all accounts of threats to humanity, either from space or from natural causes.

Froomb! (UK 1964) tells of a time traveller who sees his own future, and *Ten Million Years to Friday* (UK 1967) is another time story in which multiplication of the speed of light imposes a resurrection of the distant past upon the modern world. Other novels include *The Coming of the Strangers* (UK 1961), *A Sword Above the Night* (UK 1962) and *The Nowhere Place* (UK 1969).

Anne McCaffrey

Anne Inez McCaffrey was born in Cambridge, Massachusetts, in 1926. After an early career as an advertising copywriter she studied voice and drama, and directed opera in Delaware. Her main body of work in the genre borders on fantasy and explores the empathy existing between men and dragons in a mythical land depicted in the novels *Dragonflight* (US 1968) and *Dragonquest* (US 1970). On the same theme, her stories 'Weyr Search' and 'Dragonrider' respectively won Hugo and Nebula awards in 1968. A major contribution to the development of 'cyborgs' is *The Ship Who Sang* (US 1969), derived from her stories about a spaceship operated directly by the brain of a young girl who was born too badly deformed to lead a normal life. Other of her novels include *Restoree* (US 1967) and *Decision at Doona* (US 1969), and she has edited the anthology, *Alchemy & Academe* (US 1970), an exceptional book which brings together the ventures of some noted sf writers into the field of transmutation.

J. Francis McComas

American editor and writer, Jesse Francis McComas (born 1910) is best known in the sf field for his anthologies. He was co-editor with Anthony Boucher of *The Magazine of Fantasy and Science Fiction* from its launch in 1949 until 1954. As such, he was also co-compiler with Boucher of the first three annual anthologies from the magazine, *Best From Fantasy and Science Fiction*. Earlier he had been co-compiler with R. J. Healy of *Adventures in Time and Space* (US 1946), one of the best of the immediate post-war anthologies.

J. T. McIntosh

'J. T. McIntosh' is the pseudonym of the Scottish writer James Murdoch MacGregor, who was born in Paisley in 1925 and graduated from the University of Aberdeen. In his time he has worked in journalism and teaching, and has also been a professional musician. His first published story, 'The Curfew Tolls' appeared in *Astounding* in 1950; his début in the British market came with 'The E.S.P. Worlds' in *New Worlds* two years later.

McIntosh has written many sf novels over the past twenty years, demonstrating a considerable variety of plot ideas. Among them are *World Out of Mind* (US 1953), which deals with the admittedly not very original theme of an attempted conquest of Earth by means of a single alien disguised as a human, *The Fittest* (US 1955), telling of the horrific effects of experiments to heighten animal intelligence, and *200 Years to Christmas* (US 1961), a 'travelling ark' variation.

The idea of Earth being covered by a single metropolis is explored in the anti-utopian *The Million Cities* (US 1963), and *The Noman Way* (US 1964) depicts a planet where population control consists of killing those who fail in physical aptitude tests. *Out of Chaos* (US 1965) is a post-catastrophe story, following the world's most devastating earthquake; *Flight from Rebirth* (UK 1973) describes the complications resulting from the scientific achievement of reincarnation. Other novels include: *Born Leader* (US 1954), *Time for a Change* (UK 1967) and *Six Gates from Limbo* (UK 1968).

Vonda N. McIntyre
Vonda N. McIntyre is an American writer who studied at the Clarion Writer's Workshop in the early 1970s and won the *Clarion II* award with her first published story, 'Of Mist, and Grass, and Sand'. The same novelette brought her a Nebula in 1973. Her novel, *The Exile Waiting* (US 1975), tells of a telepathic girl pickpocket in an underground city of post-catastrophe Earth.

She is also co-compiler, with Susan Anderson, of the anthology, *Aurora: Beyond Equality* (US 1976).

R. W. Mackelworth
Ronald Walter Mackelworth is a British writer, born in London in 1930, who began contributing short stories to *New Worlds* in the early 1960s. His full-time career has been mainly in insurance and his sf output is small but thoughtful. It includes the novels: *Firemantle* (UK 1958), which pits the central character against an unseen enemy threatening Earth, and *Tiltangle* (UK 1971)—an interesting

'Ice Age' setting of a colony which has forgotten the purpose of its being in its particular surroundings.

Richard McKenna

Richard McKenna was a US author well known in other literary fields. He was born in Idaho in 1913, joined the US Navy in 1931, and died in 1964. He has written some short sf stories, noted for their excellent style. Five of them can be found in his collection *Casey Agonistes* (UK 1974), which also includes an introduction by Damon Knight. McKenna won a posthumous Nebula in 1966 with 'The Secret Place'.

Dean McLaughlin

American writer who first appeared in *Astounding* in 1951 with 'For Those Who Follow After'. He became a fairly regular contributor and also wrote for one or two other magazines. His books include *Dome World* (US 1962), which is an undersea setting, and *The Fury From Earth* (US 1963), an account of Earth's first space war. The struggle of one man to put humanity back on the road to interstellar flight is told in *The Man Who Wanted Stars* (US 1965).

Katherine MacLean

Katherine Anne MacLean is an American writer whose relatively small output has attracted favourable attention. She was born in New Jersey in 1925 and has followed a great variety of occupations ranging from food quality control to organizing the Free University of Portland. Her first short story, 'Defence Mechanism', appeared in *Astounding* in 1949. Among her subsequent tales 'Incommunicado' (1950), 'The Snowball Effect' (1952) and 'Unhuman Sacrifice' (1958) are of particular note, the last being an account of Man's misunderstanding of alien rituals. The first two can be found in her collection *The Diploids* (US 1962).

Katherine MacLean has also written a novel in collaboration with Charles V. de Vet, *Cosmic Checkmate* (US 1962), and won the Nebula Award for her story 'The Missing Man' in 1971.

Willis E. McNelly

American academic and co-editor with Leon E. Stover of *Above the*

Human Landscape: A Social Science Fiction Anthology (US 1972). It is an important selection with two searching appendices: 'Apeman, Superman—or, 2001's Answer to the World Riddle' and 'Vonnegut's *Slaughterhouse Five*: Science Fiction as Objective Correlative'.

Charles Eric Maine

The pseudonym of the British writer David McIlwain, who was born in 1921. Before serving in the Royal Air Force during the Second World War he had been a noted fan in the north of England. After the war he took up TV engineering and began writing about television and radio. His first novel, *Spaceways* (UK 1953), was adapted from his own radio play; it was also filmed.

Among his many published stories are an account of the first moon landing in *High Vacuum* (UK 1958), and the chronicle of the last man left alive in a female society, *World Without Men* (US 1958). The depletion of the seas as a result of H-bomb tests is depicted in *The Tide Went Out* (UK 1958), while Martian efforts to take over Earth feature in *He Owned the World* (US 1960).

The Darkest of Nights (UK 1962) tells of the breakdown of society following a lethal epidemic. *B.E.A.S.T.* (UK 1966) describes the dangerous effects of attempting to simulate animal evolution. Other tales include: *Timeliner* (UK 1955), *Crisis 2000* (UK 1955), *Escapement* (UK 1956), *The Isotope Man* (UK 1957), *Count-Down* (UK 1959), *Subterfuge* (UK 1960), *The Mind of Mr Soames* (UK 1961), *Never Let Up* (UK 1964) and *The Random Factor* (UK 1970).

Barry N. Malzberg

A recent American arrival, Barry N. Malzberg has shown himself both prolific and versatile during the few years he has been writing science fiction. Among his first novels were *The Falling Astronauts* (US 1971) in which a moon mission is threatened by disaster, and *Overlay* (US 1972), an alien invasion of Earth concentrated through one man. He became the first winner of the John W. Campbell Memorial Award with *Beyond Apollo* (US 1972), which tells of the return of the initial mission to Venus minus commander, and with the remaining crew member insane.

The Day of the Burning (US 1974) is a variation of the 'Man must prove himself fit for the Galactic Federation, or die' theme, only in this instance there is a 12-hour time limit; and a strange 21st-century re-enactment of J. F. Kennedy's assassination has unpleasant consequences in *The Destruction of the Temple* (US 1974). Other novels include *Revelations* (US 1972), *The Men Inside* (US 1973), *Tactics of Conquest* (US 1973) and *On an Alien Planet* (US 1974). Some of his short stories have been collected in *Out From Ganymede* (US 1974).

Laurence Manning

A popular and regular contributor to *Wonder Stories* during the 1930s, Laurence Edward Manning was born in Canada in 1899, moving to the US in 1920 as a journalist. Among his more noted stories were 'The Voyage of the Asteroid' (1932) and the two series 'The Man Who Awoke' and 'Stranger Club' which ran in *Wonder Stories* during 1933–35. The latter includes an imaginative alien robot tale, 'The Call of the Mech-Men'.

Leo Margulies

Born in Brooklyn in 1900, Leo Margulies spent more than forty years in publishing and editorial activities, almost exclusively in the magazine field. Among the publications with which he was connected were *Captain Future*, *Thrilling Wonder Stories* (which had originally been Gernsback's *Wonder Stories* before he sold it to Clayton Magazines in 1936), *Startling Stories*, *Fantastic Universe*, *Satellite Science Fiction* and a variety of crime and mystery magazines. His many anthologies include: *Three Times Infinity* (US 1958), *Three from Out There* (US 1959), *Get Out of My Sky* (US 1960), *The Unexpected* (US 1961), *The Ghoul Keepers* (US 1961), *Three in One* (US 1963), *Weird Tales* (US 1964), *Worlds of Weird* (US 1965), and the following in collaboration with Oscar J. Friend: *From Off This World* (US 1949), *My Best Science Fiction Story* (US 1949), *The Giant Anthology of Science Fiction* (US 1954) and *Race to the Stars* (US 1958). Margulies died at the end of 1975.

Harry Martinson

Writer of what became literally a 'space opera', Harry Martinson is a Swede who was born in 1904. A distinguished poet in his own country—he was elected to the Swedish Academy in 1949—he has written a 102-poem saga, *Aniara* (Sweden 1957), which tells of a Mars-bound spaceship deflected from its course so that it leaves the solar system altogether. It was set to music in 1959 by Martinson's compatriot Carl-Birger Blomdahl and the opera has subsequently been broadcast over many European TV networks and performed in Stockholm, London and West Berlin. The poems were translated into English in 1963.

Douglas R. Mason

Douglas Rankine Mason began writing science fiction a little over a decade ago, but in that time he has produced a sizable collection of space- and earth-bound adventures in a lightweight vein (both in his own name and under the pseudonym 'John Rankine'). He was born in Wales in 1918 and has spent most of his adult years in education, first becoming a junior-school headmaster in 1954. His published sf stories date from the inclusion of 'Two's Company' (using his pseudonym) in Carnell's first *New Writings in SF* (UK 1964).

Stories under his real name include: *From Carthage Then I Came* (US 1966), *Eight Against Utopia* (US 1967), *Landfall Is a State of Mind* (US 1968), *Ring of Violence* (US 1968), *The Tower of Rizwan* (US 1968), *The Janus Syndrome* (US 1969) and *Satellite 54–Zero* (US 1971).

Using the 'Rankine' pen-name, he has written three books in the 'Dag Fletcher' space adventure series: *The Blockage of Sinitron* (UK 1966; a short story collection), *Interstellar Two–Five* (UK 1966) and *One is One* (UK 1968); also *Never the Same Door* (UK 1968), *Moons of Triopus* (UK 1968), *Binary Z* (UK 1969), *The Weisman Experiment* (UK 1969) and *Operation Umanaq* (UK 1973).

David I. Masson

An antiquarian librarian, born in Edinburgh in 1915. His first sf story, 'Traveller's Rest', appeared in *New Worlds* in 1965, and he has since written a number of others. Examples can be found in his collection *The Caltraps of Time* (UK 1968).

Richard Matheson

Richard Burton Matheson is an American writer noted for his ability to write horror stories which can also be called science fiction. Born in New Jersey in 1926, he graduated as a Bachelor of Journalism from the University of Missouri and for the last twenty years has been mainly occupied with TV scripts and screenplays. He was scriptwriter on the film *The Incredible Shrinking Man*, produced by Albert Zugsmith and directed by Jack Arnold, which won a Hugo in 1958. *The Magazine of Fantasy and Science Fiction* published his first story, 'Born of Man and Woman', in 1950 and his work in this form can be found in several collections: *Born of Man and Woman* (US 1954, reprinted as *Third From the Sun* in 1955), *The Shores of Space* (US 1957), *Shock* (US 1961), *Shock II* (US 1964) and *Shock III* (US 1966). His novels include *I Am Legend* (US 1954), an interesting attempt to account for human vampires by a scientific explanation; *The Shrinking Man* (US 1956), the basis of the film; and *A Stir of Echoes* (US 1958). Matheson was Guest of Honour at the 16th World Science Fiction Convention in 1958.

Shepherd Mead

American advertising man, former Vice President of the Benton & Bowles New York agency and author of *How to Succeed in Business Without Really Trying*, Edward Shepherd Mead was born in St Louis in 1914. His contribution to the sf field is small, but noted for its strong satirical quality. It includes the novels *The Magnificent MacInnes* (US 1949), *Tessie, the Hound of Channel I* (US 1951), *The Carefully Considered Rape of the World* (US 1966) and *The Big Ball of Wax* (US 1954)—the last being a hilarious account of the confrontation between a Madison Avenue advertising man and an evangelistic ex-burlesque queen whose revivalist movement is destroying public response to high-pressure sales techniques.

S. P. Meek

Former US Army officer, Sterner St Paul Meek achieved popularity in *Amazing Stories* and *Astounding* at the beginning of the 1930s, particularly with his 'Doctor Bird' series in the latter. He was born in Chicago in 1894 and worked his way through the Army

Ordnance Department until he became its Chief Publications Officer in 1941. He also wrote two 'Lost World' serials for *Amazing*, published thirty years later in book form as *The Drums of Tapajos* and *Troyana* (both US 1961). His *Monkeys Have No Tails in Zamboanga* (US 1935) is a collection of humorous and intriguing tales.

Judith Merril

Born Josephine Judith Zissman in 1923, Judith Merril is a Canadian-based writer as well known for her irrepressible enthusiam as for her writings and anthologies in the field. Her first story, 'That only a Mother', was run in *Astounding* in 1948 and examples of her other contributions to the magazines can be found in the collections, *Out of Bounds* (US 1960) and *Daughters of Earth* (UK 1968). Her novels include *Shadow on the Hearth* (US 1950), a gripping account of a nuclear attack on North America, and *The Tomorrow People* (US 1960), in which the first expeditions to Mars are set against an East–West struggle for the conquest of space; also two collaborations with C. M. Kornbluth writing under the pseudonym of 'Cyril Judd': *Gunner Cade* and *Outpost Mars* (both US 1952).

Among her many anthologies are: *Shot in the Dark* (US 1950), *Beyond Human Ken* (US 1952), *Beyond the Barriers of Time and Space* (US 1954), *Human?* (US 1954), *Galaxy of Ghouls* (US 1955), *SF: The Best of the Best* (US 1967) and *England Swings SF* (US 1968). In 1956 she embarked on an annual series, which began as *S-F: the Year's Greatest Science-Fiction and Fantasy* (US 1956), switching to *5th Annual Edition of the Year's Best SF* (US 1960), and later changing to *SF 12* (US 1968).

Abraham Merritt

Known to pulp readers as 'Lord of Fantasy', Abraham Merritt was born in the US in 1884. Originally destined for a career as a lawyer, he turned to journalism after a decline in family fortunes. From local papers he progressed to the post of associate editor of *The American Weekly* and in 1937 took over its editorial chair which he held until his death in 1943. His first published story, 'Through the

Dragon Glass', appeared in *All-Story Magazine* in 1917, and he subsequently became a regular contributor to *Weird Tales* and other fantasy pulps.

The major part of Merritt's work was fantasy, and if his use of symbols and images was often striking, his purple prose was enough to deter some readers—and it still is, although much of his work remains popular. Even his best-known stories, such as *The Moon Pool* (US 1919) and *The Ship of Ishtar* (US 1926), have only tenuous links with science fiction, but so much of his work has appeared in sf magazines that it could hardly not be of some influence. Damon Knight's description of Merritt as 'chinless, bald and shaped like a shmoo' calls to mind what many an aspiring writer must feel about the faceless editor hiding behind the latest batch of rejection slips.

Sam Merwin Jr

American editor and writer, Samuel Merwin entered the sf pulp field in 1939 with 'The Scourge Below' in *Thrilling Wonder Stories*. In 1945 he took over the editorship for Standard Magazines of *Thrilling Wonder* and *Startling Stories* and also launched *Fantastic Story Magazine* and *Wonder Story Annual*. Leaving in 1951, he subsequently edited the early numbers of *Fantastic Universe* and was Assistant Editor of *Galaxy* and *Beyond* during 1953–54. He also edited two issues of *Satellite Science Fiction* in 1956.

His own stories in the genre include *The House of Many Worlds* (US 1951), telling of a journey to alternate worlds, and its sequel *3 Faces of Time* (US 1955). *Killer to Come* (US 1953) is a futuristic detective tale, and *The White Widows* (US 1953) takes the sex war to the limits where women plan to exterminate men.

P. Schuyler Miller

A leading sf book reviewer, Peter Schuyler Miller was born in the US in 1912. An educationalist who majored in chemistry, he won the *Air Wonder* cover story contest in 1930 with 'The Red Plague'. Among his other notable stories during the next few years were 'The Man from Mars' (1931) and 'The Sands of Time' (1937). Others can be found in his collection *The Titan* (US 1952). He also collaborated with L. Sprague de Camp on *Genus Homo* (US 1950), a setting in the far future where advanced apes have replaced man.

In 1951 Miller began his 'The Reference Library' column in *Astounding*, and it is as a reviewer that he is now chiefly known. His work in this area earned him a Hugo in 1963. He died in 1974.

Walter M. Miller Jr

A noted American writer, Walter M. Miller was born in 1923. He served with the US Air Force during the Second World War and was involved in the notorious destruction by the Allies of the monastery at Monte Cassino in Italy. His first story was 'Secret of the Death Dome' in *Amazing* in 1951, after which he wrote for many of the magazines. Two excellent collections of his work are *Conditionally Human* (US 1962), which contains his Hugo-winning story 'The Darfstellar' (1955), and *The View From the Stars* (US 1965).

Miller's striking novel *A Canticle for Leibowitz* (US 1960) is an amalgam of three stories first published in *The Magazine of Fantasy and Science Fiction*. It won a highly deserved Hugo in 1961. It tells of the new rise of civilization many centuries after a nuclear war where the Church, almost unwittingly, has been the guardian of many technological secrets from the former Age. On another level, the book is a biting satire on the qualities of good and evil inherent in the human condition. It ends with Earth's second nuclear holocaust.

Robert P. Mills

Robert P. Mills is a former editor of *The Magazine of Fantasy and Science Fiction* and the short-lived *Venture* magazine. Born in Montana in 1920, he has followed a career in publishing and in literary agencies. Already managing editor of *The Magazine of Fantasy and Science Fiction*, he took over the editorship in 1958 when Anthony Boucher left because of ill health.

Mills remained editor until 1962. As such he continued the compilation of the annual anthologies *Best from Fantasy and Science Fiction*, producing the 9th–11th in the series. He also selected the stories for *A Decade of Fantasy and Science Fiction* (US 1960).

Samuel Mines
Originally assistant to Sam Merwin at Standard Magazines, Samuel Mines edited *Thrilling Wonder, Startling Stories, Fantastic Story Magazine* and *Wonder Story Annual* after Merwin's departure in 1951, and continued until 1954. He also launched *Space Stories* and compiled the anthology *The Best From Startling Stories* (US 1953, retitled *Startling Stories* (UK 1954) and later *Moment Without Time* (UK 1956, Science Fiction Book Club edition)).

Naomi Mitchison
English writer and sister of eminent scientist the late J. B. S. Haldane, Naomi Mitchison was born in 1897. Among her many novels are a few deliberately written as science fiction. These include *Memoirs of a Spacewoman* (UK 1962), a story of symbiosis entailing the grafting of extraterrestrials on to humans to ensure the aliens' survival, and *Solution 3* (UK 1975) in which a new human society is built on the basis of cloning and homosexuality.

Michael Moorcock
Born in London in 1939, Michael Moorcock first became interested in fantasy on discovering Edgar Rice Burroughs, but has since found him unreadable, and in science fiction when he encountered *Galaxy* in the mid-1950s. He now views the genre with distaste.

Having edited *Tarzan Adventures* at age 17, he became the guiding hand behind the British *New Worlds* magazine in 1964 and a germinal influence on the 'New Wave'. He encouraged experimental styles and approaches which sometimes read more like hard-core pornography than soft-ware science. The magazine had to be rescued with an Arts Council grant in 1967 and in the following year it was proscribed by the UK's largest retail booksellers, W. H. Smith, because of the salty language gracing Norman Spinrad's *Bug Jack Barron*. Other New Wave writers cultivated by Moorcock in *New Worlds* included John Sladek, Thomas M. Disch, J. G. Ballard and Pamela Zoline.

Moorcock's own science fiction writing is relatively small compared with his copious output of 'Sword and Sorcery' fantasy. However, his 'Jerry Cornelius' novels, *The Final Programme* (UK 1968), *A Cure for Cancer* (UK 1969) and *The English Assassin* (UK 1973), have enjoyed wide popularity and the character moved over to the serial universe of *International Times* as a cartoon strip. (His collected adventures in that environment were published by Moorcock and Langdon Jones as *The Nature of the Catastrophe* (UK 1971).)

Moorcock won a Nebula in 1967 for 'Behold the Man', in which a time traveller actually impersonates Christ to fulfil the Passion when he finds that Jesus is a cretin. A later story of note is *Breakfast in the Ruins* (UK 1972).

C. L. Moore

One of the most successful and influential women writers of science fantasy, and wife until his death in 1958 of Henry Kuttner. Born in Indianapolis in 1911, Catherine Lucille Moore is said to have weaned herself on a diet of *Amazing Stories* and Edgar Rice Burroughs. Her richly inventive short story 'Shambleau', which appeared in *Weird Tales* in 1933, is still hailed by many as a masterpiece and its success led her to write several sequels featuring its central character, 'Northwest Smith'. Thereafter she became a regular contributor to both *Weird Tales* and *Astounding*.

After her marriage Catherine Moore collaborated with Kuttner on several novels and many short stories. As a solo effort she wrote *Doomsday Morning* (US 1957), which tells of a revolt against authority in a US of the near future. Her magazine stories can be read in several collections: *Judgment Night* (US 1952), *Shambleau & Others* (US 1953) and *Northwest of Earth* (US 1954).

Patrick Moore

Science writer and astronomer whose unruly hair and runaway enthusiasm are familiar to many British viewers of his *Sky at Night* TV programme. Patrick Alfred Moore was born in 1923 and served in the Royal Air Force during the Second World War. He has written a large number of 'juvenile' sf stories since the early 1950s and several popular books on the moon and planets. His survey of the genre, *Science and Fiction* (UK 1957), was a useful handbook in its time and one of the first British efforts to examine science fiction in some detail and at length.

Ward Moore
Only an occasional sf writer, to our cost, Ward Moore was born in New Jersey in 1903. He has worked in the book trade, in shipyards, farming and other occupations in between writing books. He emerged fully-fledged into the sf field with *Greener Than You Think* (US 1947), a satirical and delightfully zany account of a world overrun by mutated devil grass set off by a wonder fertilizer. Subsequently he wrote a number of stories for the magazines, one of which he expanded into *Bring the Jubilee* (US 1953), a highly successful attempt to portray an alternative US of the 1950s on the assumption that the South had won the Civil War. Echoes of the Civil War also occur in *Joyleg* (US 1962), written in collaboration with Avram Davidson.

Leo Morey
Cover artist throughout most of the 1930s for *Amazing Stories*, Leo Morey was born in Peru and later studied engineering. He did some newspaper illustrating before entering the sf field. Other magazines which occasionally used his work were *Future Science Fiction*, *Stirring Science Stories* and *Satellite*.

Dan Morgan
Former professional guitarist, Dan Morgan is a British author who was born in Cheshire in 1925. He began contributing to *New Worlds* in 1952 with 'Alien Analysis', the first of many stories for that magazine. His earliest novel was *Cee Tee Man* (UK 1955), followed by *The Uninhibited* (UK 1961). *The Richest Corpse in Show Business* (UK 1966) is a humorous send-up of the genre, and *The New Minds* (UK 1967), *The Several Minds* (UK 1969) and *The Mind Trap* (UK 1970) all deal with new states of mental perception. He has collaborated on a number of stories with John Kippax, including *Thunder of Stars* (UK 1968) and *The Neutral Stars* (UK 1973). His most recent book, *The Country of the Mind* (UK 1975), is another ESP treatment involving the fusing of people's consciousness.

Sam Moskowitz
American science fiction researcher, editor, agent, critic and

anthologist, Sam Moskowitz (born 1920) has become synonymour in name with the production of articles and introductions in which his knowledge of the genre has been demonstrated—but his accuracy has been questioned. His two volumes of painstaking appraisal, *Explorers of the Infinite* (US 1963) and *Seekers of Tomorrow* (US 1966), are useful guides to the development of science fiction based on the individual careers of many leading writers. His other published studies include a history of sf fandom, *The Immortal Storm* (US 1954); a history and anthology of early stories in popular magazines from 1891 to 1911, *Science Fiction by Gaslight* (US 1968); and *A History of The Scientific Romance in the Munsey Magazines, 1912–1920* (US 1970). He is also joint compiler of several anthologies with Roger Elwood and sole producer of *Editor's Choice in Science Fiction* (US 1954), *Doorway Into Time* (US 1966), *Masterpieces of Science Fiction* (US 1967), *The Vortex Blasters* (UK 1967) and *Microscopic God and Other Stories* (US 1968).

Terry Nation
Original scriptwriter for the BBC TV series *Dr Who* and the man who laid waste to the tranquillity of countless British homes by dreaming up the Daleks. The piping tones of 'I will exterminate you', addressed to astonished parents as their offspring endeavoured to emulate Nation's free-wheeling pepper pots, offered a cheerfully destructive counter-balance to the 'Peace and Love' Flower Power movement which their elder sisters and brothers were busy propagating in the mid-1960s. Latterly, his post-catastrophe series *The Survivors* appeared on the small screen in 1975, followed by the book of the same name (UK 1976).

Josef Nesvadba
A Czechoslovak psychiatrist who was born in 1926, Josef Nesvadba is among the leading Central European sf writers. Collections of his stories are numerous in his native land, and several tales have appeared in translation in *The Magazine of Fantasy and Science Fiction*. Translations of his work include the collection *In The Footsteps of the Abominable Snowman* (UK 1970), subsequently retitled *The Lost Face* (US 1971).

Kris Neville

Kris Ottman Neville is an American writer whose work in the sf field has been concentrated very much on the magazines. He was born in Missouri in 1925, served as a radio operator in the US Army, and has also spent some time in the Merchant Navy. His first story, 'The Hand from the Stars', appeared in *Super Science* in 1949, and was followed by many others in various magazines including several novelettes in *Imagination*. Among his full-length novels are *The Unearth People* (US 1964), *The Mutants* (US 1966), *Peril of the Starmen* (US 1967) and *Special Delivery* (US 1967).

Peter Nicholls

Peter Nicholls was born in Australia in 1939. He lectured in English Literature for seven years after graduation, and won a Harkness Fellowship in film direction in Boston and Hollywood 1968–70. Since 1971 he has been Administrator and Senior Lecturer at the Science Fiction Foundation in London. He is editor of the journal *Foundation: The Review of Science Fiction* and has written many critical articles on the subject. He has also edited *Science Fiction at Large* (UK 1976), a collection of lectures given by sf writers and others at the Institute of Contemporary Arts, London, in 1975.

Larry Niven

A noted arrival of the last decade and a sophisticated updater of space opera, Laurence Van Cott Niven was born in Los Angeles in 1938. He studied at the universities of Washburn and California and made his first sf sale with 'The Coldest Place' in *If* in 1964. Since then he has collected no less than three Hugos: for 'Neutron Star' in 1967 (included in the collection of the same name, US 1968), for *Ringworld* (US 1970) in 1971, and for 'Inconstant Moon' in 1972. *Ringworld* also won a Nebula in 1970 and tells of an expedition to a strange world by humans and puppeteers (the latter being a favoured invention of Niven which look vaguely like two-headed centaurs).

Among his other novels are the telepath story *World of Ptavvs* (US 1966), *A Gift from Earth* (US 1968) and *Protector* (US 1973). He has also written *The Mote in God's Eye* (US 1974, in collaboration with Jerry Pournelle), which recounts a mission to a very unEarthlike world via a black hole in space. A continuation of the partnership with Pournelle produced *Inferno* (US 1975).

William F. Nolan

US editor and sf reviewer for the *Los Angeles Times*, William Francis Nolan was born in 1928 in Kansas City. He has compiled the anthologies *Man Against Tomorrow* (US 1965), *The Pseudo-People* (US 1965), *Three to the Highest Power* (US 1968) and *A Sea of Space* (US 1970). He is also co-author with George Clayton Johnson of *Logan's Run* (US 1967). The novel tells of a search for sanctuary in a technological 'utopia' where no one is allowed to live beyond the age of twenty-one.

Alden H. Norton

Born in 1903 in Massachusetts, Alden H. Norton claims an ancestry reaching back to the Pilgrim Father carpenter, John Alden. In the science fiction field his reputation as a pulp magazine editor in direct competition with John W. Campbell is almost as impressive. After various junior editorial posts he became editor of *Astonishing Stories* and *Super Science Stories* in 1941. His first issues included Heinlein's early 'Lost Legion' (under the pseudonym of 'Lyle Monroe'), stories by Henry Kuttner and Alfred Bester, and 'Daughters of Eternity' by the former editor of both publications, Fred Pohl (writing as 'James McCreigh'). Among other regular contributors were 'Doc' Smith, Robert Bloch, Leigh Brackett, Wilson Tucker and Ray Bradbury, who owed to Norton the publication of his first professional story, 'Pendulum'. Both magazines were victims of the paper shortage during the Second World War, but Norton revived *Super Science Stories* in 1949 and, with its second and final demise, moved on to edit both *Argosy* and *Adventure*. He was also editor-in-chief of *Famous Fantastic Mysteries* during the 1940s.

Andre Norton

A leading woman writer in the field, Andre Norton was born in Cleveland, Ohio, in 1912, and was at one time a children's librarian there. Her real name is Alice Mary Norton, but she has also written some stories under the pseudonym of 'Andrew North'. Under that name, her first published story ran in 1947—'The People of the Crater' (in *Fantasy Book*). Since then she has written many novels, often with a fantasy slant and much melodrama. They include excursions on to unknown worlds in *The Beast Master* (US 1959) and its sequel *Lord of Thunder* (US 1962), *Sargasso of Space* (US 1955), *Plague Ship* (US 1956) and *Voodoo Planet* (US 1959)—the last three under the 'Andrew North' pen-name.

Adventures in time travel feature in *The Crossroads of Time* (US 1956) and in *The Time Traders* (US 1958) and its two sequels, *Galactic Derelict* (US 1959) and *The Defiant Agents* (US 1962). *The Sioux Spaceman* (US 1960) is one example of its author's liking for Red Indian heroes. Among her other novels are: *Star Guard* (US 1955), *Sea Siege* and *Star Born* (both US 1957), *Star Gate* (US 1958), *Catseye* (US 1961) and *Eye of the Monster* (US 1962).

Some of Andre Norton's short stories have been collected in *High Sorcery* (US 1970), and she has compiled the anthologies *Space Service* (US 1953), *Space Pioneers* (US 1954) and *Space Police* (US 1956).

Alan E. Nourse

Another of science fiction's medical contributors, Alan Edward Nourse was born in Iowa in 1928. He first studied biology before qualifying at Pennsylvania Medical School. His professional experience is put to use in several of his novels, among them *A Man Obsessed* (US 1955), which concerns brain surgery and the psychological sciences, and *Star Surgeon* (US 1960), an account of an extraterrestrial undergoing human medical training. *The Mercy Men* (US 1968) tells of humans used as guinea-pigs in sinister underground laboratories.

Rocket to Limbo (US 1957) features interstellar exploration and the discovery of a hostile planet, while a future Earth setting and the overthrow of an oppressive régime in the US can be found in *The Invaders Are Coming* (US 1959, written with J. A. Meyer).

Among Nourse's tales in the collection *Tiger by the Tail & Other Science Fiction Stories* (US 1961), both 'Nightmare Brother' and 'Brightside Crossing' are of note, the latter recounting a perilous journey across the hot face of the planet Mercury. Other collections are *The Counterfeit Man* (US 1963), *Psi High and Others* (US 1965) and *PX for Tomorrow* (US 1972). He has also written a number of novels for the juvenile market.

Philip Francis Nowlan

The originator of 'Buck Rogers', who probably never foresaw that both his own and his invention's future lay in the realm of comic strips. The die was cast with Nowlan's first story in *Amazing*, 'Armageddon 2419' (1928), which with its sequel, 'The Airlords of Han' (1929), introduced the central character 'Anthony Rogers', the prototype of 'Buck'. The two stories were combined in *Armageddon 2419 A.D.* (US 1962) twenty-two years after Nowlan's death. Nowlan stayed pretty well exclusively in the comic field once the 'Buck Rogers' strip acquired an enthusiastic following, but he had just begun what he hoped would be a new series for *Astounding* when he died. The Rogers saga was filmed in 1939 by Universal.

Fitz-James O'Brien

Along with Poe and Mary Shelley, Fitz-James O'Brien was another precursor of the modern genre. He was born in Ireland in 1828 and died from wounds sustained in the American Civil War in 1862, having emigrated across the Atlantic ten years earlier. Many of his stories are ingenious—and some, as in the case of 'The Diamond Lens', are renowned. Several were reprinted during the pulp era in such magazines as *Amazing* and *Famous Fantastic Mysteries*. Two collections were also published: *The Diamond Lens* (US 1885) and *Fitz-James O'Brien: Collected Stories* (US 1925).

Andrew Offut

Andrew Offut is a new American writer among whose first novels are *Evil is Live Spelled Backwards* (US 1970) and *The Castle Keeps* (US 1972). The former portrays a religious tyranny in 21st-century America against which a satanist underground rebels, while the latter is a graphic account of civilization tearing itself apart. Another story, *Andor on Aros* (US 1973) is mainly 'Sword and Sorcery' fantasy.

Chad Oliver

Symes Chadwick Oliver is an American anthropologist, born in Cincinnati in 1928. His work in anthropology for the University of Texas has taken him as far afield as Kenya, and his devotion to the subject is evident in many of his sf stories. It is notable in the novel *Shadows in the Sun* (US 1954) which explores the theme of human-like aliens on Earth. In *The Winds of Time* (US 1957) extraterrestrials emerge who have been in suspended animation for 150 centuries. *Unearthly Neighbours* (US 1960) is a further treatment of aliens, centred around the problems of communicating with them. Oliver's short stories are available in the collection *Another Kind* (US 1955).

Bob Olsen

An early pulp writer whose full name was Alfred Johannes Olsen Jr. He was born in the US in 1884. Olsen made his début in Gernsback's *Amazing* in 1927 with 'The Four-Dimensional Roller-Press', the first of a series of amusing tales on the fourth dimension. He also wrote a number of mystery stories with a scientific slant. He died in 1956.

Paul Orban

American illustrator whose work has appeared in the interiors of many sf magazines since the 1940s. He trained at the Chicago Academy of Fine Arts and worked for the *Chicago Tribune* before moving over to advertising. Later he became a freelance artist in New York, also contributing to a variety of publications outside the sf field.

George Orwell

'George Orwell' was the pseudonym of the British writer Eric Arthur Blair. He was born in 1903 in India, where his father was a civil servant, and was taken to Britain in 1907. Educated at Eton, he left to join the Indian Imperial Police in Burma, remaining there until 1928. He more or less starved in both Paris and London before serving and being wounded in the International Brigade during the

Spanish Civil War. He began his literary career as a book reviewer and later became literary editor of *Tribune* and a correspondent for the *Observer* and *Manchester Evening News*. He died of tuberculosis in 1950.

He achieved lasting renown with his anti-utopian novel *Nineteen Eighty-four* (US 1949). While much of the *plot* stems from Zamyatin's *We* (which in turn derives a great deal from Wells's *When the Sleeper Wakes* and 'A Story of the Days to Come'), the story is notable for its sinister communication concepts of 'Newspeak' and 'Doublethink', and for its use of violence and oppression as a political philosophy. (Orwell later confessed that the book might have been less grim had he not been so ill when he wrote it.) Five years later it was adapted for BBC Television and caused an uproar because of its torture scene (mild by comparison with what is viewed today). It was also filmed by Associated British in 1955.

His other major speculative novel, *Animal Farm* (UK 1945), is an allegorical fantasy with similar anti-utopian overtones.

Raymond A. Palmer

A controversial figure on the sf landscape, US editor Ray Palmer (born 1910) has been branded as the most sensation-seeking among the many colourful, occasionally odd, sometimes downright weird characters who have held editorial chairs during the fifty years of the sf magazines. To counter the charge he might well claim that it sold his publications—which it did—but at the cost of alienating many of the more dedicated devotees. His first move on taking over *Amazing* when Ziff-Davis bought the magazine in 1938 was to slant it towards the juvenile market. A year later he launched *Fantastic Adventures* with a similar approach. Both paid off in terms of large circulations and thereafter Palmer pulled many rabbits out of the hat when he felt like boosting sales.

The most spectacular of these was the *Shaver Mystery* stories, written by Richard S. Shaver and beginning with 'I Remember Lemuria' in *Amazing* in 1945. These so-called factual accounts of voices from the underworld brought a new occult-minded readership to the magazine and finally persuaded Palmer to enter that field at the end of 1949. Leaving Ziff-Davis he launched *Other Worlds* and *Imagination*, selling the latter after only two issues. For several years he continued with *Other Worlds*, sometimes changing its title, eventually calling it *Flying Saucers from Other Worlds*.

During his editorship of *Amazing* and *Fantastic Adventures*, Palmer wrote a number of stories for both magazines, often under such pseudonyms as 'A. R. Steber', 'G. H. Irwin' and 'Frank Patton'.

Edgar Pangborn

Edgar Pangborn was an American writer born in New York in 1909. He studied at Harvard and the New England Conservatory of Music. Setting aside music composition, he turned to writing in his twenties and freelanced for a decade before serving in the US Army during the Second World War. His first sf story, 'Angel's Egg', appeared in *Galaxy* in 1951 and he won the 1955 International Fantasy Award with *A Mirror for Observers* (US 1954). The novel tells of the battles between two opposing Martian factions over the future of Earth.

Other stories are *West of the Sun* (US 1953), recounting the struggle to colonize a strange planet after a spaceship crash, and *The Judgement of Eve* (US 1966), a post-catastrophe tale. Pangborn died in early 1976.

Alexei Panshin

A noted fan, critic and—more recently—author, Alexei Panshin was born in Michigan in 1940. His writings in the realm of fandom won him a Hugo in 1967 and in the following year he received a Nebula for his novel *Rite of Passage* (US 1968), recounting the travails of a young girl cast out from a post-catastrophe Earth on to a hostile colonial world. Two other books, *The Thurb Revolution* and *Star Well* (both US 1968), tell of the interstellar adventures of 'Anthony Villiers'.

Panshin's study of Robert A. Heinlein, *Heinlein in Dimension* (US 1968), is considered one of the most thorough investigations of any single sf writer. Dividing Heinlein's writing career into three stages, it shows very clearly how the author has moved from the brilliantly executed tales of his early years into the long, discursive, less palatable books of his third period. In 1968 Panshin also became editor of the *Science Fiction Writers of America Bulletin*.

Frank R. Paul

One of the most effective of all sf illustrators whose main work, however, was devoted to textbooks. Frank Rudolph Paul was born in Vienna in 1884. He studied art in Europe and the US and began working with Gernsback's factual publications, *Electrical Experimenter* and *Science and Invention*, before producing all the covers for *Amazing* from its launch in 1926 until 1929. Gernsback then employed him for the covers and many inside illustrations in his *Wonder Stories* magazines until they were sold in 1936. He later returned to *Amazing* under its Ziff-Davis management and produced a noted series of back covers for both it and its companion *Fantastic Adventures*.

He ceased sf illustration during the Second World War and only occasionally reappeared in the field before his death in 1963.

Emil Petaja

Emil Theodore Petaja is a US writer who was born in Montana in 1915. He was formerly a professional photographer, owning his own portrait studios. He first appeared in the sf field with 'Time Will Tell' in *Amazing* (1942) and has since written a number of novels, among them *Alpha Yes, Terra No!* (US 1965), *The Caves of Mars* (US 1965), *The Prism* (US 1968) and *The Time Twister* (US 1968). He has also produced a series of heroic fantasy tales: *Saga of Lost Earths* (US 1966), *The Star Mill* (US 1966), *The Stolen Sun* (US 1967) and *Tramotane* (US 1967).

Rog Phillips

'Rog Phillips' was one of the pen-names of Roger Phillips Graham, an American writer born in 1909 who contributed many short stories to the US magazines during the 1940s. He also wrote a fan column in *Amazing* for some five years and produced several sf novels before his death in 1965. Among these were *Time Trap* (US 1949), *Worlds Within* (US 1950), *World of If* (US 1951) and *The Involuntary Immortals* (US 1959).

H. Beam Piper

Born around 1900, former Pennsylvania Railroad-man H. Beam

Piper began contributing to the sf magazines at the end of the 1940s. Much of his work first appeared in *Astounding*, including his 'Paratime' series. He has written for the juvenile market and produced two novels in collaboration with J. J. McGuire: *Crisis in 2140* (US 1957) and *A Planet for Texans* (US 1958), the latter depicting a planet organized as if it were the early American West. Among his other stories, *Little Fuzzy* (US 1962) stands out as a picturesque account of aliens less stupid than some would have them. He died in the mid-1960s.

Charles Platt

Charles Platt was born in England in 1944. He has been organist in a pop group, a freelance photographer, and a book-jacket designer. He has also designed *New Worlds* magazine, written for it, and been its associate editor. His novel *Garbage World* (US 1967) depicts life on an asteroid used as a rubbish tip by more affluent societies. Another story is *The City Dwellers* (UK 1970), telling how declining population figures affect future urban communities. He is co-compiler, with Hilary Bailey, of the anthology *New Worlds Seven* (UK 1975).

Edgar Allan Poe

Master of the macabre, father of modern detective fiction and author of some precursory sf stories, Edgar Allan Poe was born in Boston in 1809. He led a very chequered career. His mother died while he was young and he was raised by a wealthy guardian who subsequently disowned him. He was expelled from the University of Virginia and courtmartialled at West Point for neglecting his duties. He became a journalist, enjoying success with his writing and highly individualistic poetry, but never receiving much by way of remuneration. His love life was complicated and he suffered from a brain lesion which produced disastrous consequences if he drank (it didn't stop him—at least not until 1849 when he died after one such episode).

Poe is now renowned for his elevation of the Gothic horror story to a level where it could almost be described as art. His scientific romances were few, but notable for a more realistic approach than the more usual fantasies of his time. One of his earliest, *Hans Phaal*

—*A Tale*, ran in the *Southern Literary Messenger* in 1835. It chronicles a balloon flight to the moon and was discontinued when the New York *Sun* began 'seriously' to report the discoveries of vegetation and animal life on the lunar surface—a famous hoax perpetrated by Richard Adams Locke. Another story, *The Narrative of Arthur Gordon Pym's Adventures* (US 1832), telling of an Antarctic voyage, was also left unfinished (it was later completed in 1897 by Jules Verne, who was much influenced by Poe).

A number of Poe's short stories were also written in the early sf idiom. They include a vision of a future society in 'Mellonta Tauta', an account of an individual built entirely of prostheses in 'The Man That Was Used Up', and the imaginative use of mesmerism to prolong personality after physical death in 'The Facts in the Case of M. Valdemar'. All can be found in *The Complete Tales and Poems of Edgar Allan Poe* (US 1938) and distributed at random through many subsequent collections.

Frederik Pohl

A noted American writer and editor, Frederik Pohl was born in New York in 1919. His initial contributions to the genre were made when he was in his early twenties and his first published piece was, perhaps surprisingly, a poem, 'Elegy to a Dead Planet: Luna', in *Amazing* in 1937. He edited *Astonishing* and *Super Science Stories* during 1940–41, and the *Star Science Fiction Stories* series for Ballantine from 1953 until 1959. During the period 1962–69 he edited both *Galaxy* and *If*, and compiled the *If Reader* anthologies from 1966. He has also been an authors' agent and now edits for Bantam Books.

Some of his early magazine stories were written under the pseudonym 'James McCreigh' (occasionally spelt MacCreigh), and his first short collaborations with C. M. Kornbluth were produced under the joint pen-name of 'S. D. Gottesman'.

The partnership with Kornbluth was particularly fruitful, beginning with the much acclaimed *The Space Merchants* (US 1953 —originally serialized in *Galaxy* in 1952 as *Gravy Planet*). It is one of the major anti-utopias of the modern genre, presenting an over-populated world struggling in the grips of a monstrous production-consumption complex and dominated by the non-existent ethics of the Madison Avenue advertising industry. It was followed by

Search the Sky (US 1954), relating the attempts to rediscover Earth after the far-flung colonies had lost touch with it. *Gladiator-at-Law* (US 1955) presented the vision of giant business corporations lethally at war with one another, and the last novel in the collaboration, *Wolfbane* (US 1959), combined a revolt against a repressive régime and a fight with alien robots who had forced a group of humans into a symbiotic whole to assist them in their task of conquest. The partnership of Pohl and Kornbluth finally won a Hugo in 1973 with the short story 'The Meeting', but for Kornbluth it meant little—he had already been dead for well over a decade.

Of Pohl's solo novels, *Slave Ship* (US 1957) told of the training of animals to fight in wars, and *Drunkard's Walk* (US 1960) showed a mathematics teacher being hounded to death by telepathy on a university campus. Further stories are *A Plague of Pythons* (US 1965), dealing with mind control and mental transference from body to body, and *The Age of the Pussyfoot* (US 1970). He has collaborated with Jack Williamson on *The Reefs of Space* (US 1964), *Starchild* (US 1965) and *Rogue Star* (US 1969). They have also jointly produced some novels for the juvenile sf field.

Pohl has written numerous short stories, many of which can be found in his collections: *Alternating Currents* (US 1956), *The Case Against Tomorrow* (US 1957), *Tomorrow Times Seven* (US 1959), *The Man Who Ate the World* (US 1960), *Turn Left at Thursday* (US 1961), *The Wonder Effect* (US 1962, with C. M. Kornbluth), *The Abominable Earthman* (US 1963), *Digits and Dastards* (US 1966), *Day Million* (US 1970) and *The Gold at the Starbow's End* (US 1972). In addition to the *If* anthologies, he has compiled: *Beyond the End of Time* (US 1952), *Shadow of Tomorrow* (US 1953), *Assignment in Tomorrow* (US 1954), *Star of Stars* (US 1960), *The Expert Dreamers* (US 1962), *Time Waits for Winthrop* (US 1962), *The Seventh Galaxy Reader* (US 1964—and subsequent volumes in the series), *Star Fourteen* (US 1966) and *Best Science Fiction for 1972* (US 1972).

Arthur Porges

American mathematics instructor, Arthur Porges (born 1915) has taught at Western Military Academy and the Illinois Institute of Technology. He began writing short stories in the 1950s, and first appeared with 'The Fly' in *The Magazine of Fantasy and Science*

Fiction in 1952. Since then, his sf and fantasy tales have been published in many magazines.

Festus Pragnell

Former London policeman and early British contributor to the American pulps, Festus Pragnell (born 1905) made his first bow in *Amazing* with 'The Essence of Life' in 1933. He later wrote a series of stories for the same magazine around the adventures of 'Don Hargreaves' on Mars and its two moons. His other noted tale, *The Green Man of Graypec*, originally serialized in *Wonder Stories* in 1935, later appeared as *The Green Man of Kilsona* (UK 1936). It is a miniature world setting.

Fletcher Pratt

A noted early contributor to the sf magazines, Fletcher Pratt was born in the US in 1897. In his time he was a journalist, prizefighter, *New York Times* critic and historian of the American Civil War. He entered the sf field at the close of the 1930s, collaborating for some of the time with Laurence Manning and translating many foreign tales for Gernsback's Wonder publications. He also produced a number of space travel popularizations for the juvenile market during the final years before his death in 1956.

Pratt collaborated with L. Sprague de Camp on numerous occasions (see the latter's entry) and wrote, as solo efforts, a fantasy novel, *The Well of the Unicorn* (US 1948, under the pseudonym 'George U. Fletcher') and a space opera, *The Undying Fire* (US 1953). Four short novels make up the collections *Double in Space* (US 1951) and *Double Jeopardy* (US 1952). *Alien Planet* (US 1962) was first published as 'A Voice Across the Years' in *Amazing Stories Quarterly* in 1932. He compiled the anthology, *World of Wonder* (US 1952).

Christopher Priest

A recent arrival on the British sf scene, Christopher Priest made his début with *Indoctrinaire* (UK 1970), which tells of an area in the Brazilian jungle mysteriously existing two hundred years in the future. It was followed by *Fugue for a Darkening Island* (UK 1972), an account of a three-way civil war in a future Britain.

Inverted World (UK 1974) is a well-handled 'slow perception of reality' story, and *The Space Machine* (UK 1976) is a deliberate pastiche of a Wellsian scientific romance, involving time travel from the 1890s forwards.

A selection of his short stories can be found in *Real-Time World* (UK 1974).

Tom Purdom

Thomas Edward Purdom was born in Connecticut in 1936. He has had various clerical and sales jobs, and has written about science in a public relations capacity. His first sf stories appeared in 1957: 'Grieve for a Man' in *Fantastic Universe*, and 'A Matter of Privacy' in *Science Fiction Quarterly*. Since then he has written both short stories and novels, among the latter: *I Want the Stars* (US 1964), *The Tree Lord of Imeten* (US 1966) and *Five Against Arlane* (US 1967).

James L. Quinn

US editor of *If* from 1952 to 1958. As such he collaborated with Eve Wulff on the compilation of the anthologies: *The First World of If* (US 1957) and *The Second World of If* (US 1958).

John Rackham

'John Rackham' is the pen-name of British writer John Thomas Phillifent, who was born in Durham in 1916. Formerly a seafarer—he served in the Royal Navy from 1935 to 1947—he has produced a space operatic account of interplanetary warfare in *Danger from Vega* (US 1966) and under his own name has written novelizations of the following vaguely sf-orientated episodes from *The Man from U.N.C.L.E.* television series: *The Mad Scientist Affair* (US 1966), *The Corfu Affair* (UK 1967) and *The Power Cube Affair* (UK 1968). Other stories under his pseudonym include *The Touch of Evil* (UK 1963), *We, the Venusians* (US 1965), *The Double Invaders* (US 1967), *Alien Sea* (US 1968) and *The Proxima Project* (US 1968).

Ayn Rand

Ayn Rand is a noted US novelist, playwright and screenwriter who was born in Petrograd, Russia. She is a forceful advocate of what are generally seen as right-wing views, most effectively expressed in her anti-collectivist *Anthem* (UK 1938) in which the central character rediscovers the concept of 'I' in a soulless future state that has abolished individuality. Her *Atlas Shrugged* (US 1957) is a pointed criticism of societies where, among other things, state monopolistic organizations are run according to the laws of progressively diminishing economic returns. As a prediction, it becomes increasingly more accurate as the years go by.

Ed Earl Repp

Early US pulp writer (born 1901) who was formerly an advertising man and only took to writing after the Wall Street Crash of 1929. He wrote regularly for Gernsback's Wonder magazines and contributed a series to *Amazing*, featuring the scientific detective 'John Hale', between 1939 and 1943. Examples of his longer stories can be found in the collections *The Radium Pool* and *The Stellar Missiles* (both US 1949).

Mack Reynolds

Dallas McCord Reynolds was born in California in 1917. A local newspaper editor for a brief period in the 1930s, he has also travelled widely in Africa and Europe, worked for IBM and been foreign editor for *Rogue* magazine. His first sf story was 'Isolationist' in *Fantastic Adventures* (1950). He followed it with *The Case of the Little Green Men* (US 1951), a detective tale featuring sf fans among its characters, and has subsequently written many magazine stories.

Among his novels are *The Earth War* (US 1963), telling of new methods of warfare in the 21st century, and the time-travel variation, *Time Gladiator* (US 1966). Further examples are: *Planetary Agent X* (US 1965), *Of Godlike Power* (US 1966), *The Rival Rigelians* (US 1967), *Mercenary from Tomorrow* (US 1968) and *Code Duello* (US 1968). He was co-anthologist with Fredric Brown on the humorous selection *Science Fiction Carnival* (US 1953).

Keith Roberts

A British writer, whose *Pavane* has been hailed as one of the major alternative histories of recent years. He was born in Northampton-shire in 1935, studied art, and worked as an illustrator on cartoon films and advertising visuals. He is now an advertising freelance. His early stories appeared in Carnell's *New Writings* anthologies, beginning with 'Boulter's Canaries' in 1965, and in *Science Fantasy*, a magazine he edited briefly on the departure of Bonfiglioli in 1966 (when its name had changed to *Impulse*).

His novels include *The Furies* (UK 1966), *The Inner Wheel* (UK 1970) and *The Chalk Giants* (UK 1974), the last being a post-catastrophe story, harrowing, but pertinent to the enduring human condition. *Pavane* (UK 1968) conjures a vision of present-day Britain assuming Elizabeth I had been assassinated and the Spanish Armada had been successful—an unlovely picture of today's possible society, less advanced, and still under the heel of the 'soul-saving' psycopaths of 'the Inquisition'. His short stories are collected in *Anita* (US 1970), *Machines and Men* (UK 1973) and *The Grain Kings* (UK 1976).

Frank M. Robinson

A noted writer for the US magazines during the 1950s, Frank M. Robinson was born in 1926. He worked as a junior for the Ziff-Davis publishing house before the Second World War, during which he served in the US Navy. Afterwards he returned to maga-zine publishing (but not in the sf field). His first story 'The Maze' appeared in *Astounding* in 1950, followed by many others. His novel *The Power* (US 1956), a mystery tale involving mind control, was later adapted for US television.

Gene Roddenberry

American NBC TV producer (born in Texas in 1921) and begetter of *Star Trek*, a long-staying series (it began in September 1966) which has been described by one devotee as 'the thinking man's Buck Rogers'. Not perhaps an entirely accurate description, but indicative of the response elicited in some quarters by the inter-stellar heroics of Captain James Kirk and his starship *Enterprise*—an appropriate name in view of the extraordinary commercial spin-off the programme has engendered. The revenue in the US from badges, stickers, transfers and copies of the original scripts has been prodigious; and more than three thousand 'Star Trekkies' attended their first convention in 1972. 'I Grok Spock' lapel buttons bear witness to the curious appeal of those elevated eyebrows and elfin ears; the unbending two-hearted Vulcan at one time ranked second in a British Top TV Personality poll. The series won a Hugo in 1967 for the individual episode 'The Menagerie', and again in 1968 for 'City on the Edge of Forever', scripted by Harlan Ellison.

Alva Rogers
Another cherished name in US fandom, Alva Rogers was born in New Mexico in 1923. Apart from his fan activities—although not very far apart—is his *Requiem for Astounding* (US 1964), a retrospective and nostalgic review of the magazine's days of greatness. Enough to bring tears to the eyes of the most hard-bitten devotees, which it did—and to demand a contribution from John W. Campbell himself, which it got.

Hubert Rogers
Pre-war cover artist for Campbell's *Astounding*, Hubert Rogers produced a dozen or so distinctive front illustrations for the magazine during 1939–42 before serving in the US Navy. He rmedesu contributing from 1947 for a further five years.

Mordecai Roshwald
Born in Poland in 1921, Mordecai Roshwald studied at the Hebrew University in Jerusalem and has been a professor and lecturer in Israel, the UK and the US. He has also written several books on Humanism and on education. In the sf field, and outside it, his *Level Seven* (UK 1959) received widespread praise; it has since been televised in the UK. It tells of an underground command centre during the world's first and only nuclear war, and of how lethal radiation gradually penetrates into even the deepest shelter levels. Another novel, *A Small Armageddon* (UK 1962), depicts a nuclear-armed submarine holding its country to ransom.

Franz Rottensteiner

Editor, critic and anthologist, Franz Rottensteiner shares with Sam Lundwall the distinction of having become something of a science fiction guru while still in his early thirties; he was born in Austria in 1942. Responsible for a number of collections and anthologies in Germany, including the *Polaris* series, he is also active in the United States as editorial consultant to *Science-Fiction Studies*, a periodical published by Indiana State University, and as a member of the editorial board of *Extrapolation*, a comparable publication emanating from Wooster College, Ohio. His 'illustrated history' of the genre, *The Science Fiction Book* (UK 1975), is certainly illustrated, but it is far from being a history. It consists of some four dozen one-page 'potted biographies' of leading writers and popular sf themes which *may* interest the newcomer and anyone who still has two square feet of vacant space on a coffee table.

Victor Rousseau

A man who spent most of his life, and much of his writing, obsessed with his half-Jewish parentage, Victor Rousseau Emanuel (his surname was more easily shed than his heritage) endeared himself to many pulp readers during the vintage years with his often ingenious stories in *Strange Tales* and other magazines. Born in London in 1879, he emigrated first to South Africa and then to the United States where he applied for citizenship and remained until his death in 1951. His best-known science fiction story, *The Messiah of the Cylinder* (US and UK 1917) has been likened, not unfavourably, to Wells's *When the Sleeper Wakes* and develops a similar theme, i.e. a dark interpretation of Bellamy's *Looking Backward*. Two further of Rousseau's sf novels were *Draught of Eternity* (UK 1918, originally appearing under the pen-name of 'H. M. Egbert') and *The Sea Demons* (UK 1925).

Joanna Russ

Born in New York in 1937, Joanna Russ has held various editorial jobs and has also taught English at Cornell University. Her first story 'Nor Custom Stale' appeared in *The Magazine of Fantasy and Science Fiction* in 1959. Her novel *Picnic on Paradise* (US 1968) is an account of adventures on the planet of the title; other stories are *And Chaos Dies* (US 1970) and *The Female Man* (US 1975). In 1972 she won a Nebula for 'When it Changed'.

Eric Frank Russell

The man who persuaded a suitably amazed Olaf Stapledon of the existence of sf pulp magazines, Eric Frank Russell is a veteran British writer who came into prominence in Campbell's *Astounding* just before the Second World War and has since maintained his popularity on both sides of the Atlantic. He was born in Sandhurst in 1905, son of an army instructor, and travelled abroad extensively while still a child. He, too, served briefly in the army and followed several other occupations before the appearance of his first published story, 'The Saga of Pelican West' in 1937. During the next two years he contributed a regular supply of stories to *Astounding* and other magazines; but it was with the first publication of his novel *Sinister Barrier* (UK 1943) in *Unknown*, in 1939, that his reputation was assured. It was his first major production and is still considered by many to be his best. In it he drew on an idea of Charles Fort that humans might simply be 'property', and told of the discovery that alien entities had literally been feeding on Man's emotions and were the primary cause of human conflict.

Russell's output was interrupted by the war, during which he served with the Royal Air Force, but afterwards his stories appeared in many magazines and in 1955 he received a Hugo for his humorous 'Allamagoosa'. A generous selection of his tales can be found in *Deep Space* (US 1954), *Far Stars* (UK 1960), *Dark Tides* (UK 1962) and *Somewhere a Voice* (UK 1965). Among his other novels are *Dreadful Sanctuary* (UK 1951), a Fortean-type story of an attempt to prevent the beginnings of space-flight, *Sentinels from Space* (UK 1954), and *Men, Martians and Machines* (UK 1955), an amalgamation of three magazine stories featuring the robot 'Jay Score'. *Three to Conquer* (UK 1957) reflects the then current preoccupation in sf with psi-powers, while *Wasp* (US 1957), *The Space Willies* (US 1958), *The Great Explosion* (UK and US 1962) and *With a Strange Device* (UK 1964) are further examples of interplanetary or earthbound espionage and adventure tales.

Fred Saberhagen

Fred Thomas Saberhagen was born in Chicago in 1930. A former electronics technician, he has also served four years in the US Air Force and written for *Encyclopedia Britannica*. His first science fiction novels date from the mid-1960s and include *The Golden People* (US 1964) and *The Water of Thought* (US 1965). He soon gained popularity with his 'Berserker' stories, featuring alien robot fighting machines programmed to seek out and destroy life wherever it is found. Some of the tales were collected in *Berserker* (US 1967) and the series also led to two novels: *Brother Berserker* (UK 1969) and *Berserker's Planet* (UK 1975).

Other stories are *The Broken Lands* (US 1968) and *The Black Mountains* (US 1971), both verging on fantasy in a mutant-populated Earth a thousand years hence; also *Changeling Earth* (US 1973) which goes fifty millennia ahead to a world where conventional science no longer works but magic and sorcery do.

Alexander Samalman

US editor and writer who presided over the last days of *Thrilling Wonder*, *Startling Stories* and *Fantastic Story Magazine*. He was born in 1904 and was encouraged in his literary endeavours by the dubious romancer but capable editor, Frank Harris. He worked for Standard Magazines for nearly thirty years, taking over the above three publications in 1954 on the departure of Samuel Mines. In a little over a year each of the magazines had died (not really Samalman's fault, but he followed *Startling* to an early grave only a few months later at the beginning of 1956).

H. S. Santesson

Hans Stefan Santesson was an American writer, editor and reviewer; he was also a specialist in Islamic art. He has edited several mystery magazines and began contributing reviews to *Fantastic Universe* in 1955. Subsequently he edited the publication from 1956 until 1959 and compiled the anthology *The Fantastic Universe Omnibus* (US 1960), with an introduction by Lester del Rey. Other of his anthologies are: *Rulers of Men* (US 1965), *Gods for Tomorrow* (US 1967) and *Flying Saucers in Fact and Fiction* (US 1968). A sympathetic and generous supporter of several writers in their lean years, he died in 1975.

Nathan Schachner

One of the mainstays of *Astounding* during the 1930s, Nathan Schachner was born in the US in 1895. A research chemist before the First World War, he switched to the legal profession shortly afterwards and practised as a lawyer for more than a decade before devoting his time to writing. In the non-fiction field he became a distinguished biographer of early Americans and was working on a study of the Founding Fathers when he died in 1955. His first sf story, 'In 20,000 AD', written in collaboration with A. L. Zagat, appeared in *Wonder Stories* in 1930. Thereafter he wrote many tales for *Astounding*, two of which, 'Old Fireball' and 'Jurisdiction', were combined to form his only sf novel, *Space Lawyer* (US 1953)—an intriguing account of legal processes beyond Earth which he was well qualified to write.

K. H. Scheer

A German writer born in 1928, Karl Herbert Scheer has produced many sf novels as yet untranslated into English. He is best known outside Germany for his collaboration with Kurt Mahr on the original 'Perry Rhodan' story *Enterprise Stardust* (US 1969) (*see also under* Walter Ernsting).

James H. Schmitz

James H. Schmitz was born in Hamburg in 1911 and moved permanently to the US in 1938. Originally employed in Germany on harvester and trailer building, he followed the same occupation in America after serving with the US Air Force in the Pacific during the Second World War. He became a full-time writer in 1959. His 'Vegan Federation' series, begun in *Astounding* in 1949, was later continued in the novel *A Tale of Two Clocks* (US 1962), the earlier stories being collected in *Agent of Vega* (US 1960).

His later books include *The Universe Against Her* (US 1964), *The Witches of Karres* (US 1966), and a tale of interplanetary warfare involving worlds of the galactic hub—*The Demon Breed* (US 1968). A further collection of his stories is *A Nice Day for Screaming and Other Tales of the Hub* (US 1965).

Alex Schomburg
Alex Schomburg is an American artist who contributed many cover and inside illustrations to the Standard magazines. He was born in New York in 1905, and worked as a film company artist while producing magazine illustrations as a sideline. His first sf work featured in *Thrilling Wonder* at the end of the 1930s.

Thomas N. Scortia
An American writer whose work first appeared in *Future* and *Science Fiction Stories* during the late 1950s. He also contributed some factual articles on space-flight to *Future*. His tales include *What Mad Oracle?* (US 1961), *Earthwreck!* (US 1974) and *Caution! Inflammable!* (US 1975).

Idris Seabright
'Idris Seabright' is the pseudonym of Margaret St Clair, who was born in Kansas and graduated from the University of California. She tried other fields of fiction before turning to sf stories in the 1940s and contributing a series to *Thrilling Wonder* under her real name; she adopted the 'Seabright' pseudonym for her work in *The Magazine of Fantasy and Science Fiction*. Her first story in the latter was 'The Listening Child' (1950); it was followed by many others.

Her novels include *The Green Queen* (US 1956), telling of intrigue in a rigidly structured planetary colony, *Agent of the Unknown* (US 1956), and *The Games of Neith* (US 1960), featuring the goddess of an invented religion. Other of her books are *Sign of the Labrys* (US 1963), *Message from the Eocene* (US 1964), *The Dolphins of Altair* (US 1967), *The Dancers of Noyo* (US 1973), and the collections: *Three Worlds of Futurity* (US 1964) and *Change the Sky and Other Stories* (US 1974).

Arthur Sellings
Pseudonym of the British writer Robert Arthur Ley (1921–1968), a former customs officer and book dealer. He started writing science fiction short stories in the early 1950s, many of which were taken by the American magazines and form the bases of two collections: *Time Transfer* (US 1956) and *The Long Eureka* (UK 1968). His

first novel was *Telepath* (US 1962), an account of the slow awakening to his abilities of the original man of the title. It was followed by *The Uncensored Man* (UK 1964), *The Quy Effect* (UK 1966) and *The Power of X* (UK 1968), the last being a neat variation on the matter duplicator theme.

Luis Senarens

US author of the 'Frank Reade' stories which held many American youngsters enthralled nearly a century ago, and were popular for long afterwards. Luis P. Senarens was born in 1865 and first began the tales for *Wide Awake Library* while still in his teens. For most of them he used the pseudonym 'Noname'. Frank Reade's adventures in the world of the future ran into hundreds; among their many later followers was a boy called Robert Heinlein. Senarens died in 1939.

Rod Serling

Rod Serling is a US TV writer and producer of the popular *Twilight Zone* series. He was born in 1924 and served as a paratrooper during the Second World War. He adapted many sf and fantasy stories for the series, in addition to his own scripts which can be found in the collections: *Stories from the Twilight Zone* (US 1960), *More Stories from the Twilight Zone* (US 1961) and *New Stories from the Twilight Zone* (US 1962). The programmes won Hugos in 1960, 1961 and 1962 as the 'Best Dramatic Presentation of the Year'.

Garrett P. Serviss

A turn-of-the-century American writer whose tales were later resurrected by the early pulps. Garrett Putman Serviss was born in 1851 and followed the profession of lawyer. He also wrote editorials for the New York *Sun* and many articles popularizing science. By way of recreation he scaled the Swiss Matterhorn at the age of forty-five.

His novel, *Edison's Conquest of Mars*, written as a kind of sequel to Wells's *The War of the Worlds* (which had just appeared) was run in the *New York Evening News* in 1898. In *The Moon Metal*

176

(US and UK 1900) he told of the quest for a unique lunar mineral, and foresaw the first flight to Venus in *A Columbus of Space* (UK 1911). His classic tale of a worldwide flood and the building of a new ark was entitled *The Second Deluge* (US 1912). He died in 1929.

Richard S. Shaver

The man behind the much-vaunted 'Mystery' series, which editor Raymond Palmer deftly used to boost *Amazing*'s circulation to an all-time high in the 1940s. US writer Richard Sharpe Shaver produced some twenty 'stories' allegedly based on genuine transcripts of voices emanating from a world beneath the Earth's surface. From the first appearance in *Amazing* of 'I Remember Lemuria' (March 1945) to the final 'Mer-Witch of Ether 18' (August 1947), the series attracted numerous new readers who seemed only too eager to believe the authenticity of the claim (yesterday's savants of Shaver are today's von Däniken devotees).

Shaver continued the legend intermittently in *Other Worlds* and *Fantastic*; articles about it were published in non-sf journals; and an amateur publication, *Shaver Mystery Magazine*, ran for several issues (now rare collectors' items). *I Remember Lemuria & The Return of Sathanas* (US 1948) put two of the episodes into book form. Shaver also wrote quite a number of magazine stories unconnected with the hoax.

Bob Shaw

Robert Shaw was born in Belfast in 1931. A graduate mechanical engineer who has also worked in public relations and journalism, he began writing short stories for the British sf magazines in the 1950s, but his first novels did not appear until the latter part of the 1960s, initially in the US.

They include *Nightwalk* (US 1967), in which a blinded man learns to 'see' through empathy with animals and aliens, and *The Two-Timers* (US 1968), telling of a man's search in a parallel world for the double of his murdered wife. *Other Days, Other Eyes* (UK 1972) involves the discovery of 'slow glass' which retards light rays. *Orbitsville* (UK 1975) depicts the search for a planet or other space structure to relieve the human population explosion.

Further novels are: *Shadow of Heaven* (US 1969), *The Palace of*

Eternity (US 1969) and *1 Million Tomorrows* (UK 1970), the last presenting the interesting situation where Man has arrested the ageing process but finds the result has made him both impotent and sterile—it doesn't have the same effect on women. Some of Shaw's short stories are collected in *Tomorrow Lies in Ambush* (UK 1973).

Robert Sheckley

Born in New York in 1928, Robert E. Sheckley served with the UN Forces in Korea during 1946-48 and afterwards graduated from New York University. His work in the sf field dates from 1951, and his short stories are renowned for their plot twists, off-beat humour, and idiosyncratic style. Although his reputation rests largely with his shorter fiction, several novels are of note. They include *Immortality Delivered* (US 1958), in which a dying man's mind is spirited through time to a future where immortality has been achieved, and *The Status Civilisation* (US 1960), featuring a planetary penal colony and attempts to rejuvenate Earth.

Mindswap (US 1966) relates the perturbation of a human who is switched mentally through the bodies of various odd-shaped aliens, while in *The 10th Victim* (US 1966) men are licensed to hunt and kill each other for recreation. *Dimension of Miracles* (US 1968) is a humorous account of what happens to the winner of a galactic sweepstake. *Options* (US 1975) is in a similarly amusing vein.

Sheckley's inimitable handling of the sf short story can be enjoyed in several collections, among them: *Untouched by Human Hands* (US 1954), *Citizen in Space* (US 1955) which contains the improbable utopia of 'A Ticket to Tranai', *Pilgrimage to Earth* (US 1958), *Notions Unlimited* (US 1960), *Store of Infinity* (US 1960), *Shards of Space* (US 1962) and *The People Trap* (US 1968).

Mary Shelley

Wife of the renowned British poet, daughter of Mary Wollstonecraft (a prototype Women's Liberation agitator), Mary Wollstonecraft Shelley utilized the Gothic horror idiom to present the world with a character which was later to keep Boris Karloff, Christopher Lee, and sundry other actors and painstaking make-up assistants in a lifetime of monstrous employment. She was born in 1797 and met Shelley in 1812 (while he was still married elsewhere,

178

but he had heard of poetic licence). Soon afterwards they discussed with Byron and others the idea of producing the kind of creation which she subsequently foisted on the Baron of the title: *Frankenstein: A Modern Prometheus* (UK 1818). The early part of the story was filmed by James Whale for Universal in 1931; there have been many less impressive movie sequels. Aside from the obligatory horrific trimmings, the original novel has interesting things to say about the downfall of innocence and the psychological concept of 'the stranger male'.

Mary Shelley wrote one more scientific romance, a futuristic vision of humanity destroyed by a plague in *The Last Man* (UK 1826). She died in 1851.

M. P. Shiel

An Irishman, born in the West Indies in 1865, Matthew Phipps Shiel was more or less a contemporary of Garrett P. Serviss—but of an entirely different persuasion. His *The Yellow Danger* (UK 1898) relates a racialist world war precipitated by Asia but finally won by the British, who then proceed to wholesale genocide. Shiel's apparent obsession with universal destruction and race purity continues to hold a morbid fascination for some readers. In his best-known work, *The Purple Cloud* (UK 1901), mankind is wiped out by a toxic gas and the sole survivor whiles away his solitude by laying waste to deserted cities. Other of his novels, pursuing similar themes, are *The Lord of the Sea* (US 1901) and *The Dragon* (UK 1913). A post-war collection of some of his tales is *Best Short Stories of M.P. Shiel* (UK 1948). He died in 1947.

Robert Silverberg

The man who won a Hugo in 1956 as the 'Most Promising Author', an expectation he would seem to have fulfilled, since he is reputed to have made a fortune from his writing. He was born in the mid-1930s in New York and first appeared on the sf horizon in the 1950s. He collaborated with Randall Garrett under the joint pseudonym 'Robert Randall' for the 'Nidor' series of stories in *Astounding*; it was later incorporated in the novels: *The Shrouded Planet* (US 1957) and *The Dawning Light* (US 1959). He has also used the pseudonyms 'Calvin M. Knox', 'David Osborne' and 'Ivar Jorgenson'.

During the last twenty years his production of books seems to have been never-ending, and many of them have been of a high standard. Among his earliest are *The 13th Immortal* (US 1957), which tells of an attempt to refurbish a devastated Earth, and *Master of Life and Death* (US 1957), where one man endeavours to solve the world's population crisis. They were followed by *Lest We Forget Thee, Earth* (US 1958, as 'Calvin M. Knox'), *Invisible Barriers* (US 1958, as 'David Osborne'), *Invaders from Earth* (US 1958), *Starhaven* (US 1958 as 'Ivar Jorgenson'), *Stepsons of Terra* (US 1958), *The Planet Killers* (US 1959), *The Plot Against Earth* (US 1959, as 'Calvin M. Knox'), *Collision Course* (US 1961) and *The Seed of Earth* (US 1962).

Recalled to Life (US 1962) recounted the problems involved when corpses could be restored to normal living beings (it was revised a decade later, but with few major changes). *To Open the Sky* (US 1967) presented the hysterical, fad-dominated society of the not-so-distant future, and *Nightwings* (US 1969), which won his second Hugo, depicted an Earth destroyed by alien invaders, but with one man hoping to return to it. *Vornan-19* (US 1969) portrayed more fears about the survival of Earth in the near future, while *Up the Line* (US 1969) juggled with complex time-travel paradoxes. *The World Inside* (US 1971) envisages the free-loving citizens of future one-thousand-storey-high, towered 'cities', and *A Time of Changes* (US 1971) shows an alien being led astray by the hallucinogens of a visiting Earthman, until it discovers the concept of 'I'. The story won a Nebula in the same year.

Other novels include: *The Time Hoppers* (US 1967), *Thorns* (US 1967), *Tower of Glass* (US 1970), *Son of Man* (US 1971), *Dying Inside* (US 1972), *Unfamiliar Territory* (US 1973), *Born with the Dead* (US 1974) and *The Stochastic Man* (US 1975), the last being a story about the so-called science of predicting the future. He has also written novels for the juvenile sf market.

Among his short story collections are *Next Stop the Stars* (US 1962), *Godling, Go Home!* (US 1964) and *Needle in a Timestack* (US 1966). As a compiler of anthologies he has produced: *The Mirror of Infinity* (US 1970), *Science Fiction Hall of Fame* (US 1970), *Dark Stars* (US 1971) and *Beyond Control* (US 1972). He began, and has continued, two annual series of anthologies: *Alpha* (US from 1970) and *New Dimensions* (US from 1971). He has also edited *The Mirror of Infinity, a critics' anthology of Science Fiction* (US 1970).

His first Nebula was won with 'Passengers' in 1969, and his third in 1971 with 'Good News from the Vatican', which ends with a robot becoming Pope.

Clifford D. Simak

Another veteran from the days of the pulps, Clifford D. Simak was born in Wisconsin in 1904. He studied journalism at the University of Wisconsin and then followed a newspaper career. His first sf story, 'World of the Red Sun', appeared in *Wonder Stories* in 1931, but after several years of running for the Gernsback stable he was more or less resolved to give up writing science fiction; then he heard that Campbell had become editor of *Astounding*. He believed he could write more imaginatively for Campbell, and so he could— he became an early mainstay of the magazine. It published most of the work in his 'City' series, a moving saga which tells how robots and intelligent dogs are left to inherit the Earth—they were collected in *City* (US 1952). The noted tale of robot reproduction, 'How-2', first appeared in *Galaxy* in 1954.

Many of his novels are memorable for their optimistic vision, but he has had his problems. In 1935 his presentation of the Universe without a god-like maker in *The Creator* (US 1946) was denounced by most magazine editors as blasphemous, and it ended up in *Marvel Tales*.

Two well-handled treatments of the time theme can be found in *Time and Again* (US 1951) and *Time Is the Simplest Thing* (US 1961), the latter showing how a man reaches the stars by mind-travelling, which is one way of overcoming the time obstacle in interstellar flight. More recently his *Destiny Doll* (US 1971) utilizes the well-tried theme of a space expedition trapped on an alien world.

Among his other books are *Cosmic Engineers* (US 1950—originally serialized in *Astounding* in 1939), *Empire* (US 1951), *Ring Around The Sun* (US 1953), *The Trouble With Tycho* (US 1961), *They Walked Like Men* (US 1962) and *Way Station* (US 1963). The last won a Hugo in 1964, and exemplifies Simak's compassion not only for his own species, but for all species—whether actual or invented. It tells of a stopping-off point established on Earth by a federation of many galactic races and of the one human who, as keeper of the station, is allowed to communicate with them. *Why Call Them Back from Heaven* (US 1967) portrays a future where near immortality has been achieved with the use of cryogenics for suspended animation; but the gift is available only to those who can save enough to provide adequate investment funds to finance their next lives. *The Werewolf Principle* (US 1967) is another lycan-thropic variation, presenting on this occasion a man brought back to Earth whose body is also shared by two aliens, one of them a wolf-like form. It was followed by *The Goblin Reservation* (US 1968), *Out of Their Minds* (US 1970) and *Cemetery World* (US 1973).

His short story collections include: *Strangers in the Universe* (US 1956), *The Worlds of Clifford Simak* (US 1960), *All the Traps of Earth* (US 1962), *Worlds Without Flesh* (US 1964), *Best Science Fiction Stories of Clifford Simak* (US 1967) and *So Bright the Vision* (US 1968). He also edited the sixth of the *Nebula Award* anthologies (US 1971). Simak's first Hugo was won in 1959 with the novelette 'The Big Front Yard'.

Curt Siodmak

Curt Siodmak was born in Germany in 1902 and first saw print with a fairy story at the tender age of eight. He studied at Zurich in Switzerland and wrote for some years in his native country before moving to the US in 1937. He has produced a number of sf movies in Hollywood and scripted *Creature with the Atom Brain* (a 1955 Columbia production), but he is better known for his novels in the genre. *F.P.1. Does Not Reply* (Germany 1932; US and UK trans-lations, 1933) outlined the then pertinent idea of building aircraft-landing platforms in the Atlantic to facilitate intercontinental flights. It was filmed in both Germany and the US in 1933.

His most successful story is *Donovan's Brain* (US 1943), an account of how the revived brain of a dead criminal begins to control other people. It, too, has twice been filmed: firstly by Republic as *The Lady and the Monster* (1944), and subsequently under its original title by Dowling Productions in 1953. More than two decades later, the book *Hauser's Memory* (US 1968) appeared as a sequel. Another novel, *Skyport* (US 1959), tells of an elaborate satellite complex, including a hotel and hospital, parked in a stationary orbit above the Earth. Siodmak's screenplay for the 1954 United Artists' production *Riders to the Stars* was rewritten as a novel by R. Smith and published in the US in the same year.

Joseph W. Skidmore

Another popular American name from the early, but post-Gernsbackian days of *Amazing*, particularly remembered for his series recounting the adventures of 'Posi and Nega' during 1932–35. Joseph William Skidmore also pre-empted, by some thirty years, the basic concept of the film *The Fantastic Voyage* (*see under* Asimov) when he described the journey of a micro-miniaturized man through a human's arteries in 'A World Unseen' (*Weird Tales,* 1936).

John T. Sladek

One of the fairly recent expatriate American arrivals, John T. Sladek was born in Iowa in 1937. He studied mechanical engineering and English Literature at the University of Minnesota and has since worked as a technical writer, barman, draughtsman, and on the railroads. Having hitch-hiked through Europe, he now lives in England. His writing has humour, incisiveness and a human quality comparable to the work of Vonnegut.

His first novel, *The Reproductive System* (UK 1968), tells of an autonomous metal-eating, self-reproducing mechanism that predictably gets out of hand. It was followed by *Black Alice* (US 1968, in collaboration with Thomas M. Disch) and *The Müller-Fokker Effect* (UK 1970), the latter being a joyride through American irrelevancies and indignities, with a host of zany characters and a man who is stored on computer tape.

He has also written a factual survey of current 'nut-cults', *The New Apocrypha* (UK 1973). Some of his short stories are collected in *The Steam-Driven Boy and Other Strangers* (UK 1973), and his 'The Happy Breed' can be found in Ellison's *Dangerous Visions*.

Henry Slesar

US advertising man and enthusiastic jazz-record collector, Henry Slesar wrote a great many magazine sf stories beginning in the mid-1950s. He was a regular contributor to *Fantastic* and *Amazing* and wrote a novelization of the Columbia film *20 Million Miles to Earth* which appeared in *Amazing Stories Science Fiction Novel* in 1953.

T. O'Conor Sloane

An early editor of *Amazing Stories*, Terence O'Conor Sloane was born in the US in 1851 and became a son-in-law of Thomas Alva Edison. He assisted Gernsback on *Amazing* during 1926–1929, becoming editor at the end of 1929 and continuing until the magazine was bought by Ziff-Davis in 1938. He introduced many new writers, among them John W. Campbell and John Russell Fearn, and at the opening stage of his editorship maintained a fairly high standard. This had begun to tail off by the time he left, but he was nearly ninety! He died two years later in 1940.

Cordwainer Smith

One of the mystery men of science fiction, few knowing his real identity until after his death in 1966. He turned out to be Paul Myron Anthony Linebarger, a Professor of Asiatics at Johns Hopkins University, a linguist and military adviser, an expert on psychological warfare. He was born in Wisconsin in 1913. His first sf story, 'Scanners Live in Vain' was published in *Fantasy Book No. 6* in 1950.

Many of his stories verge on full-blown fantasy, steeped in legends of humanity originating ten millennia hence. They can be lyrical, bitter-sweet, elusive, surrealistic, violent. Unlikely to appeal to the more technically-minded enthusiast, their haunting quality has nevertheless secured them a substantial following of devotees. They can be found in the collections *You Will Never Be the Same* (US 1963), *Space Lords* (US 1965) and *Under Old Earth* (UK 1970). He wrote very few novels, among them *The Planet Buyer* (US 1964), in which a youth uses a master computer to make himself the richest person in the cosmos, *Guest of Three Worlds* (US 1966) and *The Underpeople* (US 1968). The posthumously-published *Norstrilla* (US 1975) incorporates both *The Planet Buyer* and *The Underpeople*, and also includes additional material.

E. E. 'Doc' Smith

Grand Father of Space Opera, former lumberjack, bus conductor and chief chemist in a doughnut-mix company, 'Doc' Smith lives on in the almost continuous reprinting of the two monumental sagas he donated to the genre in the early days of the pulps. He was born Edward Elmer Smith in Sheboygan, Wisconsin, in 1890. His first novel, begun in 1914 and completed in 1920, during which period he acquired the PhD which featured reverently beside his name above all his tales, had to wait a further eight years before it was serialized in *Amazing*. When it finally appeared *The Skylark of Space* (US 1946) left readers agape with the prodigious backdrop against which its plot was enacted. For in *The Skylark* and its sequels Smith spread a panorama of mile-long starships, incredible battles and a formidable array of hostile aliens across the entire sweep of the galaxy.

When he attempted to come closer to Earth in 1931 with *The Spacehounds of IPC* (US 1947), the outcry of indignant fans left him in no doubt where his popularity lay; and two years later he headed back out to interstellar space with *Triplanetary* (US 1948), from which his 'Lensman' series evolved. The major part of Smith's output was thus concentrated in the 'Skylark' and 'Lensman' tales. Although they have been criticized for almost every possible failing, their gargantuan embodiment of 'Sense of Wonder' has ensured their permanence in the genre. The other 'Skylark' novels are *Skylark Three* (US 1948), *Skylark of Valeron* (US 1949) and *Skylark Du Quesne* (US 1967), the last being completed only shortly before Smith died in 1965. After *Triplanetary*, the 'Lensman' series continued with *First Lensman* (US 1950), *Galactic Patrol* (US 1950), *Grey Lensman* (US 1951), *Second Stage Lensman* (US 1953), *Children of the Lens* (US 1954) and *The Vortex Blaster* (US 1960).

Two other novels, *Subspace Explorers* and *The Galaxy Primes* (both US 1965) are products of Smith's final period and are unconnected with either of his major series. Shortly after his death a 270-page guide to his imagined worlds and characters, compiled by Ron Ellik and Bill Evans, was published as *The Universes of E. E. Smith* (US 1966).

George O. Smith

George Oliver Smith, by profession an electronics engineer, was born in the US in 1911. He began writing sf short stories in the 1940s and contributed a series set around interplanetary communications to *Astounding* (it was later published as a collection: *Venus Equilateral* (US 1947)). Among his novels are some better-than-average space operas, *Nomad* (US 1950), *Operation Interstellar* (US 1950) and *Hellflower* (US 1953). *Fire in the Heavens* (US 1958) tells of the dangers of contacting a parallel universe, and *Lost in Space* (US 1959) depicts the hunt by a starship for dispersed lifecraft.

Other stories include: *Pattern for Conquest* (US 1949), *Highways in Hiding* (US 1956), *Troubled Star* (US 1957), *The Fourth 'R'* (US 1959) and *Path of Unreason* (US 1959).

Jerry Sohl

Former newspaperman and avid reader of the early sf pulps, Gerald Allan Sohl was born in Los Angeles in 1913. His first stories were *The Haploids* (US 1952) and 'The Seventh Order' in *Galaxy* in the same year, since when he has written stories for most of the US magazines and produced a number of novels.

Costigan's Needle (US 1952) is a 'fourth dimension' variation, and *The Transcendant Man* (US 1953) develops the Fortean 'Man is property' theme. *The Altered Ego* (US 1954) tells of physical revival after death. Among his other tales are *Mars Monopoly* (US 1955), *The Time Dissolver* (US 1957), *One Against Herculum* (US 1959), *Night Slaves* (US 1965) and a literally rather nasty-smelling account of an enzyme acting on human bodies in *The Odious Ones* (US 1959).

Norman Spinrad

Former literary agent and TV writer, Norman Richard Spinrad was born in New York in 1940. He made his first appearance in *Analog* in 1963 with 'The Last of Romany', following it with other short stories and the novels *The Solarians* (US 1966), *Agent of Chaos* (US 1967) and *The Men in the Jungle* (US 1967). His one-time notorious *Bug Jack Barron* (US 1969) tells of an organization which preserves humans in liquid helium against the day when physical immortality might be achieved. The use of expletives notably undeleted in the story caused trouble in Britain during its serialization in *New Worlds* (a curious reaction in what was meant to be a swinging country at the time—the pendulum has since been mortgaged to the oil sheiks).

Some of his short stories are collected in *No Direction Home* (US 1975).

Brian Stableford

Brian Stableford is a recent British arrival who was born in Yorkshire in 1948. A regular reviewer for the sf journal *Foundation*, he is currently teaching the sociology of literature at Reading University. His first novel, *Cradle of the Sun* (UK 1969), tells of a hazardous expedition to locate what appears to be a remorseless entity but which turns out to be something rather different.

There followed *The Blind Worm* (UK 1970) and the 'Dies Irae' trilogy, a space opera involving war between Man and artificially-bred 'Beasts', and consisting of *The Days of Glory, In the Kingdom of the Beasts* and *Day of Wrath* (all US 1971). *To Challenge Chaos* (US 1972) depicts a planet having one of its hemispheres in another universe, and he has since written a series of 'Grainger' stories: *The Halcyon Drift* (US 1972), *Rhapsody in Black* (US 1973), *The Paradise Game* (US 1974), *The Fenris Device* (US 1974) and *Swan Song* (US 1975). *Man in a Cage* (US 1976) is his latest offering.

Olaf Stapledon

'The most titanic imagination ever to write science fiction' is how Sam Moskowitz has described William Olaf Stapledon, not that Stapledon himself was aware that he was writing it. He was a British Doctor of Philosophy, born in Cheshire in 1886, who lectured in philosophy and psychology at Liverpool University, served in a non-combatant ambulance unit during the First World War, and remained until his death in 1950 an active and idealistic socialist. Stapledon's science fiction is of an intellectual order rarely found elsewhere in the genre, and until recently it has fallen into inexplicable neglect. His first 'novel', *Last and First Men* (UK 1930), drew as many compliments from such writers as J. B. Priestley and Arnold Bennett as it did from the sf fraternity. In short, it tells of the entire future history of Man up to the time, two thousand million years in the future, when the last men die on Neptune. Throughout the chronicle the social mores and stances for living of each successive human civilization are worked out in impeccable detail; the scope of the book is only eclipsed by the later *Star Maker* (UK 1937), in which the author modestly set out to narrate the history of the entire universe—with equally profound effect.

In a less grandiose design, Stapledon also wrote two novels on the superman theme, *Odd John* (UK 1936) and *Sirius* (UK 1944), although in the latter it is on a dog that the advanced intelligence is bestowed. The book is also a kindly plea for sexual and other forms of tolerance and, indeed, it was on the twin virtues of intelligence and kindliness which Stapledon based his philosophy of life. With the exception of Wells, whose writing he admired, he seemed unaware of the existence of other writers in the genre until he was introduced to the pulp magazines by Eric Frank Russell in 1936. Among his other books are *Last Men in London* (UK 1932), a less ambitious sequel to his first work; *A Man Divided* (UK 1950); and *Worlds of Wonder* (US 1949) which is a collection of the three short novels *The Flames* (UK 1947), *Death into Life* (UK 1946) and *Old Man in a New World* (UK 1944).

R. F. Starzl
American newspaperman, born in 1899, who contributed some two dozen popular stories to the early pulps during their first decade. He originally appeared in *Amazing* in 1928 with 'Out of the Sub-Universe', a novel treatment of the microscopic worlds theme. His work also featured in *Argosy* and *Wonder Stories*, and his final tale, 'Dimension of the Conquered', was published in *Astounding* in 1934.

Leon E. Stover
Leon Eugene Stover is an American professor of anthropology who was born in Pennsylvania in 1929. His organizes university courses in science fiction, and is co-compiler with Harry Harrison of the anthology *Apeman, Spaceman: Anthropological Science Fiction* (US 1968). He is also joint compiler with Willis E. McNelly of *Above the Human Landscape: A Social Science Fiction Anthology* (US 1972).

Boris and Arkadi Strugatski
Since these leading Russian sf authors are brothers who normally work as a team, they can both be covered in a single entry. Boris (born 1933) is an astronomer at Pulkovo Observatory, and Arkadi (born 1925) is a linguist, translator and an expert on Japan. They first came to prominence with *Hard to Be a God* (USSR 1964; UK translation 1975), in which a historian from Earth attempts to survey the strife-torn society of a distant planet. In fact, the novel is a

thinly-disguised attack on bureaucratic tyranny, outside intervention, intolerance and corruption, as are many of their subsequent stories.

These include *The Second Invasion of the Martians* (USSR 1967), *The Snail on the Slope* (USSR 1968), *The Fairy Tale of the Troika* (USSR 1968) and *The Inhabited Island* (USSR 1969). Their use of science fiction as a means of social criticism, with frequent allegorical attacks against the Soviet régime, was almost bound to bring them into disrepute with the appropriate authorities. The gag was duly administered in 1969. Two of their short stories can be found in the anthology, *Path Into the Unknown: The Best of Soviet Science Fiction* (UK 1966).

Theodore Sturgeon

A gifted and provocative writer, almost in a school of his own, Theodore Sturgeon was born in the US in 1918. His name at birth was Edward Hamilton Waldo, but it was subsequently changed. In his time he has trained to be a trapeze artist, driven bulldozers in Puerto Rico, and run a hotel in the West Indies. He made his début in the magazine field with 'The Ether Breather' in *Astounding* in 1939, and thereafter wrote many stories for editor John W. Campbell. It could well be argued that his main talent lies in the short story idiom, but he has also produced some notable novels.

Among them are *The Dreaming Jewels* (US 1950) and *More Than Human* (US 1953). The latter is a striking tale of symbiosis, taking the form of a welding into a *Homo Gestalt* of a group of paranormally-gifted but otherwise flawed children; it won the first International Fantasy Award in 1954. Another treatment of the group-mind theme can be found in *The Cosmic Rape* (US 1958), and *Venus Plus X* (US 1960) tells of a utopian society whose members maintain their peaceful state by a self-imposed mutation which converts them into hermaphrodites. Basically it is a plea for mutual tolerance, as are so many of Sturgeon's stories. His *Voyage to the Bottom of the Sea* (US 1961) is a novelization of the Irwin Allen film production of the same year, and relates how a submarine under the polar ice helps to avert an ecological catastrophe.

Not all the tales in his many collections can be considered science fiction, but their originality frequently places them in the speculative category. Along with the genuine article, they can be read in:

Without Sorcery (US 1948), *E. Pluribus Unicorn* (US 1953), *Caviar* (US 1955), *A Way Home* (US 1955—retitled *Thunder and Roses* in the UK, 1957), *A Touch of Strange* (US 1958), *Alien 4* (US 1959), *Beyond* (US 1960), *Sturgeon in Orbit* (US 1964), *The Joyous Invasions* (UK 1965), being a collection of three stories, 'To Marry Medusa', 'The Comedian's Children' and 'The [Widget], The [Wadget], and Boff', *Starshine* (US 1966), *To Here and the Easel* (UK 1973) and *Case and the Dreamer* (US 1974). His contribution to Harlan Ellison's *Dangerous Visions* anthology means exactly what its title implies, 'If All Men Were Brothers, Would You Let One of Them Marry Your Sister?'

Sturgeon was Guest of Honour at the 20th World Science Fiction Convention in 1962. In 1970 he won a Nebula with his short story 'Slow Sculpture', which also captured a Hugo in the following year.

Jeff Sutton

Jefferson Howard Sutton was born in Los Angeles in 1913. He studied at San Diego State College and has been a news reporter, photographer and salesman. He has twice served in the US Marines. Another part of his career was devoted to research into survival at high altitudes, an area on which he has concentrated in some of his stories. They include *First on the Moon* (US 1958), which tells of a race between the Americans and the Russians to make a lunar landing, with espionage, and such, as complications. *Bombs in Orbit* (US 1959) is an arms-race intrigue involving orbital nuclear weapons, and *Spacehive* (US 1960) tells of the attempt to launch a spacecraft from a satellite station. Other novels are *Apollo at Go* (US 1963), *H-Bombs Over America* (US 1967) and *The Man Who Saw Tomorrow* (US 1968). He has also written two stories in collaboration with his wife Jean: *The Beyond* and *The Programmed Man* (both US 1968).

Leo Szilard

A distinguished scientist and physicist, Leo Szilard was born in Budapest in 1898. He worked with Enrico Fermi in Berlin during the 1920s and '30s and emigrated to the US in 1937. After the Second World War he was a noted advocate of the peaceful use of atomic energy and won the Atoms for Peace Prize jointly with

E. P. Wigner in 1959. He is known in the sf field for a single collection of intriguing stories, *The Voice of the Dolphins* (US 1961), the title piece being an account of highly intelligent dolphins which are set to work on Man's problems.

John Taine

'John Taine' was the pseudonym of Eric Temple Bell, one of the most distinguished mathematicians ever to take his mind off figures long enough to write science fiction. He was born in Scotland in 1883, but moved to the US in 1902 and studied at Stanford University. Subsequently he was a leading professor at the California Institute of Technology for nearly thirty years, being President of the Mathematics Association of America and Vice-President of the American Mathematics Society. He died in 1960.

He was a pioneer sf writer in the 1920s and '30s, breaking new ground in a variety of directions. Many of his stories concentrated on biological speculation and evolutionary themes, among them: *The Greatest Adventure* (US 1929), *The Iron Star* (US 1930), in which evolution runs rife in a 'lost world' discovered in Antarctica, and *Before the Dawn* (US 1934). *The Purple Sapphire* (US 1924) is another 'lost world' tale, set in Central Asia.

An equally noted story, *The Time Stream* (US 1946—originally serialized in *Wonder Stories* in 1931), was one of the first developments of the idea of cyclical universes and a 'speculation on the nature of time and entropy', a theme which was to occupy many later writers—and still does. Among Taine's other tales, some only appearing in book form long after they were run in magazines, are *The Cosmic Geoids and One Other* (US 1949), *Seeds of Life* (US 1951), which is another account of radiation-spawned mutants going wild, and *G.O.G. 666* (US 1954).

William F. Temple

William Frederick Temple is a British writer and one-time flatmate of Arthur C. Clarke. He was born in 1914 and worked for a time on the London Stock Exchange; he joined the pre-war British Interplanetary Society and edited its journal. During the war he served with the Eighth Army in the Western Desert. His short story 'The

Four-Sided Triangle', which originally appeared in *Amazing* in 1939, was later novelized (UK 1949) and subsequently filmed. It tells of a duplicate woman created to solve the problem of two men falling in love with the same girl. Other tales include *The Automated Goliath* (US 1962), featuring an attempted alien conquest of Earth, *Battle on Venus* (US 1963), *Shoot at the Moon* (US 1966) and *The Fleshpots of Sansato* (US 1968). He has also written some books for the juvenile market.

William Tenn

'William Tenn' is the pseudonym of the gifted American author Philip Klass. Born in 1920, he became a professional writer after the Second World War. His magazine stories are noted for their frequent wry humour, which more often than not camouflages adroitly aimed barbs at human gullibility and other failings, e.g. 'The Liberation of Earth', where the world is continuously enslaved and 'freed' by two races of warring extraterrestrials, and 'Null-P', in which the decline of humanity results from the rule of the 'average' man. Both can be found in his collection *Of All Possible Worlds* (US 1955), enhanced by an inimitable introduction.

His novel *Of Men and Monsters* (US 1968) tells of the regeneration of man in a world of giants, while the resurrection of the original malcontented deities from Mount Olympus is the theme of *A Lamp for Medusa* (US 1968).

Further collections of Tenn's short stories are: *The Human Angle* (US 1956), *Time in Advance* (US 1958), *The Seven Seas, The Square Root of Man* and *The Wooden Stars* (all US 1968). He has also compiled an unusual anthology of sf stories about children, *Children of Wonder* (US 1953), which enjoys the added bonus of tales by A. E. Coppard, D. H. Lawrence and Graham Greene.

James Tiptree Jr

An American writer who was born in Chicago and is now in his sixties. He has travelled throughout India and Africa. His arrival on the sf scene is fairly recent. Among his stories of particular note are: 'The Milk of Paradise' in Harlan Ellison's *Again, Dangerous Visions* and 'Birth of a Salesman' in *Analog* in 1968. Since then he has won a Nebula for 'Love is the Plan, the Plan is Death' in 1973, and a Hugo in 1974 for 'The Girl Who was Plugged In'. Both can be found in his collection *Warm Worlds and Otherwise* (US 1975). More of his tales are included in *Ten Thousand Light-Years from Home* (US 1973).

F. Orlin Tremaine

Editor of *Astounding Stories* before the Campbell era, Frederick Orlin Tremaine was born in the US in 1899. Graduating from Valparaiso University, he made a career in magazine publishing during the 1920s and took over *Astounding* in 1933 when it was acquired by Street and Smith. In a short time he made it the leader in the field. On promotion to editorial director in 1937, he appointed John W. Campbell Jr to succeed him. Two years later he set up his own publishing company, launching *Comet Stories* in 1940 (it ran for only five issues). Ill-health compelled Tremaine to retire prematurely, and he died in 1956.

E. C. Tubb

British writer and one-time printing machine representative, Edwin Charles Tubb was born in 1919. An sf enthusiast in his youth, he began writing regularly in the 1950s and followed H. J. Campbell as editor of *Authentic Science Fiction* in 1956 (some eighteen months before it ceased publication). Many of his short stories first appeared in *Authentic*, and he also wrote a number of pocket-novels for the Scion Press and others, sometimes as 'Carl Maddox' or 'Charles Grey'. Altogether, he has written under some fifty pseudonyms.

For Scion he produced *City of No Return, Hell Planet, The Resurrected Man* and *The Stella Legion* (all UK 1954). A number of his short stories were set on Mars, and these were run together in *Alien Dust* (UK 1955). *The Space-Born* (US 1956) is an account of the interactions between members of a starship crew.

Moon Base (UK 1964) was originally serialized in *New Worlds* in 1963 as *Window on the Moon*. *Death is a Dream* (UK 1967), tells of three twentieth-century people who awake from suspended animation in an oppressive future. It was followed by *Escape into Space* (UK 1969). In recent years Tubb has written what can be called 'formula science fiction' for the US paperback market. Among such are the adventures of 'Earl Dumarest' in his long-running conflict with a group of alien cybernetic intellects, 'the Cyclan'. Some of them have also appeared in Britain: *Derai, Toyman,* and *The Winds of Gath* (all UK 1973). There is also a short story collection: *Ten from Tomorrow* (UK 1966).

Wilson Tucker

Born in the US in 1914, Arthur Wilson Tucker (better known as 'Bob') was a noted sf fan during the 1930s, running his own amateur magazines and contributing many articles and letters to both professional and fan publications. By trade a cinema projectionist, he began producing short stories in the early 1940s. Among his first novels, *The Long, Loud Silence* (US 1952) is an impressive treatment of the post-catastrophe theme following a nuclear attack on the US. *City in the Sea* (US 1951) is another post-world-war setting, in which women have become the dominant sex in the North American interior. *The Time Masters* (US 1953) and *Time Bomb* (US 1955) are two slightly-connected tales dealing with aliens stranded on Earth, with longevity and other aspects of time.

Wild Talent (US 1954) is a variation on the advent of telepathy; and *The Lincoln Hunters* (US 1958) is another time story, linked with historical research. Other novels include *The Tombaugh Station* (US 1960), *The Year of the Quiet Sun* (US 1970) and *Ice and Iron* (US 1974), the last depicting a new Ice Age as a background to the arrival of warrior women using time-warping weapons. Ten of Tucker's short stories can be found in the collection: *Science Fiction Sub-Treasury* (US 1954).

Jack Vance

John Holbrook Vance was born in San Francisco in the 1920s. Somewhat footloose by nature, he has travelled widely, worked on construction sites, and played in jazz bands. During the Second World War he served in the US Merchant Navy. He first appeared in the sf field in 1945 with 'The World Thinker' in *Thrilling Wonder Stories*. He continued writing short stories but is better known for his considerable output of novels, some of which were done for the juvenile market.

Among his early stories are *The Space Pirate* (US 1953) and *To Live Forever* (US 1956), the latter being another variation on the human attainment of physical immortality. *Big Planet* (US 1957) tells of men stranded on a world with three times the circumference of Earth, and *The Languages of Pao* (US 1958) depicts a future colony stirred to new life by the forced introduction of different tongues. *Slaves of the Klau* (US 1958) is the familiar theme of alien races competing for the domination of Earth.

In 1963 he won a Hugo for *The Dragon Masters* (US 1963), judged on its first appearance in *Galaxy* during the previous year. The story relates a war fought between reptilian aliens and transformed humans. At about this period, Vance began writing trilogies and series, and many of his subsequent books fall into these categories. They include the trilogy beginning with *The Star King* (US 1964), in which aliens disguise themselves as humans, and followed by *The Killing Machine* (US 1964) and *The Palace of Love* (US 1967); also the 'Durdane' trilogy consisting of: *The Anome* (US 1971), *The Brave Free Men* (US 1972) and *The Asutra* (US 1973). *Servants of the Wankh* (US 1969), *The Dirdir* (US 1969) and *The Pnume* (US 1970) are a series featuring the interstellar exploits of the Earthman 'Adam Reith'. Another series centring around the gambling mania of an alien race includes *Trullion: Alastor 2262* (US 1973) and *Marune: Alastor 933* (US 1975).

Further books are *Son of the Tree* (US 1964); *The Eyes of the Otherworld* (US 1966), a novel linking stories which were first published in *The Magazine of Fantasy and Science Fiction* during 1965–66; *City of the Chasch* (US 1968); *The Houses of Iszm* (US 1974) and *Showboat World* (US 1975). Some of his short stories can be found in the collection *The Dying Earth* (US 1950). In 1967 Vance won his second Hugo with 'The Last Castle', a story which had already brought him a Nebula in the previous year.

A. E. van Vogt

Master of the semi-mystical, plot-constructor extraordinary, disciple of Hubbard in the furtherance of 'Dianetics', Alfred Elton van Vogt was born in Winnipeg in 1912. The son of Dutch parents, he left school early and did various clerical and manual jobs while writing in his spare time. His first literary successes were achieved outside the sf field, but he was a regular reader of speculative fiction and finally produced his first published story in the genre, 'Black Destroyer', for Campbell's *Astounding* in 1939. In fact, his arrival on the pulp scene more or less coincided with Campbell's rise to the editorship of *Astounding* and van Vogt's reputation as a leading writer was largely secured by his regular contributions to that publication during the following decade. (He was Guest of Honour at the 4th World Science Fiction Convention in 1946.) Many of these were later incorporated into novels. 'Black Destroyer', for example, provides a chapter in *The Voyage of the Space Beagle* (US 1950), a superior form of 'Star Trek' type adventures which introduced the science of 'Nexialism'—a forerunner of the 'psycho history' which dominates Asimov's 'Foundation' trilogy.

Slan (US 1946) has been considered the most outstanding of his novels, and its treatment of the 'persecution of mutants' theme has ensured its constant reprinting. However, it reads rather less inspiringly now than it did two decades ago. *The Weapon Makers* (US 1946) and *The Weapon Shops of Isher* (US 1951) will perhaps endure longer as chronicles of a subversive and egalitarian élite in an oppressive society. Another much acclaimed novel is *The World of Null-A* (US 1948), which led many of its original readers to the study of semantics and prompted the appearance of a sequel, *The Pawns of Null-A* (US 1956).

In the mid-1940s van Vogt's output began to slow as a result of his failing eyesight, but his inventiveness continued practically unabated. It can be found in all its variety in his many other books, among them: *The House That Stood Still* (US 1950), *The Mixed Men* (US 1952), *The Universe Maker* (US 1953), *Empire of the Atom* (US 1957), *The Mind Cage* (US 1958), *The War Against the Rull* (US 1959), *The Wizard of Linn* (US 1962), *The Beast* (US 1963), *Rogue Ship* (US 1965), *The Winged Man* (US 1966, in collaboration with his wife E. Mayne Hull), *The Silkie* (US 1969), *Quest for the Future* (US 1970), *Children of Tomorrow* (US 1970), *The Battle of Forever* (US 1971) and *Darkness on Diamondia* (US 1972).

His stories appear in the following collections: *Out of the Unknown* (US 1948, with E. Mayne Hull), *Destination Universe* (US 1952), *Away and Beyond* (US 1952), *Planets for Sale* (US 1954, with E. Mayne Hull), *The Far-Out Worlds of A. E. van Vogt* (US 1968) and *The Best of A. E. van Vogt* (UK 1970). His brief autobiography, *Reflections of A. E. van Vogt* (US 1975), contains a complete bibliography of his work to date.

Vercors
Behind the pseudonym of 'Vercors', which was his code-name in

the French Resistance during the Second World War, lies writer and painter Jean Bruller. Born in 1902, he followed an early career in electrical engineering before the war. He has written a number of fantasies but his major work of science fiction, and highly praised as such, is *You Shall Know Them* (France 1952). It tells of the discovery of a living species of what could be one of the missing links in Man's ancestry, and of the problem in determining whether the killing of such a being is murder in 'human' terms.

Jules Verne

The French claimant to the title 'Founding Father of Science Fiction', who was obliged to stand down during the last ten years of his life in favour of a cross-channel upstart by the name of H. G. Wells. Jules Gabriel Verne was born in Nantes in 1828. Originally destined for a legal career, he attempted to run off to sea as a boy, later became involved in the theatre and wrote several plays before embarking on the series of *voyages extraordinaires* which was to earn him lasting recognition. Subsequently he was also concerned in local government. By the time of his death in 1905 he was renowned far beyond his native France; he had received the Papal Blessing (not a distinction sought by many succeeding sf writers); and had lived to see the first factual flying machines (they bore little resemblance to those he had depicted in some of his tales).

Verne's *forte* in his early period was 'Sense of Wonder' coupled with glorification of the machine. He began with *Five Weeks in a Balloon* (France 1863), followed by *Journey to the Centre of the Earth* (France 1864) and *From the Earth to the Moon* (France 1865). This last, with its sequel *Round the Moon* (France 1870), established him as a writer of noted scientific romances; and if the idea of firing a spacecraft as a shell from a huge cannon is considered quaint today (it was still apparently viable in the 1936 Wells-inspired film *Things to Come*), it proved a notable advance on the many earlier ideas for getting Man to the moon. It was filmed in 1902 by Verne's compatriot and pioneer movie-maker, Georges Méliès, and again more than fifty years later by RKO in 1958.

Originally influenced by Poe, whose *Arthur Gordon Pym* narrative he completed in *The Ice Sphinx* (France 1897), Verne took pains to ensure the plausibility of his futuristic machines. This he achieved by an intelligent reading of scientific journals and by what were frequently overlong technical explanations in his stories. His nearest approach to a robot tale, however, centred around a steam-driven metal elephant in *The Demon of Cawnpore*, the first volume of his novel *The Steam House* (France 1880).

Many of *les voyages extraordinaires*, though highly adventurous, cannot be classed as science fiction. Among those that do qualify is the epic submarine story, *Twenty Thousand Leagues Under the Sea* (France 1870), the central character of which (Captain Nemo) later reappeared towards the end of *The Mysterious Island* (France 1875). Both have been filmed: the former as a Walt Disney production in 1954, the latter in 1929 by M-G-M and again in 1961 by Columbia. *Hector Servadac* (France 1877) told of a comet narrowly missing Earth and carrying off the eponymous hero for a tour of the solar system. *The Clipper of the Clouds* (France 1886) features one of Verne's most impressive inventions—a hundred-foot-long airship bearing seventy-four masts topped by rotor blades. Its owner, Robur, returned eighteen years later in a sequel, *Master of the World* (France 1904), in which he had degenerated into a power-hungry megalomaniac.

The change in Robur's personality is indicative of a shift in Verne's own outlook. Whilst in his early tales the gifts of technology were employed in pursuit of fabulous adventures, they came increasingly to be shown in his later work as misused. The *Begum's Fortune* (France 1879) combined industrial power with Prussian militarism in an oppressive anti-utopian vision. *Propeller Island* (France 1895) is an account of the struggle for domination between two ruling factions on a superb floating city—an internecine strife that literally tears the giant craft apart and sinks it. *For the Flag* (France 1896) presents the reader with the archetypal mad inventor of a guided missile, which he puts to piratical use against Atlantic shipping. These darker visions of Verne's are regarded as reflections on the conflicts he saw developing in Europe and farther afield as the nineteenth century drew to its close. To that extent they are allegorical, and add to his stature as a pioneer of modern speculative writing.

Among many French studies of his work, one of the most authoritative is Jean Chesneaux's *The Political and Social Ideas of Jules Verne* (UK translation 1972).

A. Hyatt Verrill

Renowned US explorer, archaeologist and early pulp writer, Alpheus Hyatt Verrill was born in 1871. He spent half a century in penetrating the depths of Central and South America and the West Indies. He wrote assiduously of his travels and research and had become a recognized authority in various anthropological and archaeological areas before his death in 1954. Many of the short stories he contributed to the sf magazines in the 1920s and 1930s drew on his experience, as did his novel *The Bridge of Light* (US 1950), which first appeared in *Amazing Stories* in 1929 and tells of a 'lost world' discovery in South America.

Harl Vincent

Harl Vincent Schoepflin—to give him his full name—was born in the US in 1893. A cherished writer in the early pulps, like Murray Leinster he was writing science fiction well before the advent of the sf magazines in 1926. However, it was not until 1928 that he first appeared in Gernsback's *Amazing* with 'The Golden Girl of Munan'. Thereafter he contributed regularly to *Amazing* and its quarterly companion—and to many others, including *Science Wonder Stories* and *Astounding*. He abandoned the field in the early 1940s, but returned only shortly before his death in 1968.

Erich von Däniken

Another dabbler in economically profitable guesswork whose researches are dismissed by scientists as 'science fiction'—and cut even less ice in the sf field itself. He was born in Switzerland in 1935 and first came to public notice with his best-selling *Chariot of the Gods?* (Germany 1968). In it he linked together a variety of early cultural phenomena intended to show that Earth had been visited by extraterrestrials in ancient times. The book caused a stir in the same quarters as Adamski's *Flying Saucers Have Landed* and offered as little real proof of anything. However, its success has prompted further offerings in the same vein: *Return to the Stars* (Germany 1968), *The Gold of the Gods* (Germany 1972) and *In Search of Ancient Gods* (Germany 1973).

Kurt Vonnegut Jr

An idiosyncratic voice on the sf horizon who now prefers to dis-associate himself from the genre, Kurt Vonnegut was born in the US in 1922. He studied biochemistry at Cornell University and served in the European theatre during the Second World War. He was captured by the Germans and witnessed the infamous allied bombing of Dresden while he was a POW, an experience he later portrayed as the central event in his novel *Slaughterhouse Five* (filmed in 1971 by director George Roy Hill and a Hugo-winner of 1973). After the war he specialized in anthropology at the University of Chicago before turning to freelance writing. Having achieved considerable success with a handful of sf novels he declared he had abandoned the field, but there are still elements of the genre in much of his later work.

His first novel, *Player Piano* (US 1952), has been hailed as a major sf anti-utopia. Set in a US of the near future, it depicts the futility of an industrially-automated society where those people who actually are still employed—including management—lead essentially purposeless lives. The tragi-comic elements which came to charac-terize his stories were already evident in his next book, *The Sirens of Titan* (US 1959), an ingenious blend of satire and conventional science fiction which finally shows how all human history has been manipulated by aliens for an utterly trivial purpose.

Cat's Cradle (US 1963), an unusual cataclysmic tale, features a homely Caribbean religion propagated by calypsos and includes many pointed observations on the human condition before it ends with the instant crystallization of all Earth's water. The attempt to describe his Dresden nightmare was presented in *Slaughterhouse Five* (US 1969) by way of a central character adrift in time. It reintroduced the aliens of *The Sirens of Titan*, who are able to see every period in time simultaneously. Personalities from other Vonnegut stories also made fleeting appearances—a device he has used frequently. It is employed again in *Breakfast of Champions* (US 1973), which is not so much science fiction as a sadly humorous story about an invented sf writer, Kilgore Trout, who had featured in Vonnegut's earlier tales (*See also under* Philip José Farmer).

Whatever brand of fiction he claims to be writing, Vonnegut's commitment to humanity, and his concern for its more fallible specimens, illumines his work. It is just as evident in his short stories, some of which are collected in *Welcome to the Monkey House*

(US 1968). His work is reviewed by various contributors in *The Vonnegut Statement* (US 1963), edited by Jerome Klinkowitz and John Somer.

F. L. Wallace
American magazine writer, Floyd L. Wallace first appeared in *Astounding* in 1951 with 'Hideaway'. He contributed regularly to the field during the 1950s (frequently in *Galaxy*) with such stories as 'Big Ancestor' (1954), a notable explanation of how Man came to be the most widespread lifeform in the Milky Way. His novel *Address: Centauri* (US 1955) tells of the first starship to leave the solar system—manned by a crew of physically crippled volunteers.

George C. Wallis
Another early UK contributor to *Amazing* in the 1920s, mainly under the pseudonym of 'B. & G. C. Wallis'. He followed a career in printing at the beginning of the century and later moved on to cinema management. He also wrote frequently for the British *Tales of Wonder*. His novel, *The Call of Peter Gaskell* (UK 1947), is a 'lost world' variation.

Bryce Walton
Bryce Walton was born in the US in 1918. He served as a Navy correspondent during the Second World War and was present at the bitter assaults on the Japanese islands of Iwo Jima and Okinawa. Afterwards he became a full-time writer, with science fiction as only a part of his output. He has written for the juvenile sf market, and had a number of short novels published in the adult magazines, among them: 'Man of Two Worlds' and 'Too Late for Eternity' (in *Space Stories* during 1952 and 1955 respectively).

Donald Wandrei
Joint-founder with August Derleth of the Lovecraft survival industry, Donald Wandrei seemed always more at home in *Weird Tales* during the 1930s than in Tremaine's *Astounding* where his genuine sf stories were often published. (He was born in the US in 1908.) In retrospect his contribution to the genre elicits jaded

expressions in some quarters, but such tales as 'The Black Fog', 'The Blinding Shadows' and 'The Red Brain' may commend themselves to the reader of his collection *The Eye and the Finger* (US 1944). He has also produced a collection of fantasy verse and the odd (deliberately so) novel in the Lovecraft tradition.

Ian Watson

Ian Watson is a former British lecturer in Tanzania and Tokyo who has recently become a full-time writer. He was born on Tyneside in 1943 and studied English at Balliol College, Oxford. His first sf short stories were stimulated by his three-year stay in Japan, and he made his début with 'Roof Garden Under Saturn' in *New Worlds* in 1969. Since then his stories have appeared in various magazines and anthologies, including *Science Fiction Monthly* and *New Writings in SF 26*.

His novel *The Embedding* (UK 1973) defies any brief description, dealing as it does with linguistics, a threatened Brazilian tribe, aliens pursuing an ancient quest, and new ways of perceiving reality. He became a member of the governing council of the Science Fiction Foundation in 1974 and has been features editor of the journal *Foundation* since 1975.

Stanley G. Weinbaum

Generally credited as the man who rehabilitated the image of the BEM in the sf magazines of the mid-1930s, Stanley Grauman Weinbaum was only just past the lift-off stage in his sf trajectory at the time of his early death. He was born in 1900 and graduated from the University of Wisconsin in chemical engineering. His first contribution to *Wonder Stories*, 'A Martian Odyssey', received widespread acclaim in 1934; but by the end of the following year, during which hardly a month had passed without at least one of his stories appearing in either *Wonder* or *Astounding*, Weinbaum was dead.

What he did for the BEM was to reverse the longstanding concept imposed in Wells's *The War of the Worlds* of extraterrestrial life-forms being both hostile and physically repellent. He introduced in 'A Martian Odyssey', and in such tales as 'Valley of Dreams' and 'Parasite Planet', a collection of fascinating, often lovable aliens whose very last intention was to make mincemeat of *Homo sapiens*. After his death a limited memorial collection of his work, *Dawn of Flame and Other Stories* (US 1936), was issued, followed by the further collections *A Martian Odyssey and Others* (US 1949) and *The Red Peri* (US 1952). A number of his earlier unpublished manuscripts were also printed, among them the novels *The New Adam* (US 1939), *The Black Flame* (US 1948) and *The Dark Other* (US 1950).

Mort Weisinger

One-time editor for Standard Magazines, Mortimer Weisinger has distinguished himself with a sale of over two million copies of his practical *1001 Things You Can Get Free* (original copies of the vintage pulps he produced are *not* included). Born in the US in 1915, he was a fan from an early age, editing amateur sf magazines before joining Standard as a graduate from New York University. During the period 1936–41 he edited *Thrilling Wonder* for five years, *Startling Stories* for some eighteen months, *Strange Stories* for a year, and *Captain Future* for three quarterly issues. He served in the US Army during the Second World War and subsequently entered the sf comics field, where he has been much involved with 'Superman'.

Manly Wade Wellman

US author who, like so many other writers, has 'enjoyed' a variety of occupations. Manly Wade Wellman was born in West Africa in 1905, the son of a then medical researcher in the former Portuguese territory. Very successful in the crime-writing area, he has also produced many sf and fantasy tales, beginning with 'When Planets Clashed' in *Wonder Stories Quarterly* (1931). His magazine contributions continued into the 1960s, with a series featuring 'John, the Minstrel' that spanned over a decade in *The Magazine of Fantasy and Science Fiction*.

His sf novels, which frequently verge on fantasy, include a parallel worlds treatment in *The Beasts from Beyond* (UK 1950) and a Martian setting in *The Devil's Planet* (UK 1951), both originally appearing in *Startling Stories* some years earlier. Other books published long after magazine débuts include *Twice in Time* (US 1957), being an excursion backwards to Leonardo's Florence, *The Dark Destroyers* (US 1959), *Giants from Eternity* (US 1959) and *Island in the Sky* (US 1961). *The Solar Invasion* (US 1968) is a further offering. Some of his stories can also be read in the collection *Who Fears the Devil?* (US 1963).

H. G. Wells

Described by Brian Aldiss as 'the Shakespeare of Science Fiction', Herbert George Wells comes near to defying categorization in the range and diversity of his writing. He was born in Bromley, on the outskirts of London, in 1866, the son of a domestic housekeeper and a gardener-cum-failed-shopkeeper-cum-professional-cricketer. After defeating several attempts to turn him into a tailor's and chemist's apprentice, he won a scholarship to the Normal School of Science (now the Imperial College of Science and Technology) where he studied for a year under Darwin's fiercest apostle, Thomas Henry Huxley (the grandfather of Aldous). Wells then tried his own hand at teaching, but was dogged by almost fatal ill-health. As a last resort he turned to writing and enjoyed immediate success. Within a few years he was a leading light of the popular intellectuals, a charisma he was to retain until shortly before his death in 1946. His influence extended far beyond the realm of science fiction.

Probably no other individual did more to establish the basic plot structures and thematic material of the modern sf genre. In the space of a mere dozen years, Wells wrote the great majority of his sf stories and stamped his imprint ineradicably on the culture which was to come. He began with *The Time Machine* (UK 1895), still the most powerfully evocative of all time-travel stories, and an essentially pessimistic view of what might become of Man. It embodied completely the basic Wellsian message and technique— the sombre warning clothed in glittering words and delivered in breathtaking flights of imagination. He followed it with the deliberately blasphemous *The Island of Dr. Moreau* (UK 1896), in which animals are surgically altered in an attempt to make them men—an allegorical comment on the beast lurking close beneath the surface of human civilization.

A year later came *The Invisible Man* (UK 1897), telling how a discovery that might be thought a unique advantage eventually proved an insurmountable handicap. Allowing the reader little time to collect his wits, Wells subjected him successively to the Martian invasion of *The War of the Worlds* (UK 1898), the oppressive anti-utopia of *When the Sleeper Wakes* (UK 1899), the chillingly-efficient Selenite society in *The First Men in the Moon* (UK 1901), and the giant children with their equally big ambitions in *The Food of the Gods* (UK 1904). In the following year he published what many regard as the definitive utopian story; but it was significant that he set *A Modern Utopia* (UK 1905) on a parallel Earth, a device he was to use again in his other utopian treatment, *Men Like Gods* (UK 1923). *In the Days of the Comet* (UK 1906) might be described as the coming of a utopia, since peace descends on Man as a result of a hallucinogenic gas released from the comet's tail. *The War in the Air* (UK 1908), with its remarkable forecast of aerial combat, marked the end of his main period as a writer of science fiction, although he was still to produce a handful of other notable tales in the genre.

Of these, *The World Set Free* (UK 1914) told of a future atomic war, which, unlike the factual world conflict which was just beginning, led to an enduring and constructive peace. *Mr Blettsworthy on Rampole Island* (UK 1928) was an excursion into 'Inner Space' and a horrifying account of a protracted state of hallucination experienced by an Englishman living in New York. *The Croquet Player* (UK 1936) is also allegorical in intent, depicting the psychological effects of the mass haunting of a village by a brutish, caveman-like 'prescence' in the nearby marshes.

Among his other late stories which fall into the sf category was *The Shape of Things to Come* (UK 1933), which in its telling fell below his usual standard but served as a basis for Alexander Korda's epic film production *Things to Come* in 1935 (Wells's screenplay of the same title was published in the UK during the same year). *Star Begotten* (UK 1938) also bore signs of fatigue, and the idea of humans being genetically influenced by radiations directed at Earth from an entity in space was hardly developed beyond its initial statement.

Novels aside, many of Wells's seventy-odd short stories are firmly placed in the sf category, and illustrate his ability to combine both 'Sense of Wonder' and 'willing suspension of disbelief'. Unlike Verne, he was never particularly interested in technical explanations, but relied almost entirely on the 'imaginative jump'. He stuck rigidly to the introduction of only one far-fetched assumption in any single story and developed each plot from there. Among his classics—given in the order in which they appear in the first edition of *The Complete Short Stories of H. G. Wells* (UK 1927)—are 'The Empire of the Ants' (1905), 'The Land Ironclads' (1903) which forecast the invention of the armoured tank, 'The Door in the Wall' (1906), 'The Country of the Blind' (1904), 'The Lord of the Dynamos' (1894), 'The Sea Raiders' (1896), 'The Crystal Egg' (1897), 'The Star' (1897), 'A Story of the Days to Come' (1897), 'The Man Who Could Work Miracles' (1898), 'The Valley of Spiders' (1903) and 'The New Accelerator' (1901).

Numerous collections of his short stories appeared before the 'definitive' Ernest Benn edition of 1927 (which itself missed out at least eight tales). They included *The Stolen Bacillus and Other Incidents* (UK 1895), *The Plattner Story and Others* (UK 1897), *Tales of Space and Time* (UK 1899), *Twelve Stories and a Dream* (UK 1903) and *The Country of the Blind and Other Stories* (UK 1911). There have been many since.

In addition to Korda's *Things to Come* (directed by William Cameron Menzies) several other film adaptations of Wells's sf stories have been made, among them: *The Invisible Thief* (a silent 1909 production by Pathé, France, based on *The Invisible Man*), *The First Men in the Moon* (a silent Gaumont production of 1919 directed by J. L. V. Leigh), *The Island of Lost Souls* (Paramount 1932, featuring Charles Laughton and Bela Lugosi and based on *The Island of Dr. Moreau*), *The Invisible Man* (United Artists 1932, directed by James Whale of *Frankenstein* renown), *Man Who Could Work Miracles* (a Korda production of 1935—Wells's script was published in the UK in the same year), *The War of the Worlds* (Paramount 1952, an updating of the original story and set in the US), *The Door in the Wall* (an experimental Associated British and Pathé production in 1953), *The Time Machine* (M-G-M 1960, directed by George Pal) and *The First Men in the Moon* (American British 1964).

There was also the notorious Orson Welles US radio broadcast of 30th October, 1938, during which numerous listeners were persuaded that *The War of the Worlds* had *actually* begun—they took to the hills in droves (Wells himself was not amused: 'Unwarranted liberties were taken with my work', he cabled). The full story of the fiasco is told in Hadley Cantril's *The Invasion from Mars* (US 1940).

Of the many studies written on Wells and his work, few are devoted solely to his science fiction. Bernard Bergonzi's *The Early H. G. Wells: A Study of the Scientific Romances* (UK 1961) is the most authoritative to date.

Hans Wesso

A well-known illustrator who first appeared as the cover artist of *Amazing*'s September 1929 issue. He was born in Germany in 1882 (as Hans Waldemar Wessolowski) and moved to the US in 1914. He produced thirty-four covers for *Astounding* during 1930–33 when it was owned by Clayton Magazines, and afterwards contributed to many publications in the field.

James White

James White is a British writer who was born in Belfast in 1928. He spent part of his early life in Canada, returning to Northern Ireland to go into management with a tailoring business. In the mid-1960s he became publicity director of an aircraft company. His first short story, 'Assisted Passage', appeared in *New Worlds* in 1953, and he subsequently wrote a popular series for the magazine featuring a hospital in space which treated aliens. (Five of the stories were later connected to make *Hospital Station* (US 1962), and *Star Surgeon* (US 1963) pursued the theme. White has admitted that he has always wanted to be a doctor.)

His first novel, *The Secret Visitors* (US 1957) involves alien warfare over the misuse of Earth. *The Second Ending* (US 1962) tells of the last man left alive in a world run by robots, and in *The Watch Below* (US 1966) humans engage in underwater conflict with a race of aquatic aliens. *All Judgment Fled* (UK 1968) presents Earth with a vast extraterrestrial spaceship containing many strange life-forms. The problem for the men who encounter them is to discover which one is in charge. *The Dream Millennium* (UK 1974) recounts the dreams of a starship captain during long periods in suspended animation on an interstellar journey. It enables White to review the human condition with the compassion for which his work is well known, and also to linger on spacecraft technology at which he is generally adept.

Among his other books are *Open Prison* (UK 1964—retitled *The Escape Orbit* for US 1965), *Major Operation* (US 1971), *Tomorrow is Too Far* (US 1971), and the short story collections: *Deadly Litter* (US 1964) and *The Aliens Among Us* (US 1969).

Ted White

US author and editor, who won a Hugo in 1968 as 'Best Fan Writer'. He was assistant editor of *The Magazine of Fantasy and Science Fiction* from 1963 until 1968, moving on to the full editorship of *Amazing* and *Fantastic* in 1969. His novels, some of which verge on fantasy, include *Android Avenger* (US 1965), *Phoenix Prime* and its sequel *The Sorceress of Qar* (both US 1966), *The Secret of the Marauder Satellite* (US 1967) and *The Spawn of the Death Machine* (US 1968).

Kate Wilhelm

Kate Wilhelm is an American freelance writer who was born in Ohio in 1928. Among her sf novels are *The Clone* (US 1965, in collaboration with Theodore L. Thomas), *The Nevermore Affair* (US 1966) and *Abyss* (US 1971). *The Killing Thing* (US 1967) tells of a murderous alien device on a far planet, while *Where Late the Sweet Birds Sang* (US 1976) is a post-catastrophe setting in which the last real humans are threatened by clones.

In 1968 she won a Nebula with 'The Planners', and she is noted for several other acclaimed short stories. The title piece in her collection, *Andover and the Android* (US 1966), is one such, and shows a man falling in love with an android which he has already married for commercial reasons. Other collections are: *The Mile-Long Spaceship* (US 1963) and *The Downstairs Room and Other Speculative Fiction* (US 1968). She was also editor of the ninth in the series of *Nebula Award* anthologies (US 1974). Kate Wilhelm is married to Damon Knight.

Robert Moore Williams

A prolific contributor to the sf magazines during the 1940s. Robert Moore Williams was born in the US in 1907 and graduated from the University of Missouri School of Journalism in 1931. He has also written under several pseudonyms, among them 'John S. Browning'. Since the 1950s he has produced a number of novels in the Ace paperback series, including *Conquest of the Space Sea* (US 1955), in which aliens attempt to prevent Man's space exploration, and the parapsychology variations: *The Chaos Fighters* (US 1955) and *Doomsday Eve* (US 1957). Others in the series are *The Blue Atom* (US 1958), *The Day They H-Bombed Los Angeles* (US 1961) and *The Darkness Before Tomorrow* (US 1962).

More recently he has written the 'Zanthar' stories: *Zanthar of the Many Worlds* (US 1967), *Zanthar at the Edge of Never* (US 1968) and *Zanthar at Moon's Madness* (US 1968). Eleven of his short stories can be found in the collections: *The Void Beyond* (US 1958) and *To the End of Time* (US 1960).

Jack Williamson

An eminent long-stayer in the field, John Stewart Williamson was born in Arizona in 1908. As a child he travelled with his family by covered wagon to a homestead in New Mexico, where he later studied at the State University. He began writing early, and his first story, 'The Metal Man', appeared in *Amazing* in 1928. He was soon a regular contributor, collaborating briefly with Miles J. Breuer on 'The Girl from Mars' (1929) and 'Birth of a New Republic' (1931), and striking up a lasting friendship with Edmond Hamilton, with whom he travelled widely. He served in the US Air Force during the Second World War as a weather forecaster in the Pacific and afterwards worked for a while as a newspaperman. Ultimately he took to teaching English, obtaining his Ph.D. at the University of Colorado and setting up a course of studies in science fiction at the University of Eastern New Mexico in 1964. His Ph.D. thesis, a penetrating evaluation of the work of H. G. Wells, was serialized in the amateur *Riverside Quarterly* during the late 1960s and subsequently published as *H. G. Wells: Critic of Progress* (US 1973).

Many of his books are revivals of original magazine serials, among the earliest of which was his classic space opera *The Legion of Space* (US 1947, first serialized in *Astounding* in 1934). It was followed by a sequel, *The Cometeers* (US 1950, serialized in *Astounding* in 1936), and later by the equally well-received *The Legion of Time* (US 1952, an *Astounding* serial in 1938). His 'Gateway to Paradise' (1941), telling of a force field built to enclose the entire US, became the book *Dome Around America* (US 1955). *The Humanoids* (US 1949) first appeared in *Astounding* as '. . . And Searching Mind', but the noted robot story to which it was a sequel, 'With Folded Hands . . .', has not been printed separately as a book. His two anti-matter tales, *Seetee Shock* (US 1950) and *Seetee Ship* (US 1951), published under the pen-name 'Will Stewart', should rightfully be read in the reverse order.

Darker Than You Think (US 1948) is an intriguing attempt to explain werewolves scientifically, and *Dragon's Island* (US 1951) describes the discovery of mutants in New Guinea. *Star Bridge* (US 1955), written in collaboration with James Gunn, depicts the domination of a planetary race who have discovered the secret of a faster-than-light spacedrive. A further collaboration, on this occasion with Frederik Pohl, produced the trilogy: *The Reefs of Space* (US 1964), *Starchild* (US 1965) and *Rogue Star* (US 1969). *Bright New Universe* (US 1967) is a variation on the theme of Man encountering a galactic civilization.

Other stories include: *The Green Girl* (US 1950, first serialized in *Amazing* in 1930), *After World's End* (UK 1961, originally in *Marvel Stories* in 1939), *The Trial of Terra* (US 1962), *Golden Blood* (US 1964), *Trapped in Space* (US 1968) and *The Moon Children* (US 1972). Some of his short stories can be found in the collections: *The Pandora Effect* (US 1969) and *People Machines* (US 1971).

Richard Wilson

American news chief Richard Wilson was born in New York in 1920. He contributed a few stories to *Astonishing* in the early 1940s before departing for war service. Afterwards he became the New York Bureau Chief of Trans-radio Press. His novels in the genre include *The Girls from Planet 5* (US 1955), recounting the invasion of the US by extraterrestrial Amazons, and *30 Day Wonder* (US 1960), which tells of a non-violent conquest of Earth. *And Then the Town Took Off* (US 1960) is an amusing account of the effects on an American urban population when they discover their environment is more elevated than they had thought.

Some of Wilson's stories can be found in the collections: *Those Idiots From Earth* (US 1957) and *Time Out for Tomorrow* (US 1962). In 1968 he won a Nebula for his 'Mother to the World'.

Russell Winterbotham

Russell Winterbotham was a US bridge-columnist, cartoon-strip writer, news-service editor, and author of both western and sf stories. He was born in Kansas in 1904 and was educated at Kansas University. He read his first science fiction in 1934 and promptly decided to write it, initially appearing with 'The Star That Would Not Behave' in *Astounding* (1935). He produced many stories in the genre before the Second World War, and returned to it later when his contributions included *The Space Egg* (US 1957), telling of a dangerous symbiote invasion of Earth, *The Red Planet* (US 1962), *The Men from Arcturus* (US 1963) and *The Puppet Planet* (US 1964). He died in 1971.

Bernard Wolfe

Another American newsman, Bernard Wolfe is also a qualified psychologist and contributor of many articles and stories to magazines both in and outside the sf field. He was born in 1915 and studied at Yale University. For a while he was Night City Editor of Paramount Newsreel, and the war correspondent for *Popular Science*. He has also edited *Mechanix Illustrated*. In addition to his sf short stories, he has written the novel *Limbo* (US 1952, retitled *Limbo 90* in the UK, 1953). It is an anti-utopian vision of a future Earth, with physically reshaped people dominated by cybernetics.

Donald A. Wollheim

A noted American editor, anthologist and writer. He entered the field in 1934 with 'The Man from Ariel' in *Wonder Stories*, and subsequently became a very regular contributor to the early pulps. In 1941 he edited both *Stirring Science Stories* and *Cosmic Stories*, but unhappily neither magazine lasted very long. After the Second World War he worked for a while with Avon Books and later became editor for Ace Books; with the former he edited the *Avon Science Fiction* series. He has also written for the juvenile sf market, and since 1961 has produced many stories featuring the astronaut 'Mike Mars'.

Wollheim has been an industrious anthologist for more than thirty years. His first two, *The Pocket Book of Science Fiction* (US 1943) and *Portable Novels of Science* (US 1945), were an early break-through into what is now a common publishing form. Among his many successive compilations are: *Flight Into Space* (US 1950), which includes his own 'Planet Passage', *Prize Science Fiction* (US 1953), *Adventures in the Far Future* (US 1954), *Tales of Outer Space* (US 1954), *The Ultimate Invader & Other Science Fiction* (US 1954), *Adventures on Other Planets* (US 1955), *The End of the World* (US 1956), *The Earth in Peril* (US 1957), *Men on the Moon* (US 1958), *The Hidden Planet* (US 1959), *More Adventures on Other Planets* (US 1963), *Swordsmen in the Sky* (US 1964) and *Operation: Phantasy; the Best from the Phantagraph* (US 1967). In 1965 he began compiling the annual *World's Best Science Fiction* series in collaboration with Terry Carr. The latter dropped out after the first few issues, and Wollheim has continued the series into the 1970s on his own.

His study of the genre, *The Universe Makers: Science Fiction Today* (US 1971), is an effective appraisal by one whose knowledge of the field is exhaustive.

Farnsworth Wright
US editor who took over *Weird Tales* in 1924, some eighteen months after its launch, and guided it capably until his death in 1940. He encouraged many early writers who also acquired reputations in the genuine sf magazines, among them Ray Cummings, Edmond Hamilton, David H. Keller and Murray Leinster. The magazine, however, was primarily devoted to the macabre in the Lovecraft vein, to 'ooze' tales of deranged scientists creating slippery monsters and to unlimited flights of fantasy.

S. Fowler Wright
Sydney Fowler Wright (1874–1965) was a veteran British writer of many detective mysteries and one or two notable sf tales. His novels *The World Below* (UK 1924) and *The Amphibians* (UK 1929; which includes the former work) are the first two parts of an unfinished trilogy telling of an Earth three thousand centuries hence. They have been much reprinted. His other notable contributions to the field are *Deluge* (US 1928) and its sequel *Dawn* (US 1929), relating the onset and aftermath of a cataclysmic flood.

Further stories are *The Adventures of Wyndham Smith* (UK 1938) and *Spiders' War* (US 1954). Many of his shorter pieces have been collected in *The New Gods Lead* (UK 1932), *The Witchfinder* (UK 1946) and *The Throne of Saturn* (US 1949).

Philip Wylie

Philip Gordon Wylie was born in the United States in 1902. Coming from a literary family, he wished to concentrate on English during his education but was made to study science at Princeton. In 1925 he joined the staff of *The New Yorker* and subsequently followed a writing career. His first science fiction novel, *Gladiator* (US 1930), utilized the persecuted mutant theme in the form of a chemically-induced physical superman. It ended with one of the most glaringly inappropriate pieces of *deus ex machina* that can ever have found its way into print. Perhaps it was inevitable that Wylie then moved rapidly into the Hollywood arena, scripting the adaptation of Wells's *The Island of Doctor Moreau* which was filmed, impressively, by Paramount as *The Island of Lost Souls* (1932). His best-known work, *When Worlds Collide* (US 1932, written with Edwin Balmer), was filmed by George Pal for Paramount in 1951.

Wylie caused a stir by the inclusion of views on the inferiority and unreliability of women in such books as *The Savage Gentleman* (US 1932), and in his subsequent attack on 'Momism' in a polemical work (not sf), *Generation of Vipers*. However, he came down in support of the interdependence of the sexes in *The Disappearance* (US 1951). His *Tomorrow!* (US 1954) drew on his own experiences as a civil defence adviser in its vivid descriptions of a nuclear attack on the US. Wylie died in 1971.

John Wyndham

'John Wyndham' was the best-known pseudonym of the British writer John Wyndham Parkes Lucas Beynon Harris (during his career he made use of all his forenames in pseudonyms). He was born in Warwickshire in 1903 and educated at Bedales School. He made attempts at several occupations during the 1920s, from farming and law to commercial art and advertising. He began writing in 1925 and sold his first sf short story, 'Worlds to Barter', to *Wonder Stories* in 1931. Virtually all his early work appeared in American magazines and he became a popular contributor. He was a civil servant at the beginning of the Second World War, but later joined the Royal Corps of Signals and took part in the D-Day invasion in 1944. Afterwards he continued writing until his death in 1969.

His style has a distinctive quality, perhaps 'Englishness' is the word, which makes it readily identifiable. However, his scientific approach was also sound and he developed many themes, but usually with a slant towards characterization. His first novel, *The Secret People* (US 1935) was followed by *Stowaway to Mars*, serialized in *Modern Wonder* in 1937. His best-selling *The Day of the Triffids* (US 1951) is a gripping account of how mobile and deadly plants threaten a population blinded by a radiation storm. It was filmed—not very effectively—by Security Pictures in 1963.

Then came *The Kraken Wakes* (UK 1953), telling of extra-terrestrials concealed in the depths of Earth's oceans, and *The Chrysalids* (UK 1955—retitled *Re-birth* in the US, 1955), a notable post-catastrophe story. *The Midwich Cuckoos* (US 1957) related an invasion by aliens achieved by the impregnation of women who subsequently gave birth to paranormal children. It also was filmed, as *Village of the Damned*, by M-G-M in 1960, a well-conceived production but lacking the subtle air of menace of the original (M-G-M filmed a sequel, *Children of the Damned*, in 1963). *The Outward Urge* (UK 1959) was published, for convoluted reasons, as being written in collaboration with 'Lucas Parkes', a further combination of Wyndham's own names. His last stories included *The Trouble with Lichen* (UK 1960) and *Chocky* (US 1968), a touching tale of a boy in communication with an extraterrestrial child. *Sleepers of Mars* and *Wanderers of Time* (both UK 1973) are book collections of earlier magazine stories written under the name of John Beynon Harris.

His stories are available in several more collections: *Jizzle* (UK 1954), *Tales of Gooseflesh and Laughter* (US 1956), *The Seeds of Time* (UK 1956), *Consider Her Ways* (UK 1961), *The Infinite Moment* (US 1961), *The Best of John Wyndham* (UK 1973) and *The Man From Beyond and other stories* (UK 1975).

Ivan Yefremov

Ivan Antonovich Yefremov was born in Russia in 1907. He came to prominence with *The Andromeda Nebula* (USSR 1957, US translation in 1959 as *Andromeda*), a utopian story set in the year 3000 AD. It is an imaginative vision but sometimes turgid by Western standards, and somewhat heavy on the eulogies to 'heroic effort' and 'creative work'. His later *The Hour of the Bull* (USSR 1970) is disappointing by comparison. Two collections of his short stories have been translated: *A Meeting Over Tuscarora and Other Adventure Tales* (UK 1946) and *Stories* (US 1954), the latter repeating several of the tales from the earlier volume and including three or four new ones.

Robert F. Young
Robert Franklin Young was born in New York State in 1915. He served with the US Army in the Pacific during the Second World War and engaged in a variety of jobs, including pouring metal in a foundry. Subsequently he became a full-time writer, producing many short stories for the sf magazines. His work is noted for a deftness of touch and frequent charm. It can be effectively sampled in his collections: *The Worlds of Robert F. Young* (US 1965) and *A Glass of Stars* (US 1968).

Evgenii Zamyatin
A celebrated Russian writer who was imprisoned and finally exiled following the Communist Revolution. He was born in Lebedian in 1884 and died in Paris in 1937. His renowned anti-utopian novel *We* was written in 1920, but never published in Russia (a Russian language version printed in Prague was the reason for his exile). Its first English translation appeared in the US in 1924. The story portrays a grimly uniform Welfare State on the verge of space colonization, with the hero eventually betraying his mistress with whom he had attempted to rebel. Much of it is influenced by Wells's *When the Sleeper Wakes*, and in its turn it provided Orwell with ideas for *Nineteen Eighty-four*.

Roger Zelazny
A new star among recent American sf writers, Roger Zelazny was born in Ohio—of Polish, Irish, American and Dutch origins. He studied at Western Reserve University and at the University of

Columbia, and has worked in the US Government's Social Security Administration. He came to prominence in 1965 by winning two Nebulas in the same year with his stories, 'He Who Shapes' and 'The Doors of His Face, the Lamps of His Mouth'. The former was later extended into the novel *The Dream Master* (US 1966), telling of the development of dream analysis with some chilling results. The latter is an account of the hunting of an immense sea-monster on another world; it can be found in his collection *Four for Tomorrow* (US 1967).

Zelazny is noted among other things for the sureness of his style. Not only does he have good ideas, but he is also a good writer. Some enthusiasts have branded his early work as being too intellectual, which leads to speculation regarding what they might make of the latest writers in the genre. In *Lord of Light* (US 1967) he offers a subtle blending of science fiction and Indian folklore and mythology, while *Creatures of Light and Darkness* (US 1969) pursues mythology into the realm of fantasy. *Damnation Alley* (US 1969) is a post-catastrophe story presenting a radioactive wasteland inhabited by mutants.

Other books include *And Call Me Conrad* (US 1965), with which he won his first Hugo (the second being for *Lord of Light*), *Isle of the Dead* (US 1969), *Nine Princes in Amber* (US 1970), *Jack of Shadows* (US 1971), *The Guns of Avalon* (US 1972), *Sign of the Unicorn* (US 1975) and *Doorways in the Sand* (US 1976), the last being a humorous and fast-moving tale involving intrigue and blackmail between interstellar communities. His 'Auto-da-Fe' is in Ellison's *Dangerous Visions*, and he has also edited the anthology *Nebula Award Stories 3* (US 1968).

A Select Bibliography of books on Science Fiction

Aldiss, Brian W., *Billion Year Spree: The history of Science Fiction.* London and New York, 1973. (ed) *Science Fiction Art.* London and New York, 1975.

Amis, Kingsley, *New Maps of Hell: A Survey of Science Fiction.* New York and London, 1960.

Appel, Benjamin, *The Fantastic Mirror: Science Fiction Across the Ages.* New York, 1969.

Armytage, W. H. G., *Yesterday's Tomorrows: A historical survey of future societies.* London, 1968.

Ash, Brian, *Faces of the Future: The lessons of Science Fiction.* London and New York, 1975.

Ashley, Mike, *The History of the Science Fiction Magazines.* London: *Part 1: 1926–1935,* 1974; *Part 2: 1936–1945,* 1975; *Part 3: 1946–1955,* 1976.

Atheling, William, Jr (James Blish), *The Issue at Hand. Studies in contemporary magazine Science Fiction.* Chicago, 1964. *More Issues at Hand. Critical Studies in contemporary Science Fiction.* Chicago, 1972.

Bailey, J. O., *Pilgrims Through Space and Time: Trends and Patterns in Scientific and Utopian Fiction.* New York, 1947.

Baxter, John, *Science Fiction in the Cinema.* New York and London, 1970.

Bretnor, Reginald, (ed), *The Craft of Science Fiction. A Symposium on Writing Science Fiction and Science Fantasy.* New York, 1976. (ed) *Modern Science Fiction: Its Meaning and Its Future.* New York, 1953. (ed) *Science Fiction, Today and Tomorrow.* New York, 1974.

Clareson, Thomas D., (ed) *SF: The Other Side of Realism. Essays on Modern Fantasy and Science Fiction.* Ohio, 1971.

Clarke, I. F., *Voices Prophesying War, 1763–1984.* New York and London, 1966.

Davenport, Basil, *Inquiry Into Science Fiction.* New York, 1955.

(ed) *The Science Fiction Novel: Imagination and Social Criticism.* Chicago, 1964.

de Camp, L. Sprague, *Science-Fiction Handbook: The Writing of Imaginative Fiction.* New York, 1953. (Revised edn., 1975.)

Eshbach, Lloyd Arthur, *Of Worlds Beyond: The Science of Science Fiction Writing.* Chicago, 1964.

Franklin, H. Bruce, *Future Perfect: American Science Fiction of the Nineteenth Century.* New York, 1966.

Goulart, Ron, *An Informal History of the Pulp Magazines.* New York, 1972.

Green, Roger Lancelyn, *Into Other Worlds: Space Flight in Fiction from Lucian to Lewis.* New York, 1958.

Hay, George (ed), *The Disappearing Future. A Symposium of Speculation.* London, 1970.

Hillegas, Mark R., *The Future as Nightmare: H. G. Wells and the Anti-Utopians.* New York, 1967.

Johnson, William (ed), *Focus on the Science Fiction Film.* Englewood Cliffs, 1972.

Ketterer, David, *New Worlds for Old. The apocalyptic imagination, Science Fiction, and American literature.* New York, 1974.

Knight, Damon, *In Search of Wonder.* Chicago, 1956. (Enlarged edn., 1967.)

Kyle, David, *A Pictorial History of Science Fiction.* London and New York, 1976.

Lundwall, Sam J., *Science Fiction: What It's All About.* New York, 1971.

Moore, Patrick, *Science and Fiction.* London, 1958.

Moskowitz, Sam, *Explorers of the Infinite: Shapers of Science Fiction.* Cleveland, 1963. *The Immortal Storm. A history of science fiction fandom.* Atlanta, 1954. *Science Fiction by Gaslight. A history and anthology of Science Fiction in the popular Magazines, 1891–1911.* Cleveland, 1968. *Seekers of Tomorrow: Masters of Modern Science Fiction.* Cleveland, 1966. *Under the Moons of Mars. A history and anthology of 'The Scientific Romance' in the Munsey magazines, 1912–20.* New York, 1970.

Nicolson, Marjorie Hope, *Voyages to the Moon.* New York, 1948.

Philmus, Robert M., *Into the Unknown: The Evolution of Science Fiction from Francis Godwin to H. G. Wells.* Berkeley, 1970.

Rogers, Alva, *A Requiem for Astounding.* Chicago, 1964.

Rose, Lois and Stephen, *The Shattered Ring. Science Fiction and the quest for meaning*. Richmond, 1970.

Silverberg, Robert (ed), *The Mirror of Infinity. A critics' anthology of Science Fiction*. New York, 1970.

Walsh, Chad, *From Utopia to Nightmare*. New York, 1962.

Warner, Harry, Jr, *All Our Yesterdays*. Chicago, 1969.

Wertham, Frederic, *The World of Fanzines. A special form of communication*. Carbondale, 1973.

Wollheim, Donald A., *The Universe Makers: Science Fiction Today*. New York, 1971.

Reference works, indexes and check-lists

Bleiler, Everett F., *The Checklist of Fantastic Literature. A Bibliography of Fantasy, Weird, and Science Fiction Books Published in the English Language*. Chicago, 1948.

Briney, Robert E. and Edward Wood, *SF Bibliographies. An Annotated Bibliography of Bibliographical Works on Science Fiction and Fantasy Fiction*. Chicago, 1972.

Clareson, Thomas D., *Science Fiction Criticism: An Annotated Checklist*. Kent, 1972.

Clarke, I. F., *The Tale of the Future*. London, 1961. (Revised edn. 1972.)

Cole, Walter R., *A Checklist of Science Fiction Anthologies*. Brooklyn, 1964.

Day, Bradford M., *The Checklist of Fantastic Literature in Paperbound Books*. Denver, 1965. *The Complete Checklist of Science Fiction Magazines*. New York, 1961. *The Supplemental Checklist of Fantastic Literature*. Denver, 1963.

Day, Donald B., *Index to the Science-Fiction Magazines, 1926–50*. Portland, 1952.

Evans, Bill and Bob Pavlat, *Fanzine Index*. New York, 1965.

Hall, H. W., *Science Fiction Book Review Index, 1923–1973*. Michigan, 1975.

Lee, Walt, *Reference Guide to Fantastic Films, Science Fiction, Fantasy and Horror*. Los Angeles, *Vol. 1, A–F*, 1972; *Vol. 2, G–O*, 1973; *Vol. 3, P–Z*. 1974.

Metcalf, Norm, *The Index of Science Fiction Magazines, 1951–65*. El Cerrito, 1968.

New England Science Fiction Association, *Index to the Science Fiction Magazines* 1966–70. Cambridge (Mass.), 1971.

Owings, Mark and Jack L. Chalker, *The Index to the Science-Fantasy Publishers*. Baltimore, 1966.

Reginald, Robert, *STELLA NOVA: The Contemporary Science Fiction Authors*. Los Angeles, 1970.

Siemon, Frederick, *Science Fiction Story Index 1950–68*. Chicago, 1971.

Strauss, Erwin S., *The MIT Science Fiction Society's Index to the SF Magazines, 1951–65*. Cambridge (Mass.), 1966.

Tuck, Donald H., *The Encyclopedia of Science Fiction and Fantasy. Vol. 1, Who's Who A–L*. Chicago, 1974. *A Handbook of Science Fiction and Fantasy*. Hobart, 1959.

213 John Wyndham aliases